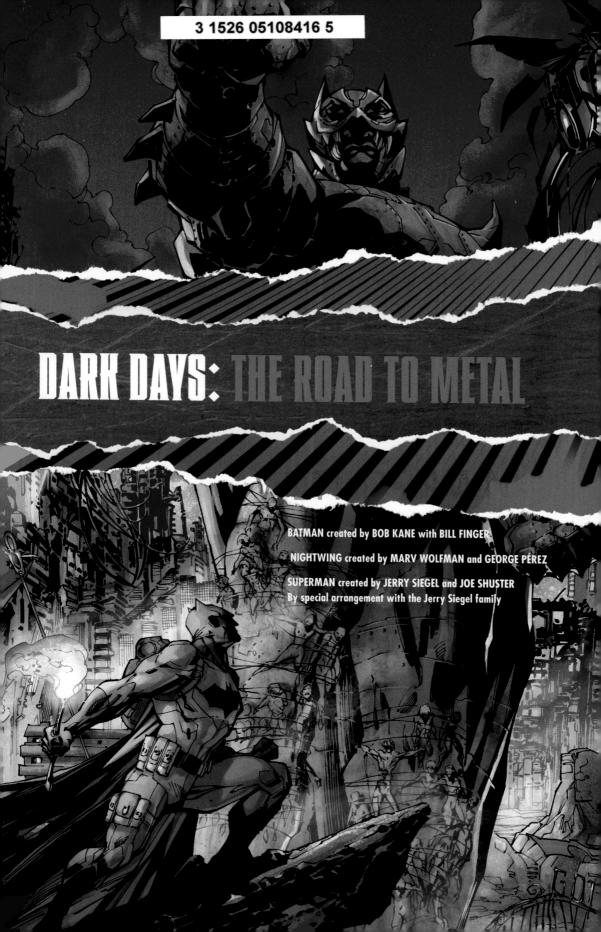

DARK DAYS: THE ROAD TO METAL

BATMAN created by BOB KANE with BILL FINGER

NIGHTWING created by MARV WOLFMAN and GEORGE PÉREZ

SUPERMAN created by JERRY SIEGEL and JOE SHUSTER
By special arrangement with the Jerry Siegel family

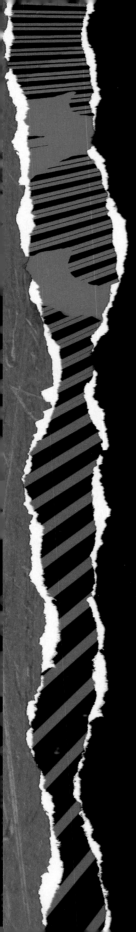

MARK DOYLE | EDDIE BERGANZA | MIKE MARTS
CHRIS CONROY | RICKEY PURDIN | REBECCA TAYLOR Editors – Original Series
ADAM SCHLAGMAN Associate Editor – Original Series
DAVE WIELGOSZ | JANELLE SIEGEL | MATT HUMPHREYS Assistant Editors – Original Series
JEB WOODARD Group Editor – Collected Editions
ROBIN WILDMAN Editor – Collected Edition
STEVE COOK Design Director – Books / Cover Design
MONIQUE NARBONETA Publication Design

BOB HARRAS Senior VP – Editor-in-Chief, DC Comics
PAT McCALLUM Executive Editor, DC Comics

DIANE NELSON President
DAN DiDIO Publisher
JIM LEE Publisher
GEOFF JOHNS President & Chief Creative Officer
AMIT DESAI Executive VP – Business & Marketing Strategy, Direct to Consumer & Global Franchise Management
SAM ADES Senior VP & General Manager, Digital Services
BOBBIE CHASE VP & Executive Editor, Young Reader & Talent Development
MARK CHIARELLO Senior VP – Art, Design & Collected Editions
JOHN CUNNINGHAM Senior VP – Sales & Trade Marketing
ANNE DePIES Senior VP – Business Strategy, Finance & Administration
DON FALLETTI VP – Manufacturing Operations
LAWRENCE GANEM VP – Editorial Administration & Talent Relations
ALISON GILL Senior VP – Manufacturing & Operations
HANK KANALZ Senior VP – Editorial Strategy & Administration
JAY KOGAN VP – Legal Affairs
JACK MAHAN VP – Business Affairs
NICK J. NAPOLITANO VP – Manufacturing Administration
EDDIE SCANNELL VP – Consumer Marketing
COURTNEY SIMMONS Senior VP – Publicity & Communications
JIM (SKI) SOKOLOWSKI VP – Comic Book Specialty Sales & Trade Marketing
NANCY SPEARS VP – Mass, Book, Digital Sales & Trade Marketing
MICHELE R. WELLS VP – Content Strategy

DARK DAYS: THE ROAD TO METAL

DC Comics, 2900 West Alameda Ave., Burbank, CA 91505
Printed by LSC Communications, Kendallville, IN, USA. 4/13/18. First Printing.
ISBN: 978-1-4012-7819-9

Library of Congress Cataloging-in-Publication Data is available.

PEFC Certified
Printed on paper from
sustainably managed
forests, controlled
sources
PEFC/29-31-337   www.pefc.org

DARK DAYS: THE FORGE Nº 1
cover by Jim Lee, Scott Williams and Alex Sinclair

There is a feeling you get at the beginning of an adventure...
...you feel it in your veins, the channels, your heart starts pounding...
...beating only for discovery...
My name is Carter Hall and this is my final journal.
I have lived many lives. But I still remember that night like it was yesterday.
A young boy had spied something in the sky, a light, and we rode out together, my princess, my advisor, our guards, all to see what it was.
We could feel it in the air, the start of something big.
Something was coming... something wondrous.
A message from the gods, perhaps? A sign?

But it was no sign.
It was a clue to the greatest mystery in the history of mankind.
And it was written in metal.

NOW.
THE BERMUDA TRIANGLE.
R-RECORD MESSAGE.
THE TREMORS STARTED FORTY MINUTES AGO AND HAVE ONLY GROWN WORSE... I DON'T KNOW IF THE REST OF THE RESEARCH TEAM MADE IT OUT IN TIME. IT'S TOO LATE FOR ME. THE LAVA WILL ENGULF THE BASE IN MINUTES.
I STAYED TO PROTECT WHAT WE'VE JUST LEARNED. I KEEP READING AND REREADING THE DATA, HOPING IT COMES TOGETHER. HOPING WHAT I THOUGHT I SAW WASN'T TRUE.
PEOPLE NEED TO KNOW. PEOPLE NEED TO UNDERSTAND.
THERE'S SOMETHING... THERE'S SOMETHING WRONG WITH THE EARTH'S CORE.
THERE'S SOMETHING IN THE METAL...
AHH!

DR. MADISON...
THE ONLY WAY OUT IS THROUGH THE VOLCANO.
GET IN.
B-BATMAN?

OH GOD, OH GOD...
PRESSURE MOUNTING.
COMPENSATE.
WE JUST NEED TO BREAK THROUGH INTO THE OPEN OCEAN...
TEMPERATURES SURPASSING SAFE LEVELS. SUIT WILL NOT HOLD.
I SAID COMPENSATE, DAMN IT!
KRAKATOW
I SEE THEM.
AQUAMAN! GET HIM TO THE SURFACE!
WHAT ABOUT YOU?
I NEED TO RETRIEVE THE DATA CARD FROM MY PRESSURE SUIT.
THE LAVA FLOW WILL CONSUME THAT BEHEMOTH IN SECONDS! LEAVE IT!
I CAN'T.
CRRRUNCH
THERE...

THE OTHERS?
MY FRIENDS ARE PULLING THEM TO SHORE NOW. NO CASUALTIES.
THANK YOU, AQUAMAN.
BATMAN. THIS WAS A WAYNE ENTERPRISES BLACK SITE. AN OFF-THE-BOOKS DRILLING OPERATION IN MY DOMAIN.
YOU WEREN'T JUST KEEPING THIS PLACE HIDDEN FROM THE SURFACE WORLD. YOU WERE KEEPING IT HIDDEN FROM ATLANTIS. FROM ME.
WHAT ARE YOU LOOKING FOR, BRUCE?
WITH WHAT I KNOW IS LOCKED UNDERNEATH ATLANTIS...IS THAT REALLY A QUESTION YOU WANT TO ASK ME?
WHAT WE NEED TO BE ASKING IS SIMPLER THAN THAT, ARTHUR...
WHAT ARE THEY HIDING?
HE CAN LOOK ALL HE WANTS, BUT HE WON'T FIND OUT. LADY BLACKHAWK TO CONTROL. BRING ME HOME.

HOME OF THE GREEN LANTERN CORPS.
HAL JORDAN OF EARTH. I AM TEMPORARILY PULLING YOU FROM ACTIVE DUTY. I HAVE A PRIVATE MISSION FOR YOU OF PARAMOUNT IMPORTANCE.
THIS MISSION MUST REMAIN SECRET FROM YOUR FELLOW LANTERNS. PARTICULARLY YOUR FELLOW EARTH MEN.
THOSE HAPPY SECRET MISSIONS, IS IT, GANTHET?
THERE ARE RUMBLINGS IN EVERY CORNER OF THIS UNIVERSE. WHISPERS OF A STIRRING IN THE DARK. A TERRIBLE TRUTH IS COMING TO LIGHT ON YOUR HOME PLANET.
AND WE MUST NOT LET IT.
WAIT, THESE ARE THE COORDINATES? THIS IS THE SOURCE OF THE THREAT?
IS THERE A PROBLEM, HAL JORDAN?
WAYNE MANOR. GOTHAM CITY.
NO. NO PROBLEM AT ALL.

THERE'S MORE SPOOKY CRAP IN THIS PLACE EVERY TIME I VISIT...

ALL RIGHT, LET'S FIND WHAT'S GOT GANTHET'S ROBES UP IN A BUNCH AND GET THE HELL *OUT* OF THIS MAUSOLEUM.

I DON'T *THINK* SO.

SORRY, GREEN LANTERN. I'M ON STRICT ORDERS FROM BATMAN.

NOBODY IS ALLOWED IN THE CAVE RIGHT NOW. NOT EVEN FAMILY.

YEAH, THAT'S NOT SUSPICIOUS AT ALL.
THOUGHT I READ THAT LITTLE RING OF YOURS DIDN'T WORK ON YELLOW...
IT DOES IF YOU KNOW WHAT YOU'RE DOING.
THAT DOESN'T MAKE ANY SENSE.
GLAD TO SEE BATMAN'S STILL RECRUITING TEENAGERS. YOU'RE NEW, AREN'T YOU? WHAT'S YOUR NAME? YELLOW ROBIN? CANARY? BIG BIRD?
ALL YOU NEED TO KNOW IS THAT BATMAN LEFT ME HERE WITH A JOB TO DO.
AND THAT IF YOU DON'T GET OUT OF HERE RIGHT NOW, YOU'RE GOING TO REGRET IT.
AW, YOU'RE DOING THE VOICE AND EVERYTHING.
SERIOUSLY, KID. WHAT'S YOUR NAME?
DUKE THOMAS. I DON'T HAVE A CODE NAME YET.
WHAT ARE YOU DOING?
SCANNING FOR SOMETHING...
THERE.
H-HEY!
COME BACK HERE!

THE CAMPUS: ONE MILE BENEATH PHILADELPHIA.
DIE...DIE... DIE...
HER NAME IS ELAINE THOMAS.
SHE SEEMS CHARMING.
SHE WAS, ONCE. BEFORE THE JOKER TOXINS RIPPED HER MIND APART. BEFORE HER SON, DUKE, HAD HER MOVED INTO WAYNE MANOR.
I MADE HER THE OFFER, MANY YEARS AGO.
THE OFFER TO JOIN A SECRET BATTLE THAT STRETCHED BACK TO THE DAWN OF TIME.
AN OFFER TO LIVE FOREVER.
SHE DIDN'T TAKE YOU UP ON IT, I'M GUESSIN'.
SO, WHY IS THE GREAT AND POWERFUL IMMORTAL MAN WALKING DOWN MEMORY LANE?
MRS. THOMAS... REACTIVATED, BRIEFLY, A FEW WEEKS AGO.
I'VE BEEN MONITORING TO MAKE SURE SHE HASN'T REVEALED ANYTHING SHE SHOULDN'T TO ANYONE SHE SHOULDN'T.
BUT SHE REMAINS INCAPABLE OF DIVULGING OUR SECRETS, NO MATTER HOW HARD THE BATMAN PRIES. WE NEEDN'T WORRY ABOUT HER.
OUR SECRECY IS PARAMOUNT TO OUR SUCCESS.
THE WORLD OF THE PUBLIC HEROES IS CAREENING TOWARD A CRISIS UNLIKE ANYTHING THEY'VE SEEN BEFORE.
AND IT WILL BE UP TO THE IMMORTAL MEN TO PRESERVE MANKIND'S FUTURE.
IF ANY OF US SURVIVE LONG ENOUGH TO SEE IT...

From that night on, that fateful night in the Egyptian desert, my story is well known.

The ship was made of a mysterious substance called **Nth metal**. It gave me, my wife, and our mortal enemy, Hath-Set, eternal life, sending us into a cycle of reincarnation-- Shiera and I fighting on the side of good, Hath-Set on that of evil.

We were born hundreds, even thousands of times over, cast against each other.

But the truth is, sometimes, in those dark moments, those moments in between lives, before being born again, I would catch glimpses...

...glimpses of something bigger, a mystery behind our lives, our story.

Something terrifying. Something on a scale I'd never seen before. A dream... no, not a dream. A **nightmare**, echoing through the metal.

NNAAAH!

So I began following a mystery of my own. Something I told no one about. Not until now.

Here in these pages.

A mystery that would take me places I never dreamed.
LUNAR BATCAVE. THE MOON.
COMPUTER.
SEND A MESSAGE TO LUCIUS.
BLACK SITE 14 IS DOWN. I WANT SITE 15 UP AND RUNNING WITHIN THE WEEK. KEEP THIS ONE AWAY FROM THE OCEANS.
CREATE UPLINK TO THE SHADOW DRIVE. ADDING NEW GEOLOGICAL DATA FOR COMPARISONS.
SO, IT WAS AS BAD AS YOU THOUGHT IT WOULD BE?

What did my **T-SPHERES** ever do to **YOU?**

Throw off the calibration of my computers. I didn't realize you were back in **OUR** universe, Michael.

This mystery of yours has made me a little queasy about crossing back and forth. It seemed time I came home for **GOOD.**

But **MR. TERRIFIC** keeps his promises. Here's all the data I could gather from the **OTHER** world.

Have you told **ANYONE** what we've been working on? On either **EARTH?**

I didn't put "FAIR PLAY" on my jacket for laughs. I **KNOW** what's at stake. When the Batman comes and says he needs a second set of eyes to help see the big picture, you **DON'T** break that trust.

FAIR PLAY

AND NOW, HOW IS THAT BIG PICTURE LOOKING?
I'LL BE HONEST, BATMAN. I HAVE AN IQ OF 179, BUT I HAVE NO IDEA WHAT ANY OF THIS MEANS. THE FREQUENCY THAT'S BEING GENERATED ACROSS THE WORLDS IS GROWING STRONGER, BUT IT'S NOT STEADY AT ALL. IT SEEMS RANDOM.
LIKE A COMPASS, SPINNING WILDLY OUT OF CONTROL...
TERRIFIC
HH...
THAT JUST SPARKED SOMETHING, DIDN'T IT?
THERE'S NOTHING ON THIS EARTH THAT I KNOW OF THAT COULD GET YOU A CLEAN READING ON THIS DATA. IT WOULD TAKE SOMETHING MASSIVE.
SOMETHING PRACTICALLY COSMIC IN SCALE.
YES. IT WILL. AND WHERE IT LEADS ME, THERE MIGHT NOT BE ANY COMING BACK.
AND MICHAEL...I'M GOING TO NEED YOU TO DO SOMETHING WHILE I FOLLOW THIS PATH TO THE END. I'VE ALREADY EXTRACTED THE MOLECULES I NEEDED FROM HIS BODY.
WE ALL AGREED HE WAS TOO UNSTABLE... THAT THERE WAS NO END TO WHAT HE COULD DO IF WE WEREN'T CAREFUL. BUT I'M GOING TO NEED HIM FOR WHAT COMES NEXT.
IT'S TIME TO LET HIM OUT OF THE BOX.
YOU'RE DAMN RIGHT IT IS.

SERIOUSLY. ONLY BATMAN WOULD HAVE A SECRET CAVE INSIDE HIS SECRET CAVE.

I TOLD YOU, YOU'RE NOT SUPPOSED TO BE HERE.

WHAT *IS* THIS PLACE?

OH, I CAN CLEAR THAT UP FOR YOU...

DON'T LOOK AT ME! I DIDN'T SAY ANYTHING!

RING, HOW MANY LIFE SIGNATURES AHEAD...?

--ZZZT-- CANNOT COMPLY --ZZZT-- INTER- FERENCE--

THIS DOESN'T MAKE ANY SENSE...

IT WOULDN'T, WOULD IT? A MYSTERY NEVER DOES AT FIRST...

MYSTERY?

OH YES, OUR FRIEND WITH THE POINTY EARS HAS BEEN FOLLOWING IT FOR YEARS NOW.

ALFRED, IS THAT YOU?

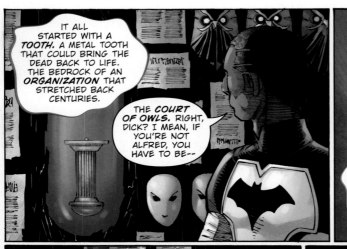

IT ALL STARTED WITH A *TOOTH*. A METAL TOOTH THAT COULD BRING THE DEAD BACK TO LIFE. THE BEDROCK OF AN *ORGANIZATION* THAT STRETCHED BACK CENTURIES.

THE *COURT OF OWLS*. RIGHT, DICK? I MEAN, IF YOU'RE NOT ALFRED, YOU HAVE TO BE--

YOU SEE, A METAL SHOULDN'T BE ABLE TO *DO* WHAT THIS *"ELECTRUM"* COULD DO. NO COMPOUND OF GOLD AND SILVER COULD MAKE THE DEAD TALONS WALK AGAIN...AND SO BATMAN HAD HIS *THREAD*, AND HE PULLED...

AND HE *EXTRACTED* SOMETHING FROM THE METAL...A STRANGE SUBSTANCE HE HAD NEVER SEEN BEFORE. A METAL THAT SCIENCE *COULDN'T* EXPLAIN.

AH...

WHAT'S WRONG?

MY RING...IT'S BURNING...

OH, YOU CAN *FEEL* IT, CAN'T YOU? THE POWER. SO COULD HE. AND IT *CONSUMED* HIM. WHAT WAS THIS STRANGE METAL? WHAT WAS ITS CONNECTION TO THE OWLS?

WHY DID IT SHARE AN ENERGY SIGNATURE WITH SO MANY OF THE MOST POWERFUL ARTIFACTS ON THE PLANET?

AND SO HE FORMED THE *FIRST* TEAM. THE FIRST OF MANY TASKED WITH INVESTIGATING ALL OF THIS.

A TEAM THAT COULD MOVE *OUTSIDE* BATMAN'S USUAL REALM OF INFLUENCE.

TOGETHER THESE **OUTSIDERS** WOULD OPERATE WITHOUT THE KNOWLEDGE OF THE JUSTICE LEAGUE, THE GOVERNMENT OR EVEN HIS **PRECIOUS** BAT-FAMILY, UNCOVERING MORE HIDDEN TRUTHS ABOUT THE METALS...

WAIT A SECOND... BATMAN HAS A **BLACK-OPS** TEAM?

SOMETHING'S REALLY WRONG IN HERE. I'VE BEEN TO EVERY CORNER OF THE UNIVERSE, AND MY RING'S NEVER DONE THIS BEFORE.

WE SHOULD FALL BACK.

OH, NO NO NO... YOU CAN'T DO THAT...

I'VE BEEN **DYING** FOR THE CHANCE TO SEE YOU BOTH FACE TO FACE. WE'RE ALL CONNECTED, YOU SEE. I WAS HOPING SOMEONE WOULD COME MEDDLING.

IT'S BEEN SO **LONELY** DOWN HERE.

LOOK, I'M **DONE** KIDDING AROUND. WE'RE TALKING ABOUT **BATMAN.** YOU THINK I DON'T **KNOW** HE HAS **SECRETS?** IF HE'S BEEN PUTTING TOGETHER SOME KIND OF MYSTERY FOR YEARS AND HE HASN'T TOLD ME, HE HAS A **REASON.**

OH, YOU CAN'T TURN BACK NOW...

THE **NEXT** BIT'S THE **BEST** PART.

IT ALL HAS TO DO WITH A LIQUID METAL, SHIMMERING AND GREEN. A METAL THAT CHANGED EVERYTHING.

THEY CALLED IT **DIONESIUM.**

BUT HE WASN'T THE ONLY ONE WHO FOUND IT, WAS HE?

NO.

WHAT THE **HELL** IS GOING ON IN HERE? WHO **ARE** YOU?

OH, I THINK **HE'S** STARTING TO PUT THE PIECES TOGETHER.

JUST LIKE I DID.

YOU SEE, HE WAS DRAGGED INTO THIS WORLD FOR A REASON. THE SAME REASON I'M SURE YOUR CELESTIAL BOSSES SENT YOU DIGGING FOR ANSWERS.
SHOW YOURSELF.
BECAUSE BATMAN IS GETTING CLOSER TO THE TRUTH.
-ZZZT- CANNOT COMPLY -ZZZT- ANOMALY DETECTED -ZZZT-
AAAHHHHHH!
MY ARM'S ON FIRE. LET'S GO BACK TO THE CAVE. I CAN BRING IN THE LEAGUE...SOMETHING'S VERY WRONG HERE.
NO.
WE KEEP GOING.
OH, MR. GREEN LANTERN. ARE YOU AFRAID?
I DON'T GET AFRAID.
OH, I THINK YOU DO...I THINK WE ALL DO...IT'S ALL IN THAT MOMENT OF DISCOVERY...
WHEN YOU'RE ABOUT TO LEARN SOMETHING YOU WILL NEVER BE ABLE TO UNLEARN.
SOMETHING THAT PUTS ALL THE PIECES TOGETHER, AND YOU FINALLY SEE THE TRUTH, AND THE WORLD CHANGES.
AND YOU KNOW IT'LL NEVER GO BACK THE WAY IT WAS BEFORE.
BUT IF YOU'RE SO VERY BRAVE, THEN JUST OPEN THE DOOR.

You don't even realize when it happens. One minute you're following the clues, and the next, they're pulling you forward, dragging you.
For years I studied Nth metal alone, trying to unlock the secret of its abilities. What I came to understand was that it was conducting energy...powerful energy from somewhere beyond my understanding.
I dug deeper. Followed every clue I could find...
Until one day I got a glimpse.
A glimpse of a story that began with the first men to walk the Earth. Three tribes...
Or rather...four.

And something else...
I was part of something bigger, something beyond my control.
And I would do everything in my power to uncover what had been taken from me. The secret that stretched back to the dawn of my species.
No matter what the cost.

THE ARCTIC CIRCLE.
THE FORTRESS OF SOLITUDE.
HH.
CLARK. I KNOW YOU'RE IN THERE. LET ME IN.

YOU KNOW, IT WOULDN'T KILL YOU TO SAY *PLEASE* EVERY NOW AND THEN.
I THINK IT ACTUALLY *MIGHT.*
WHAT'S WRONG, BRUCE?
YOU LOOK WORRIED. YOUR HEART'S RACING.
I'M FINE.

BRUCE.

THERE'S A ROOM YOU GAVE ME, YEARS AGO, DEEP UNDER THE FORTRESS. I ASKED YOU NEVER TO LOOK AT WHAT I PUT INSIDE.

AND I NEVER HAVE. NOT ONCE.

I TOLD YOU THAT THE DAY WOULD COME WHEN I WOULD NEED TO OPEN THAT DOOR. AND THAT I WOULD HAVE TO WALK THROUGH IT *ALONE.*

BRUCE...IF THIS IS TOO BIG FOR YOU, I'M RIGHT HERE. YOU KNOW THAT, DON'T YOU?

I DO. THANK YOU, I DO.

IT WON'T BE LONG NOW. I'M NOT TRYING TO KEEP PEOPLE AWAY THIS TIME. I *SWEAR* THAT'S NOT WHAT I'M DOING. I JUST NEED TO *UNDERSTAND* WHAT I'M LOOKING AT FIRST.

I'VE SEEN THAT DOOR, BRUCE. THERE'S NOTHING FROM THIS WORLD THAT COULD OPEN IT.

I THINK THAT'S WHY HE CALLED *ME.*

YOU BUILT A *SECRET ROOM* AT THE *TOP* OF THE WORLD WITH *ONE* DOOR AND A LOCK THAT NO HUMAN COULD *EVER* UNLOCK.

WHAT DID YOU DO TO THE *KEY?*

I SHOT IT INTO THE SUN.

THAT'S A JOKE, RIGHT?

RIGHT?

CAN YOU OPEN IT?

THEY DON'T CALL ME *MISTER MIRACLE* FOR NOTHING.

BATMAN.
THAT CAN'T BE WHAT I THINK IT IS. YOU CAN'T HAVE BEEN STUPID ENOUGH TO HOLD ONTO--
THANK YOU, SCOTT. THAT WILL BE ALL.
BATMAN. WHATEVER HAS BROUGHT YOU HERE, YOU NEED TO TURN BACK NOW.
THAT WILL BE ALL.
BOOOOM

I wish I could go back to that moment and warn myself.
I write this journal for anyone foolish enough to pick up my trail.
Whatever you do, do not follow in my footsteps.
LIKE A COMPASS...
COMPUTER. RUN ALL VIBRATIONAL DATA THROUGH THE TOWER. WE SHOULD BE ABLE TO TRACK THE EXACT DIMENSIONAL FREQUENCY OF THE DARK ENERGY.
RECEIVING DATA...
IT'S TIME, THEN...
TIME TO SEE WHAT'S IN THE DARK ONCE AND FOR ALL.

I beg of you, whoever might be reading this, however many generations might have passed...
BATMAN, WHAT THE HELL HAVE YOU GOTTEN YOURSELF INTO THIS TIME...?
OH, I CAN TELL YOU THAT.
Do not follow the mystery of the metals.
THIS IS A MYSTERY THAT STRETCHES BACK TO THE DAWN OF TIME. IT'S BIGGER THAN ALL OF US.
AND IT SURE AS HELL IS BIGGER THAN YOU.
Some mysteries are best unsolved. Some doors best left unopened...
YOU DON'T UNDERSTAND. ALL THAT WAS JUST A CRUEL JOKE.

Because through them, all you'll find is horror.
YOU'RE JUST ANOTHER COUPLE OF PIECES IN BATMAN'S PUZZLE.
JUST LIKE ME.
HAHAHA HAHAHAHAHA HAHAHAHAAA HAHA
DARK DAYS THE FORGE
SCOTT SNYDER & JAMES TYNION IV writers
JIM LEE, ANDY KUBERT & JOHN ROMITA JR. pencils
SCOTT WILLIAMS, KLAUS JANSON & DANNY MIKI inks
ALEX SINCLAIR with JEREMIAH SKIPPER color STEVE WANDS letters
JIM LEE, SCOTT WILLIAMS & ALEX SINCLAIR cover
DAVE WIELGOSZ asst. editor
REBECCA TAYLOR associate editor
MARK DOYLE editor

DARK DAYS: THE CASTING № 1
cover by Jim Lee, Scott Williams and Alex Sinclair

In Cairo, they had called me an adventurer. In Athens they called me a philosopher.

But at my small museum in the quiet American city of St. Roch in the first decades of the twentieth century, I was an **archaeologist**.

The job itself never changed. The human story is a mystery told by a billion unreliable narrators, and for the duration of our species I have been nothing more than a **detective**.

THE EGYPTIAN WING

The Jewels of Nabu Kandhaqi Artifacts

←

THE TOMB OF CHAY-ARA

→

The mission was always the same. To carry forward the torch of discovery and reveal the secrets hiding in the darkest shadows.

The truth buried deep beneath millennia of human memory.

We had found them over many lifetimes, lurking out of sight in human history, unchanging, all-seeing.

We had long heard rumors of the Rhyming Demon of Camelot. Brothers who kept secrets and mysteries. The man as old as America. The grove of ancient humanoid plants. Of Sorcerers, Shining Knights, Cavemen, and Phantom Strangers of all stripes.

DARK DAYS

THE CASTING

SCOTT SNYDER & JAMES TYNION IV writers
JIM LEE, ANDY KUBERT & JOHN ROMITA JR. pencils
SCOTT WILLIAMS, KLAUS JANSON & DANNY MIKI inks
ALEX SINCLAIR & JEREMIAH SKIPPER color
STEVE WANDS letters
DAVE WIELGOSZ assistant editor
REBECCA TAYLOR associate editor
MARK DOYLE editor

None had ever thought to bring them together.

The Immortals.

I told them what I now knew. That our lives did not begin in Egypt. That they began generations earlier...The dark priest Hath-Set, he had not cast us down this path of reincarnation.
He had taken our pasts away from us.
He had obscured the truth behind the metal we wore in our wings and belts in service of something darker than any mortal could comprehend.
A figure stepped from the back. His voice was like the low rumble of thunder.
He spoke of the metal that changed everything, and the terrible being that it had brought forth.
The being from beyond all our understanding.
AL GHUL... DO YOU SEE WHAT I SEE?
YES, MS. SEWARD. I DO.
The being that was cast out, and sought desperately to return.
To tear down all that was light in the world, and drag it into the dark.
And the truth would hit us like lightning.

METHANA, GREECE.
SKWEEEEEEEEEE
KRAK
ENOUGH, AMPHITRION.
THIS HUMAN FALLS UNDER THE PROTECTION OF THEMYSCIRA.
I AM CERTAIN BATMAN WAS ABOUT TO POLITELY ASK FOR SAFE PASSAGE TO YOUR PATRON'S TEMPLE.
(I WAS GOING TO DO THAT NEXT.)
GRRRR
YOU SHOULD HAVE CALLED ME, BRUCE. THIS IS NOT A PART OF THE WORLD ANY MORTAL SHOULD WALK ALONE.

I PROMISE YOU, DIANA. I WOULDN'T BE HERE IF IT WEREN'T ABSOLUTELY NECESSARY. I'M SO DAMN CLOSE TO THE ANSWERS I NEED TO MAKE SENSE OF ALL I'VE SEEN...
I NEED SOMEONE WITH A GREATER PERSPECTIVE. SOMEONE WHO WAS THERE, WHEN THIS WAS ALL SET IN MOTION.
HOW DID YOU DISCOVER THE ENTRANCE TO THIS PLACE?
I FOUND A SCROLL FROM A DEATH CULT OF SMITH WORKERS BURIED IN THE ALPS, DATING BACK TO 200 A.D..
THEY DESCRIBED THE TREACHEROUS PATH TO THE GREAT FORGE OF HEPHAESTUS.
THEY WOULD THROW THEMSELVES IN THE FIRE WHEN THEY REACHED IT. THEY WOULD BECOME THE FUEL OF HIS CREATIONS THEMSELVES.
AND THAT'S WHAT YOU WISH, BRUCE? MAKE YOURSELF A SACRIFICE TO THE GODS? THERE ARE EASIER WAYS.
DIANA... I NEED TO SPEAK WITH HIM.
I'M SORRY, BRUCE...BUT YOU'RE TOO LATE.
THE GODS HAVE ABANDONED EARTH.
THEY HAVE BARRED THE GATES OF OLYMPUS BEHIND THEM.
WHY WOULD THEY LEAVE?
I SHOULDN'T BE TELLING YOU ANY OF THIS, BRUCE...
THEY BELIEVE A WAR IS COMING. A WAR THAT WILL NOT ONLY SHAPE THE EARTH, BUT THE COSMOS THEMSELVES. A CRISIS THAT WILL SHAKE THE VERY FIRMAMENT AND DOUSE THE LIGHT OF CREATION.
I CAN SEE IN YOUR EYES THAT YOU SEE IT COMING, TOO... HOW CAN YOU KNOW THE THINKING OF THE GODS?

I KNOW FEAR, DIANA. USE YOUR LASSO IF YOU THINK I'M HIDING ANYTHING FROM YOU. I'M NOT. THE FURTHER I FOLLOW THIS MYSTERY, THE MORE FRIGHTENED I BECOME. EVERY QUESTION LEADS TO MORE QUESTIONS.
I HOPED HEPHAESTUS WOULD BE ABLE TO SHINE A LIGHT INTO THE DARKNESS...
HE MAY STILL.
BEFORE I CAME TO YOU I HAD A VISION. THE GREAT HOUND, WAR-FORM OF HEPHAESTUS, SAT BEFORE ME WITH EYES OF FIRE AND TOLD ME I WOULD NEED TO COME HERE.
AND THAT I WOULD NEED TO GIVE YOU THIS.
THIS IS THE SUNBLADE, BRUCE. IT WAS CREATED FOR APOLLO AT THE DAWN OF HUMAN CIVILIZATION. ONE OF TWELVE WEAPONS, CREATED FOR EACH OF THE PANTHEON.
HUMANS ARE NOT MEANT TO KNOW THESE WEAPONS EVEN EXIST. LET ALONE WIELD THEM. THEY WERE FORGED WITH THE MOST POWERFUL METAL HEPHAESTUS EVER WORKED WITH.
HE CALLED IT THE EIGHTH METAL. IT IS NOT THE PURE FORM YOU SEEK. BUT IF YOU FOLLOW ITS LIGHT, IT WILL GUIDE YOU WHERE YOU NEED TO GO.
THE EIGHTH...
MARK MY WORDS, BRUCE. THE GODS HAVE GIVEN YOU THE SUN TO LIGHT YOUR WAY. DO NOT THROW IT AWAY FOR THE DARKNESS.
AND MOST OF ALL, BE WARY OF THE GODS. THEY HAVE THEIR OWN AGENDAS.
SO DO I.
THERE'S SOMETHING BEGINNING IN THE WORLD, AND SOMEHOW I'VE FOUND MYSELF AT ITS CENTER.
IT'S AS THOUGH I CAN HEAR A MESSAGE CALLING OUT FROM THE SHADOWS. BUT THE MORE I TRY TO LISTEN...

THE BATCAVE.
GOTHAM CITY.

"...THE MORE IT SOUNDS LIKE *LAUGHTER.*"

HEHEHEHEHE...

DO YOU SEE THE BIG PICTURE, YET, GREEN LANTERN, OR AM I GOING TO HAVE TO SPELL IT ALL OUT FOR YOU IN BIG PLAIN LETTERS?

WE'VE LISTENED TO *ENOUGH* OF YOUR INSANITY, JOKER. THERE ISN'T A SINGLE REASON WE SHOULD TRUST A DAMN WORD YOU SAY.

JUST THINKING ABOUT BATMAN LOCKING YOU AWAY DOWN HERE FOR GOD KNOWS HOW LONG...

TRUST ME, G.L. I'M GOING TO HAVE A *TALK* WITH BATMAN WHEN HE GETS BACK.

WHY SO ANGRY, DUKE? IS IT BECAUSE YOU'RE THE ALSO-RAN? THE NOT-GOOD-ENOUGH-TO-GET-THE-REAL-JOB ROBIN?

OR IS IT BECAUSE THE LAST TIME I SAW YOU I POISONED YOUR PARENTS PAST THE BRINK OF SANITY AND TRIED TO HAVE THEM SHOT RIGHT IN FRONT OF YOUR IMPRESSIONABLE EYES?

HAHAHA HAHHAHA HAHA!

I'LL... I'LL HURT YOU...

GET BACK, DUKE... YOU DON'T WANT TO MESS WITH THAT ENERGY FIELD!

HAHAHAHAHAHA... SEE, I HAVEN'T HAD FUN LIKE THIS IN AGES.

THAT'S HOW IT ALL STARTED, YOU KNOW. A BIT OF FUN. I CUT OFF MY FACE AND THOUGHT I'D KILL HIS WHOLE FAMILY. YOU KNOW HOW IT IS. GET RID OF THE KIDS AND REKINDLE THE ROMANCE. THE OLD FLAME.

BUT IT TURNS OUT HE **LIKES** THE BRATS, SO THERE I WAS TUMBLING DOWN INTO THE DARK OF THE DEEPEST CORNER OF THE BATCAVE, AND **SPLASH**, I MUST ADMIT, I THOUGHT I WAS A GONER...

"UNTIL I WOKE UP IN THE DARK...AND THIS SHIMMERING GREEN METAL WAS RUNNING ALL OVER ME...STITCHING MY WOUNDS BACK TOGETHER. PUTTING MY FACE BACK JUST RIGHT.

"AND THEN I SAW IT... TOWERING OVER ME... A MARKING ON THE WALL, OLDER THAN GOTHAM. OLDER THAN CIVILIZATION...

"THE BAT **BEHIND** THE BAT.

I NEEDED TO KNOW MORE... AND THERE WERE PEOPLE, THEY KNEW...THE OWLS KNEW...THAT LUNATIC CRAZY QUILT KNEW...

YOU SEE? IT WAS ALL A GREAT CONSPIRACY. THE PIECES PLANTED FOR GENERATIONS. BIRDS HAD BECOME BATS. LIGHT HAD BECOME DARK. SANITY HAD BECOME INSANITY.

IT WAS COMING. I COULD FEEL IT IN ME. EVEN WHEN I WASN'T MYSELF, I COULD **STILL** FEEL IT IN MY HEAD. AN ECHO IN THE SHADOWS CALLING THE REAL ME BACK TO THE SURFACE...

I'M SURE YOU KNOW WHAT I MEAN, DUKE. YOU MUST HAVE FELT IT, TOO. YOU'RE PROBABLY FEELING IT NOW...

THAT PESKY LITTLE FORCE FIELD SURE IS REACTING STRANGELY TO YOUR BODY, DON'T YOU THINK?

YOU DID THIS...I DON'T KNOW HOW, YOU KNEW...

THEN YOU'RE NOT LISTENING!

IT'S STILL IN ME. IT'S IN YOU. IT'S ALL AROUND US!

I JUST NEEDED TO CREATE A CIRCUIT TO ESCAPE, AND YOU DID THE JOB WONDERFULLY!

NO... WON'T LET YOU GET FREE...

DEFENSIVE MEASURES ACTIVATING.

CUTTING POWER TO SUB-CAVE ALPHA. SMILE PROTOCOL IN EFFECT.

SEE?! THE DARK IS COMING. HA!

GL! LIGHT UP THE ROOM! WE CAN'T LET HIM GET AWAY!

DAMMIT, I CAN'T...RING'S STILL SHORTING OUT. I DON'T KNOW WHAT THE HELL IS HAPPENING.

OH, I KNOW HOW THIS STORY IS GOING TO END.

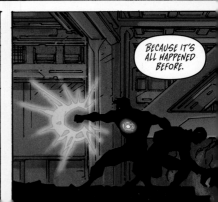

BECAUSE IT'S ALL HAPPENED BEFORE.

The Immortals spoke of the tribes at the dawn of man.

The arrival of the strange metal that would change everything, brought to this world by a tear in the fabric of reality, and the demon that rose from the dark and nearly conquered us all.

At first, we didn't believe. The scale of what they were telling us was too huge, too frightening. We set out to confirm their story. To find any evidence that it was all a lie.

But instead, we found countless paintings on every continent, hidden in the deepest cave systems. All telling the same dark story.

They spoke of the Hawk Tribe, where my story had truly begun, though I did not remember it. They spoke of the betrayal by the Judas of the birds...who sided with the demon.

The demon who took the sigil of the great and terrible **bat**. The plague bringer. The scourge of mankind.

My wife and I, we died fighting it back into the dark from whence it came. Shuttering the door between its world and ours.

That was the truth Hath-Set severed us from by recreating the scene millennia later. He, the emissary of the same dark forces that nearly fell humanity before it could begin.

Birds and Bats, forever at war.

The Immortals told us the metal was cursed. It needed to be eliminated, as its power came from the same darkness that begat this great destroyer.

But this strange metal, it had been so much more to us. It had brought us wonders, brought us wings, and countless lives.

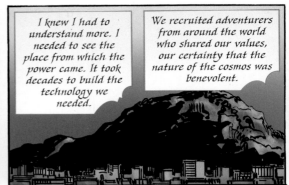

I knew I had to understand more. I needed to see the place from which the power came. It took decades to build the technology we needed.

We recruited adventurers from around the world who shared our values, our certainty that the nature of the cosmos was benevolent.

We wouldn't allow ourselves to be beaten down by the unknown.

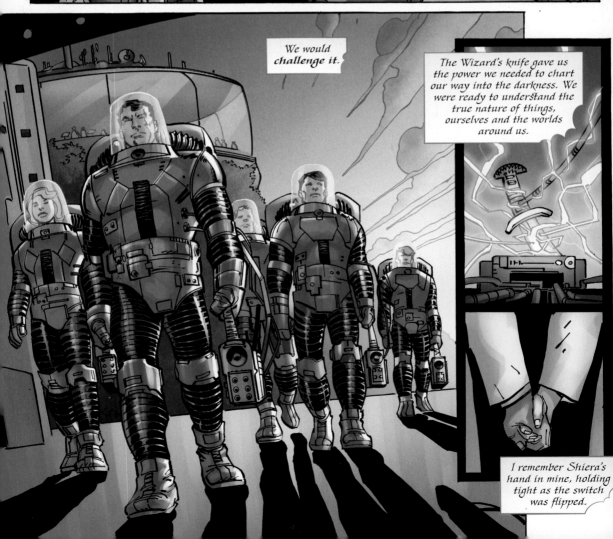

We would **challenge it.**

The Wizard's knife gave us the power we needed to chart our way into the darkness. We were ready to understand the true nature of things, ourselves and the worlds around us.

I remember Shiera's hand in mine, holding tight as the switch was flipped.

Then I remember the Earth shaking, as if it had been torn apart.
And the screaming.
As I stared into the darkness where Challengers Mountain had stood, I felt a chill down my spine...
And I saw the eyes of something great and terrible staring back at me through the abyss...
Eyes. Waiting in the dark.
Waiting for **something**.
Someone.

SONORAN DESERT.
ARIZONA.
COMPUTER. ACCESS THE SHADOW DRIVE. RECORD NEW AUDIO FILE.
I FEEL LIKE I'M RUNNING OUT OF TIME.
SIXTY MILES FROM THE COAST OF GREECE, THE SUNBLADE BEGAN TO VIBRATE IN REACTION TO AN UNKNOWN SOURCE THAT HAS LED ME HERE. TO A SECRET BASE OF UNKNOWN ORIGIN DEEP UNDER THE SONORAN DESERT.
SEARCHING FOR ANSWERS, AND ALL I FIND ARE MORE MYSTERIES. SEND AN ALERT TO **BLACK LIGHTNING.** I'LL NEED **THE OUTSIDERS** TO SCOUR THE SURROUNDINGS AND--
BATMAN.
YOU **MUST** TURN BACK.
DUBBILEX? THIS IS A **CADMUS** BASE?
NO, BATMAN. THAT IS WHAT IT **WAS.** WHAT IT HAS BECOME IS FAR DARKER. THE **DNA PROJECT** HAD TRACKED THE BEINGS WITH IT IN THEIR BLOOD. AND THEY BEGAN TO **ACTIVATE** THEM WITH A POWER SOURCE THEY DID NOT UNDERSTAND.
WHAT ARE YOU SAYING? WHAT CAUSED THIS?
THE **METAL** YOU SEEK IS CURSED, BATMAN. THE ENERGY IN IT IS ROILING AND DARK. EVERYTHING IT TOUCHES, IT CORRUPTS.
SEE FOR YOURSELF. SEE THE **DAMAGE** IT HAS WROUGHT.
TOO...WEAK... CANNOT HOLD THE PSYCHIC PROJECTION...
YOU MUST TURN BACK NOW. BEFORE IT CORRUPTS YOU, TOO...I FEEL ITS GRIP TIGHTENING ON YOU.
YOU NEED TO TELL ME WHERE THIS METAL IS...I NEED IT TO SEE WHAT'S COMING!

...NO, BATMAN...

...RUN...

HE FOUGHT SO BRAVELY TO PREVENT ME FROM TAKING MY BIRTHRIGHT. I ALMOST PITY THE CREATURE.

HELLO, BELOVED.

IT'S BEEN A LONG TIME SINCE "BELOVED."

WHAT ARE YOU DOING HERE, TALIA?

THE SAME THING AS YOU, I SUPPOSE. YOU SEEK SOMETHING OF GREAT POWER, AND IT ELUDES YOUR GRASP.

BUT NOTHING ELUDES THE GRASP OF THE DEMON, BRUCE.

WHAT DOES *RA'S AL GHUL* KNOW, TALIA?

AT THE DAWN OF THE TWENTIETH CENTURY, MY FATHER AND OTHERS OF HIS ILK CAME TOGETHER TO DISCUSS A GREAT MYSTERY. ONE OF THEM PRODUCED A POWERFUL *DAGGER* MADE FROM THE STRANGE METAL YOU SEEK.

MY FATHER SPENT DECADES TRYING TO REACQUIRE IT.

HE ULTIMATELY SUCCEEDED, PICKING IT FROM THE RUINS OF A PRIVATE MILITARY BASE IN THE ROCKY MOUNTAINS.

HE SUPPOSED THE RIGHT PEOPLE WOULD PAY GOOD MONEY TO TAP INTO ITS POWER.

SO, YOU'VE COME TO DO YOUR FATHER'S BIDDING.

NO, BATMAN. THERE HAVE BEEN SECRET BATTLES TO SUPPRESS THE POWER OF THIS METAL FOR DECADES. BUT ITS POWER HAS ONLY GROWN WITH TIME, TAINTING MORE AND MORE. *TRUE WAR* IS NOW INEVITABLE

YOU MUST KNOW THIS. YOU HAVE ONE OF THE POTENTIALS LIVING UNDER YOUR ROOF.

I CAME FOR THE KNIFE TO READY MYSELF FOR WAR. IT DARKENS DAY BY DAY, ITS TERRIBLE POWER GROWING.

I'VE HEARD RUMBLINGS... *LEVIATHAN* MOVING AGAINST YOU...THE GREAT *ASSASSIN* YOU'VE BROUGHT BACK INTO THE FOLD...

YOU HAVE NOTHING TO FEAR FROM THE *SILENCER*, BRUCE.

NOR FROM ME.

TALIA... WHAT IF I COULD OFFER YOU A TRADE...

THE EIGHTH FORM OF THE METAL FOR THE *NINTH*.

YOU WOULD TRADE LIGHT FOR DARKNESS? YOU WOULD GIVE ME THE POWER OF A GOD?

THE WORLD IS AT A MOMENT OF GREAT IMBALANCE...

I HELP THE MOTHER OF MY SON, THE DAUGHTER OF MY ENEMY, SO THAT SHOULD THE MOMENT COME WHERE I NEED TO CALL UPON HER FOR A GREATER FAVOR... PERHAPS SHE'LL ANSWER.

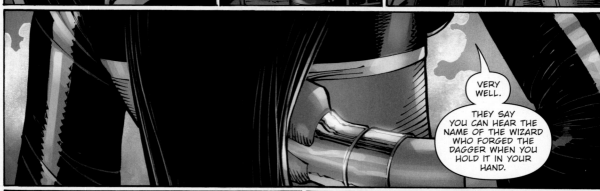

VERY WELL.

THEY SAY YOU CAN HEAR THE NAME OF THE WIZARD WHO FORGED THE DAGGER WHEN YOU HOLD IT IN YOUR HAND.

THAT IT CARRIES A SMALL PIECE OF *HIS* GREAT POWER.

THE POWER OF SHAZAM!

WE NEED LIGHT, DAMMIT!
I'M TRYING!
CLANG
JOKER, SHOW YOURSELF!
CLANG CRASH CLANG
I CAN'T LET HIM DIG ANY DEEPER. THERE'S NO TELLING WHAT WILL HAPPEN NEXT IF HE DOES...
HE DOESN'T UNDERSTAND HOW IMPORTANT HE IS. NOT LIKE I DO...
WHAT IS THAT THING...
IT'S...IT'S SOME KIND OF MACHINE.
I DON'T GET IT, JOKER...WHERE'S THE JOKE IN ALL OF THIS?
THIS ISN'T FUNNY!
GET AWAY FROM...
AAAGHHHH!!

DON'T YOU UNDERSTAND?!

THIS IS WHAT YOUR ALIEN BOSSES SENT YOU HERE TO STOP. IF HE USES THE MACHINE, THAT'LL BE THE END OF EVERYTHING!

NO!

UNNF!

OH, DUKE. I SEE WHY YOU'RE SO ANGRY. YOU'VE NEVER QUITE FIT IN HERE, HAVE YOU? NO MATTER HOW MUCH BATMAN PRETENDS YOU BELONG, LIKE THE GIANT PENNY OR THE T. REX. THERE'S SOMETHING DIFFERENT ABOUT YOU.

SHUT UP!

AREN'T YOU CURIOUS? ISN'T THERE A PART OF YOU THAT WANTS TO KNOW WHY BATMAN PICKED YOU? WHY I PICKED YOU?

DID YOU KNOW, AT GOTHAM MERCY HOSPITAL, THERE'S AN AUTOMATIC FLAG THAT GOES UP WHEN SOMETHING UNUSUAL IS DETECTED IN A BLOOD SAMPLE...

IT'S A KIND OF METAL TOXICITY, BUT THEY CAN'T REALLY TRACK ANY OF THE EFFECTS. BECAUSE IT SURE AS HELL ISN'T IRON. IT'S NOT EVEN MERCURY...

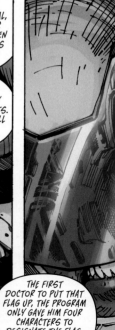

THE FIRST DOCTOR TO PUT THAT FLAG UP, THE PROGRAM ONLY GAVE HIM FOUR CHARACTERS TO DESIGNATE THE FLAG. BUT HE DID THE BEST HE COULD.

AND I'VE SEEN THAT FILE FOR BOTH YOU AND YOUR MOM.

M-E-T-A.

AND **BATMAN'S** BEEN TRACKING AS MANY OF YOU AS HE CAN FOR **YEARS** NOW. DON'T YOU **SEE**?

A WHOLE NEW GENERATION OF SUPERHEROES AND SUPER-VILLAINS! THE SOLDIERS OF THE WAR THAT WILL RIP THIS WORLD APART!

TELL THE COMPUTER TO PULL UP THE META-FILE SOMETIME. YOU CAN SEE THEM ALL FOR YOURSELF!

PEOPLE WITH THAT CRAZY METAL RUNNING THROUGH THEIR VEINS...YOU'VE SEEN WHAT IT CAN DO IN ITS OTHER FORMS...

CAN YOU IMAGINE WHAT IT DOES TO PEOPLE? WHAT AM I SAYING? OF **COURSE** YOU CAN.

I KNOW **THE TRUTH**, DUKE. I KNOW WHAT YOU ARE HERE TO DO. YOU'LL LET HIM **SEE** IN THE **DARK**.

THAT'S **ALL** YOU ARE, DUKE. THAT'S THE ROLE YOU'RE DESTINED TO PLAY.

YOU ARE **THE SIGNAL**.

AND I CAN'T ALLOW THAT. SO I'M GOING TO HAVE TO KILL YOU, NOW.

NO...I WON'T LET YOU...

AAHHH!

AND THE SIGNAL GOES DARK.

HAHAHAHAHAHAHA...

AND NOW, TO WRITE THE GRAND FINALE OF THIS SORDID TALE. SO WE CAN GET BACK TO THE GOOD STUFF.
BATS AND CLOWNS. NOT BATS AND BIRDS. THIS HAS GONE ON LONG ENOUGH.
YOU'RE DAMN RIGHT, JOKER.
HM?
RMMMBLL
THERE'S SOMETHING YOU PROBABLY SHOULD HAVE KNOWN BEFORE YOU KNOCKED ME INTO BATS' UNDERGROUND HANGAR.
I'M A DECORATED MEMBER OF THE UNITED STATES AIR FORCE.
YOUR STORY TIME IS OVER.
NO!

There was a time I believed that the world got a little better every time we solved one of the great mysteries.

When we mastered a law of nature with our wit and our science, I felt like we were marching onward and upward.

Toward the kind of utopia of science and wonder that first captured my imagination when I saw the Thanagarian ship crashing in my life as Khufu. They were scientists, we would discern. We thought they came bearing gifts and knowledge.

Now I know the reason they brought the Nth metal here. They came to warn us of what they **knew** was on the other side.

They didn't come to help us move forward into the light. They were here to stop us in our tracks, so the universe would never fall prey to the ambitions of a small world that even millennia later can barely get past its own moon.

This is the final entry in my journal. I believe I have found a way to penetrate the barrier of our reality and enter the dark myself.

I still believe, in my heart, that there is wonder and hope out there in the unknown, at the center of all this incredible power. But that hope seems more foolish with every passing day. I feel the encroaching darkness planting doubt deep in my soul.

The others, even my wife, believe that the mystery is and has always been a trap... A trap dragging us into nightmares, begging us to let those nightmares free and destroy our world.

And it is true. Our enemy has grown stronger than I ever could have imagined...they keep killing my spies, as I get closer to determining their plans.

I've done my best to avert their endgame...

I am entrusting this journal, and the terrible secrets with the family that has always been most **loyal** to the birds. With the command to hide it unless I fail and the beast comes again. Then and only then will the journal reveal itself.

They know how important this is. That they must stay far from the dark and frightening truth lurking under the world, trying to force itself through.

I stand with my torch, facing the dark. I believe I will find something out there. A glimmer of potential. But I know that I am likely wrong. That all I will find is the darkness itself.

I walk towards my end alone, so that no man could ever be foolish enough to follow.

HA! HAHAHAHAHAHAHAHA...
WHAT'S SO FUNNY?
IT'S HAPPENING AGAIN! NO MATTER WHAT I DO, IT JUST KEEPS ON COMING! EVERYTHING IS GOING BACKWARDS, AND NEITHER OF YOU UNDERSTAND!
YOU DON'T EVEN REALIZE THAT THIS TIME I WAS BEING THE GOOD GUY!
A DARK CRISIS IS COMING, AND HERE YOU ARE, TWO BRIGHT BURNING LIGHTS CALLING IT FORWARD!
GL... SOMETHING'S WRONG...
I MEAN, COME ON! HOW IS THAT NOT FUNNY!

IT'S LIKE I CAN FEEL SOMETHING GETTING CLOSER...
ALL THE PIECES ARE CONNECTED, AND THE PUZZLE ALWAYS COMES TOGETHER IN THE FORM OF A BAT.
NO...
NOOOO!
DUKE!
THE JOKER... WHERE DID HE...
JORDAN.

WHAT THE HELL DID YOU DO TO MY CAVE?
WHAT DID I DO?! THIS WAS THE JOKER!
YOU LET HIM OUT? DO YOU HAVE ANY IDEA--
--HOW MANY JUSTICE LEAGUE BYLAWS YOU'RE BREAKING FOR LOCKING UP ONE OF THE MOST DANGEROUS PEOPLE ON THE PLANET IN YOUR BASEMENT WITHOUT TELLING ANYONE? YEAH, BRUCE, I DO.
I NEEDED HIM.
FOR WHAT? TO FILL EVERY GAP IN THIS INSANE CONSPIRACY THEORY WITH LIES? SECRET METALS WITH INCREDIBLE POWER SHAPING HUMAN HISTORY...I MEAN, COME ON!
AND BASED ON WHAT YOU TOLD THE LEAGUE. YOU CAN'T EVEN BE SURE THAT WAS THE REAL JOKER!
BRUCE. WE NEED YOU TO EXPLAIN WHAT'S GOING ON HERE.
...I'VE SPENT A LONG TIME PUTTING THESE PIECES TOGETHER. FINDING WHAT I NEEDED TO LOOK BACK INTO THE DARK.
BACK?

I CALLED THIS MY *FINAL INVENTION.* IT WAS DESIGNED TO HELP ENSURE THIS CITY WOULD ALWAYS HAVE A BATMAN. BUT BEFORE IT WAS FINISHED, I DIED AT THE HANDS OF THE JOKER...

...AND THAT WOULD HAVE BEEN THE END OF MY STORY, IF NOT FOR THE METAL. IF NOT FOR THE DIONESIUM, I WOULD HAVE LOST MY LIFE, NOT JUST MY MEMORY. ULTIMATELY, I USED THE MACHINE TO RECONSTITUTE MYSELF.

"BUT THE METAL WAS STILL NESTLED IN THE CRACKS IN MY SKULL. AND WHEN THE MACHINE ACTIVATED...I SAW SOMETHING *IMPOSSIBLE.*

"IMPOSSIBLE VERSIONS OF MYSELF, DYING OVER AND OVER AGAIN.

NOTHING IN THE MACHINE I BUILT COULD HAVE GIVEN ME THOSE VISIONS. IT WAS THE METAL. THIS INCREDIBLE, POWERFUL METAL.

THIS METAL I COULDN'T ESCAPE IN ANY FACET OF MY LIFE. AS THOUGH IT WERE TARGETING ME, OVER AND OVER FOR SOME UNKNOWN REASON. AS THOUGH IT WANTED ME TO UNDERSTAND IT.

I BEGAN TO REBUILD THE MACHINE FROM THE GROUND UP. I WANTED TO LOOK INSIDE THE DARK, TO THE SOURCE OF THE METAL'S POWER. I KNEW THAT ONCE I DID, IT WOULD ALL COME TOGETHER. IT WOULD ALL MAKE *SENSE.*

WHATEVER YOU'VE BEEN DOING IN HERE CAUGHT THE ATTENTION OF THE *GUARDIANS OF THE UNIVERSE,* BATMAN.

AND DOESN'T THAT GIVE YOU PAUSE? WHY WOULD A MORTAL MAN ON A BACKWATER WORLD DOING A LITTLE BIT OF ARCHAEOLOGY REQUIRE INTERFERENCE BY INTERGALACTIC PEACEKEEPERS?

WHY DOES YOUR RING, THE MOST POWERFUL WEAPON IN THE UNIVERSE, COWER IN THE FACE OF A PURE STRAIN OF THIS STRANGE, IMPOSSIBLE METAL?

THE JOKER SAID YOU BROUGHT ME IN...TO STUDY ME LIKE SOME KIND OF EXPERIMENT.

THE JOKER *LIES,* DUKE. I NEVER TRIED TO SHAPE YOU. I ONLY WANTED TO BE THERE WHEN YOU DECIDED WHAT YOU WERE GOING TO BECOME.

THIS WAS SUPPOSED TO BE THE END OF ALL OF THIS. I HAVE THE DIMENSIONAL FREQUENCY OF THE ENERGY LOCKED...AND WITH THIS DAGGER, I HAVE THE POWER TO SEE THE TRUTH AT THE HEART OF THE MYSTERY.

WHOA... THAT DAGGER...IT'S DOING SOMETHING TO ME...

IT'S LIKE, I CAN SEE THE WHOLE MACHINE, STILL TOGETHER, MADE OF LIGHT...I SEE WHERE THIS BELONGS...HOW IT ALL FITS TOGETHER...

I CAN SEE WHERE THE *LIGHT* WAS...I DON'T KNOW HOW TO EXPLAIN.

THE JOKER SAID THIS WOULD HAPPEN...

HOW COULD HE KNOW?

HAL...I KNOW THIS MAKES YOU UNCOMFORTABLE. BUT THE *NIGHT* IS GETTING *BLACKER* EVERY MINUTE. AND THIS *EVIL* IS FAR OUT OF *SIGHT.*

YEAH, BATMAN. I KNOW MY OATH...

ALL RIGHT, KID. THIS DUPLICATE RING'S JUST A LOANER, OKAY? AND IF WHAT I'VE BEEN GOING THROUGH TODAY IS ANY INDICATION, THIS IS GOING TO HURT A *LOT.*

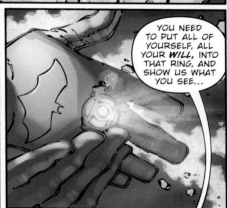

YOU NEED TO PUT ALL OF YOURSELF, ALL YOUR *WILL,* INTO THAT RING, AND SHOW US WHAT YOU SEE...

AAAAHHH...

WHOA...BATMAN IT'S ALL HERE. PSYCHO PIRATE'S MASK...THE OWL'S ELECTRUM
HYPER-ELASTIC MOLECULES. ANCIENT THEMYSCIRAN AND ATLANTEAN ARTIFACTS. RELICS OF ORDER AND CHAOS.
TOGETHER, WITH YOUR HELP, DUKE, THEY WILL SHOW ME THE WAY.
WHATEVER YOU SEE IN THERE, BRUCE... I'M TELLING THE GUARDIANS. IF THIS STUFF CAN AFFECT OUR RINGS, THERE'S NO TELLING HOW POWERFUL IT COULD BE.
I UNDERSTAND, HAL. AND THANK YOU.
There is a feeling you get at the end of an adventure.
You feel it in the anxious quickening in your heart. In every tentative footstep you take.
It's the fear of what you've done to bring you to that point. The knowledge that whatever mistakes you've made are yours to own from here into eternity.
It is the knowledge that there is **no** way back.

At the beginning, your story burned white hot with possibility. You felt the fire in your veins. The need to know. To explore. To understand.
And more than that, the knowledge that you can chart your own course toward that greater knowledge.
That you, and only you, control your destiny.
But with every step forward, your story cooled and hardened.
Pulling you inexorably toward a singular ending. An ending you can no longer choose.
An ending that chooses **you**.
BRUCE!
--FROM THE JOURNAL OF CARTER HALL
BRUCE... WHAT DID YOU SEE...?
DARKNESS...
WHAT?
I DON'T UNDERSTAND. I DID EVERYTHING RIGHT... BUT ALL I SAW WAS ***DARKNESS.***

NOW.
THREE-THOUSAND MILES BELOW GOTHAM CITY.
IT IS DONE. HE HAS STARED INTO THE ABYSS.
AND WE HAVE HIDDEN WHAT LIES WITHIN.
THE FINAL SEAL IS BROKEN.
AFTER ALL THESE GENERATIONS, THE SACRIFICE IS AT HAND.
LET US SEE THEM.
LET US SEE WHAT HE SHOULD HAVE SEEN, IF WE HAD NOT PREPARED HIM CORRECTLY...
THE DARK DAYS ARE OVER...

THE DARK KNIGHTS ARE COMING.

AND WITH THEM, THE TRUE FATHER OF BATMAN.

ANDY KUBERT BA

DARK DAYS: THE FORGE Nº 1
variant cover by Andy Kubert and Brad Anderson

DARK DAYS: THE FORGE № 1

variant cover by John Romita Jr., Danny Miki and Alex Sinclair

DARK DAYS: THE CASTING Nº 1
variant cover by Andy Kubert and Brad Anderson

DARK DAYS: THE CASTING N°1
variant cover by John Romita Jr., Danny Miki and Alex Sinclair

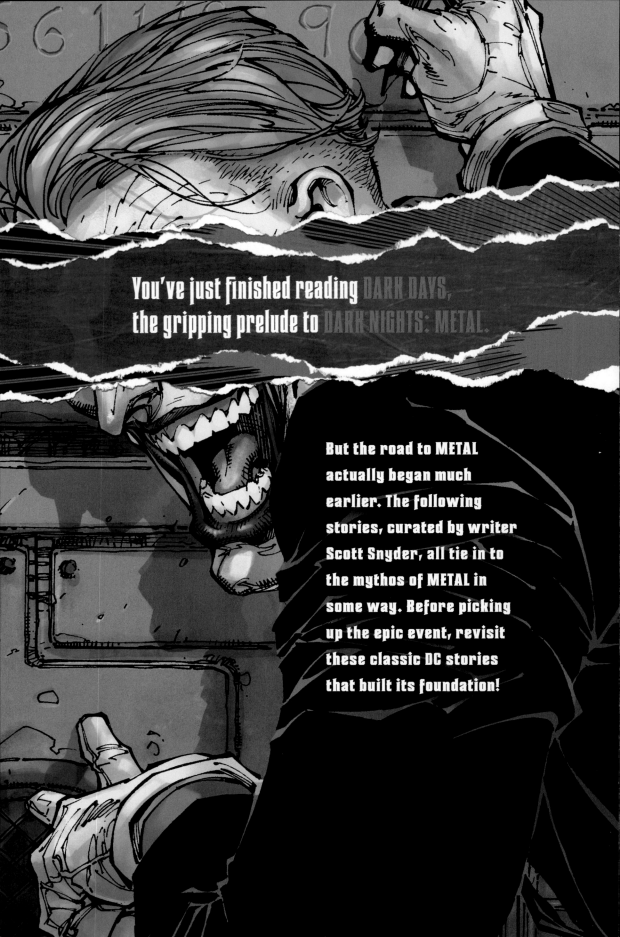

You've just finished reading DARK DAYS,
the gripping prelude to DARK NIGHTS: METAL.

But the road to METAL
actually began much
earlier. The following
stories, curated by writer
Scott Snyder, all tie in to
the mythos of METAL in
some way. Before picking
up the epic event, revisit
these classic DC stories
that built its foundation!

FINAL CRISIS № 6
cover by J.G. Jones

FINAL CRISIS № 7

cover by J.G. Jones

HURRY, SUPERMAN!
I CALCULATE WE HAVE EXACTLY 72.4 SECONDS BEFORE TIME BREAKS DOWN AND THIS SENTENCE BECOMES MEANINGLESS.
WHAT IS THIS, BRAINIAC 5?
FIRST I'M DRAGGED TO SOME HYPERWORLD WHERE PARALLEL REALITIES ARE BLEEDING TOGETHER
THEN HERE TO THE 31ST CENTURY.
I GAVE YOU MY HELP!
YOU PROMISED YOU COULD RETURN ME TO THE EXACT INSTANT I LEFT!
THAT WAS... BEFORE.
THIS CRISIS IN YOUR ERA IS OF ABSOLUTE MAGNITUDE, THREATENING ALL OF REALITY!
TIME AND SPACE ARE FRACTURING AROUND US, AS YOU'LL SHORTLY BECOME AWARE.
EXCUSE ME, ONE MOMENT.
...IT'S VITAL I REMEMBER THE EXACT SEQUENCE OF TILES TO OPEN THE LEGION OF SUPER-HEROES ARSENAL.
WHAT ARE WE DOING, BRAINIAC 5?
HOW DO I GET BACK HOME IN TIME TO STOP THIS?
LISTEN CAREFULLY...
IN 2960 THE CONTROLLERS DISCOVERED A WAY TO REFINE GUARDIANS WILL-POWERED TECHNOLOGY TO CREATE THE FINAL MACHINE.
THE ULTIMATE TECHNOLOGICAL ARTIFACT, SUPERMAN.

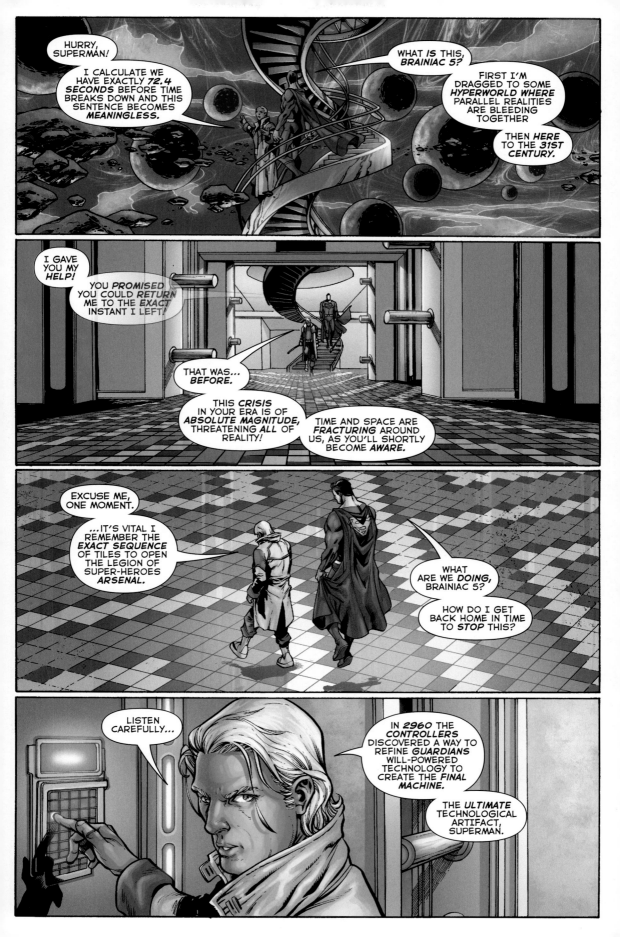

A MACHINE THAT TURNS THOUGHTS INTO THINGS.
WHY ARE YOU TELLING ME THIS?
IF A MACHINE LIKE THAT EXISTS, WHY CAN'T WE USE IT TO PROTECT OURSELVES NOW?
I'M AFRAID IT'S NOT THAT SIMPLE.
WHEN WE REALIZED THE HORRIFIC POTENTIAL OF A SINGLE STRAY THOUGHT TO COMPLETELY ALTER REALITY, WE SWITCHED THE DEVICE OFF PERMANENTLY.
WE SEALED THE MACHINE, FOR ALL TIME, IN A BLOCK OF INERTRON.
VERY FEW PEOPLE KNOW OF ITS EXISTENCE.
AND THE ONLY PERSON I'D TRUST TO EVEN LOOK AT IT IS YOU.
DO YOU UNDERSTAND WHAT I'M SAYING, SUPERMAN?
I'M ABOUT TO SHOW YOU THE GOD-WEAPON,
DO YOU UNDERSTAND?
MAKE IT FAST, BRAINIAC 5.
I'M BEING PULLED BACK TO MY OWN TIME.

GREAT KRYPTON.
IN CONTROLLER LANGUAGE ITS NAME IS GEH-JEDOLLAH-THE ABSOLUTE.
THERE'S NO TRANSLATION THAT REALLY MAKES SENSE.
WE CALL IT THE MIRACLE MACHINE.

BUT I CAN'T REACH IT!
I'M FADING...
YOU DON'T NEED TO REACH IT.
LOOK AT IT, SUPERMAN!
JUST LOOK!

...I NEVER THOUGHT I'D GET TO SEE THE EARTH FROM *SPACE*.

SURE IS A BEAUTIFUL THING.

PRETTY PATHETIC IT TOOK THE *END OF THE WORLD* TO SHOW ME WHAT WAS RIGHT.

WHAT I *HAVE*... THIS *TATTOO THING* I TOOK FOR GRANTED... THIS POWER...

IT'S A *GIFT*.

IT'S WHAT YOU *MAKE* IT, MR. RICHARDS.

AND AS CHAIRMAN OF THE *JUSTICE LEAGUE* I'M MAKING *YOU* AN HONORARY MEMBER AS OF NOW, WITH FULL PRIVILEGES *AND* RESPONSIBILITES.

*#%¢@#

HONORARY JUSTICE LEAGUE?

YEAH.

SO NOW YOU'RE TAKING ORDERS FROM *ME*.

WE HAVE CIVILIANS AND KIDS ON BOARD, AND WE NEED TO GET *RAY* BACK TO *EARTH* WITH THAT CIRCUIT OF YOURS...

...GUYS FIND ANYTHING *COOL* IN THE ARMORY?

LOTS OF WEIRD STUFF.

BUT MOM FOUND A STING-GUN FROM THE PLANET KORLL.

WAIT A MINUTE.

...WHAT'S THAT LIGHT, OUTSIDE?

DEAR GOD NO.

OH NO.

...I CAN'T LEAVE YOU GUYS...I CAN'T JUST...

MOM?

@$*¢@@$#

...EVER SINCE I BECAME A SUPERHERO.

PEACE WENT OUT THE WINDOW.

RAY, YOU HAVE TO LEAVE!

NOW!

THAT'S AN ORDER!

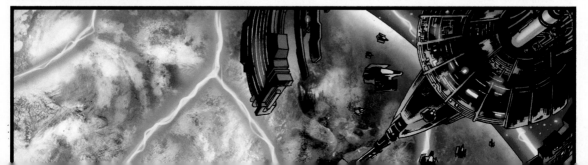

...OH, SUPERGIRL.
YOU'RE LOVING THIS!
PARKING
SUBMIT
YUKK
PARKING
PARK
HOW YOU DOING, HONEY?
GOT ABOUT A FULL HALF HOUR MIRACLO JUICE LEFT IN ME!
LOOKING GOOD.

WHAT IS THIS, TYLER, "ROMEO AND JULIET"?
SHUT UP AND HOLD THE LINE!
OUFF
SLUT.
GURRG

YOU?
CALLING ME A SLUT?
NNRRAA
...POWERS... FADE...MY GODS ARE FAR, FAR FROM HERE...BUT STILL I HEAR...
...THE VOICES OF THE NEW GODS...
...SNEERING... SHRIEKING...OVER AND OVER...IN HER HEAD...
DESAAD!
WHAT NAME IS THIS?
LET GO OF ME!

KUKK!
LET GO!
GNN
THAT'S IT.
YOU AND ME!
TOGETHER!
GTT!
SUPERGIRL!
I HAVE AN *IDEA.*
IT MIGHT TAKE THE *LAST* OF MY *MAGICAL ENERGY* BUT I THINK I CAN *STOP* HER!

WHAT ARE YOU!
TELL KALIBAK BEFORE I SMASH OUT YOUR BRAINS!
RRNNN
...MY FRIENDS...
...MY *FRIENDS,* SIR...CALL ME "TAWKY"...KRRF...
...MY NAME IN MY *OWN* TONGUE TRANSLATES AS... *"TAWNY"*...
...BUT DON'T...
...DON'T LET MY CULTURED TONES *DECEIVE* YOU...
TAWNY BITES!
AND KALIBAK IS A

GGGGAUUURRRRRR
GRAAUU!
I'LL BEAT YOU TILL YOUR BONES ARE PASTE!
KALIBAK WILL BEAT YOU
AND BEAT YOU
AND BEAT YOU BLIND!
...DON'T BE TOO SURE I WON'T JUST BREAK YOUR NECK!
HEEHEEHEEE
GOODY-GOODY-GOODY-GOODY
GREAT DARKSEID, SPARE YOUR SERVANT!
NO.
NO, I DON'T WANT TO HURT YOU.
BUT
I
AM
DARKSEID.

I WILL HURT YOU IF I MUST.
SUPERGIRL!
LEAVE THIS TO ME!
YOU AGAIN!
UH-HUH.
AND THIS TIME I'M COUNTING ON MY MAGIC LIGHTNING BEING STRONG ENOUGH TO TRANSFORM BOTH OF US!
SHAZAM!
RRRNN?
LOOK!
HAVE NO FEAR!
DARKSEID OWNS THE LIGHTNING...
GAUURRR
I BEG TO DIFFER.

HELP...
...HELP ME...
HELP
NO "HELP."
BE NOT STRONG.
HHHH
*
WHAT HAVE I DONE? OH NO, WHAT HAVE I DONE?
OH GOD, I DIDN'T MEAN THIS.
I DIDN'T MEAN ANY OF THIS.
SHH
IT WASN'T YOU. IT WASN'T YOU, MARY.
I CAN NEVER SAY IT AGAIN.
NEVER SAY THE WORD NEVER SAY IT EVER.
TELL 'EM WE SECURED THE BRIDGE, BRING UP THE...
...SECOND WAVE.
ALGO SE ACERCA
COMO EL SONIDO DE UNOS CABALLOS

...HURRN... LEGENDARY TIGER TEA, AS I WAS SAYING.
CONFERS THE STRENGTH OF TEN.
AT LEAST FOR...HRR...A LITTLE WHILE.
I'M SORRY WE ALL HAD TO MEET UNDER SUCH APPALLING CIRCUMSTANCES, BUT...
HRRN
DO YOUR WORST, GENTLEMEN.
?

...YOU ARRIVED IN YOUR *BOOM TUBE*, SO YOU MAY NOT HAVE SEEN WHAT IT'S *LIKE* OUT THERE.

THIS IS THE *LAST REDOUBT*...

NOTWITHSTANDING THE FACT THAT THERE ARE POTENTIALLY *NO MORE* THAN 1 1/2 BILLION FREE *HUMANS* ALIVE ON THIS PLANET, YOU SAY YOU CAN HELP WITH A *SOLUTION*, MR. NORMAN.

I SAY YOU CAN START WITH *THIS*.

THE SAME WARNING SIGN APPEARED EVERYWHERE ALL AT ONCE...CROP CIRCLES...CAVE PAINTINGS...

BEFORE ALL THIS.

SO THIS THING WE *PAINTED* ON OUR HEAD?

IT APPEARS TO BE A *LETTER* FROM THE *ALPHABET* OF THE *NEW GODS*.

A LIVING *SYMBOL* THAT MEANS "FREEDOM FROM RESTRICTION"... AND PROTECTS AGAINST *ANTI-LIFE*.

HM.

WHITE KING.

THE SHIELDS ARE *HISTORY*.

COUNTDOWN HAS BEGUN.

GUESS I'LL HAVE TO GET *BACK* TO YOU ON THAT ONE, MISTER NORMAN.

BLACK GAMBIT STATUS.

DID I TELL YOU ABOUT CHECKMATE'S *ENDGAME* IF THE SUPERHEROES *FAILED*, IF *HOPE* RAN OUT?

"THAT DAY HAS COME."

...SONNY.

MOTHER BOXXX SAYS YOU'RE FROM A..."LATERAL UNIVERSE"?

MOTHERBOXXX KNOWS TOO MUCH.

MAYBE THAT'S WHAT *YOU* CALL IT.

SONNY SUMO WENT BACK IN *TIME* AND DIED A HAPPY MAN IN *FEUDAL JAPAN.*

I STUMBLED THROUGH A HOLE IN *MY* LIFE, INTO *HIS* LIFE.

WITH THE END OF THE WORLD AT MY HEELS.

YOU WERE *SENT* HERE, SONNY.

ME, I DON'T GENERALLY GET INTO *FIGHTS...*

WE HAVE *NEVER* BEEN IN A FIGHT EITHER.

MOST OF OUR POWERS ARE *COSMETIC!*

EH!

THIS IS *IT!*

YOU *HAVE* TO TELL *AQUAZON* HOW MUCH I LOVE HER, KEIGO.

TELL HER I'VE *ALWAYS* LOVED HER, LIKE THE TREE LOVES TO *GROW*, LIKE THE SUN LOVES THE *DAY...*

DOOMSDAY IS COMING, TEN MINUTES TOPS!

TELL HER *YOURSELF.*

MAKE A DATE.

OH, THIS IS *TERRIBLE*.

I CAN'T SEEM TO TELL *SONIC LIGHTNING FLASH* HOW I *FEEL* ABOUT HIM.

I'M STILL *TOO SHY!*

WAIT UNTIL WE'VE SAVED THE WORLD!

THEN TELL HIM!

SO, TEAM...

LANTERN BOY, *YOU* GOT THAT *RAY THING* COMING OUT OF YOUR CHEST.

YOU CAN SCREAM YOURSELF RAW, *YOU* CAN *SWIM* LIKE A *!**@¢#!*

SUPERBAT, YOU NEVER TOLD ME WHAT *YOUR* POWER WAS....

I HAVE THE GREATEST POWER OF *ALL*, MISTER MIRACLE.

I AM *SO RICH* I CAN DO *ANYTHING*.

...SUBMIT OR WE GUT THE BRATS.
NO. NO.
JEFFERSON! OLLIE! DON'T DO THIS.
YOU SAVED MY FAMILY, DUDE!
LIGHTNING MAN!
SHOW ME THAT GUY!
ALL IS ONE IN DARKSEID.
ACCEPT ANTI-LIFE AND YOU'LL SEE.
SUBMIT.
AWWW $@"%$
NAAAARRR
ALL IS ONE IN DARKSEID.
DON'T DO THIS!
IT'S ME, OLIVER! I LOVE YOU!
I LOVE YOU SO MUCH!
GNNN
LOVE IS PAIN.
ANTI-LIFE IS THE ANESTHETIC.
SUBMIT.
NO!
YOU LET HER ALONE, YOU HEAR?!
AUUUGHH!!

STATION! VOICE ACTIVATE!
BLACK CANARY!
GRAVITY OFF!
THE CIRCUIT!
THE TATTOO JAMS THEIR SIGNAL!
YAAA!
...ANTI-LIFE... ANTI-LIFE'S SO EASY...
LOOK AT ME, OLIVER QUEEN!
LOOK AT ME AND FIGHT, DAMN IT!
SNAP OUT OF IT!
NOW!
...GNN...

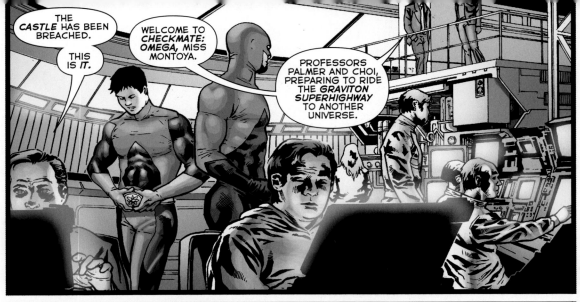

THE *CASTLE* HAS BEEN BREACHED.

THIS IS *IT*.

WELCOME TO *CHECKMATE: OMEGA,* MISS MONTOYA.

PROFESSORS PALMER AND CHOI, PREPARING TO RIDE THE *GRAVITON SUPERHIGHWAY* TO ANOTHER UNIVERSE.

HEY GUYS.

BETTER YOU THAN ME.

RAY PALMER, *THE ATOM,* HI.

PROFESSOR *RYAN CHOI,* ALSO KNOWN AS THE ATOM.

RAY, I NEED A *NEW NAME.*

THIS IS EMBARRASSING.

HERE IN *ROOM 90,* OUR PSYCHICS ARE ATTEMPTING TO *PURGE* THE HUMAN MASS CONSCIOUSNESS OF THE *ANTI-LIFE EQUATION.*

AND HERE, OUR *MYSTICS* ATTEMPT TO CONTACT *THE SPECTRE* IN THE AFTERWORLDS.

NAME SOUND FAMILIAR?

YOU HAVE A VERY UP-TO-DATE *DOSSIER.*

WHAT DO YOU WANT ME TO *SAY?*

SO WHAT GOES ON OVER *HERE?*

NOTHING.

IT'S THROUGH *THIS WAY,* MISS MONTOYA.

THIS IS WHERE THE BLACK GAMBIT WILL BE PLAYED.
THE OMEGA OFFENSIVE.
I'D LIKE YOU TO MEET LORD EYE.
WHAT?
ENOUGH OF THIS SENSORY %$%@$ OVERLOAD!
THERE'S NOTHING LEFT OUT THERE!
IN CASE YOU HADN'T NOTICED, IT'S ALL OVER FOR THE HOME TEAM!
we live within a multiverse of possibilities, miss montoya.
the choices we make decide worlds.
you have unprecedented levels of law enforcement experience--with particular regard to superhuman and crime-fighting activities, renee.
you are the template for something new.
we have already identified a target earth into which we will make our retreat.
if professors palmer and choi are successful, we will core through the bulk into a parallel universe.
we want you to lead the global peace agency that will establish the remnants of this world on another.
WAIT A MINUTE.
SAY THAT WHOLE BIT AGAIN.

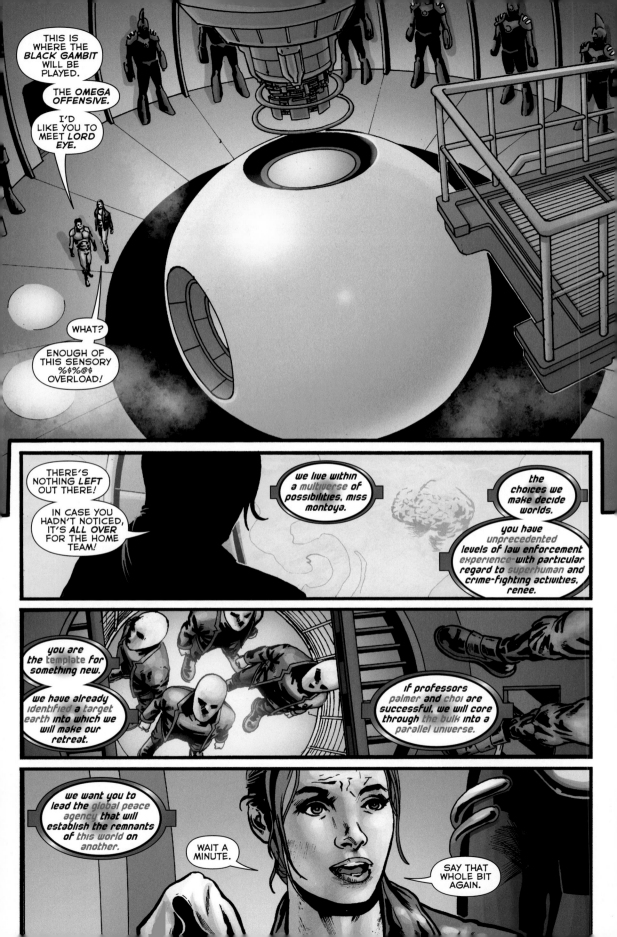

AMAZING.

HOW DOES HE KEEP THEM ALIVE?

...I *HATE* YOU, LUTHOR, DON'T *EVER* FORGET IT.

BUT THEY MADE ME WATCH MY OWN DEAR DAUGHTER SUBMIT TO THE "ANTI-LIFE EQUATION" AND *THAT* WAS THE *LAST STRAW.*

THE *VERY* LAST STRAW.

TALK *FAST,* LIBRA'S RIGHT BEHIND ME.

THE HELMETS ARE *MAD HATTER* DESIGN, PRACTICALLY MEDIEVAL.

I CONVERTED MY *WATCH* INTO A SHORT-RANGE *SIGNAL JAMMER.*

GOOD.

THEY FINALLY ALLOWED ME TO POWER UP MY *WARSUIT* IN ANTICIPATION OF TODAY'S "BATTLE."

CHARITABLE OF THEM.

...CALCULATOR WILL DIE THERE *FOREVER,* PROTESTING HIS INNOCENCE...

...BEGGING *FORGIVENESS.*

READY?

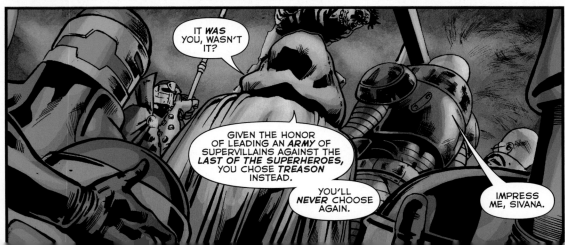

IT *WAS* YOU, WASN'T IT?

GIVEN THE HONOR OF LEADING AN *ARMY* OF SUPERVILLAINS AGAINST THE *LAST OF THE SUPERHEROES,* YOU CHOSE *TREASON* INSTEAD.

YOU'LL *NEVER* CHOOSE AGAIN.

IMPRESS ME, SIVANA.

EASY.

YOU.

///???///

LIBRA, THE MAN WHO BECAME THE *GLOVE PUPPET* OF THE GODS. A HOLLOW VESSEL.

I'LL SHOW YOU *BALANCE*...

HMMPH

AND THAT'S A CLASSIC "WE HAVEN'T HEARD THE LAST OF HIM!" IF *EVER* I SAW ONE.

THIS IS A WAR AGAINST *LIFE*, SIVANA.

I'M SOMEWHAT *FOND* OF LIFE, FOR ALL ITS UPS AND DOWNS....

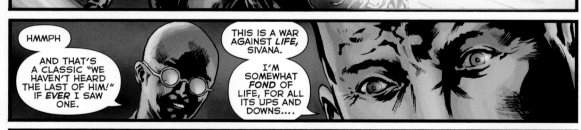

MEH! MEH! SENTIMENTAL MEH!

...THEY'LL HEAR *YOUR* VOICE AS THE VOICE OF *DARKSEID* IF YOU SPEAK INTO *THIS*.

DON'T *SHOUT*, YOU'LL BREAK IT.

...AT RELATIVISTIC SPEEDS AS YOU KNOW SPACE, TIME, LIGHT, IT ALL RUNS TOGETHER AND BECOMES *ONE THING.*

BEYOND THE SUPERLUMINAL BARRIER, MATTER CONVERTS TO *PURE INFORMATION.*

I WAS SENT BACK FROM *BEYOND* THAT BARRIER *KNOWING* THINGS.

I KNOW WHAT I HAVE TO *DO* TO STOP DARKSEID THIS TIME.

AND I NEED YOUR HELP.

...NOW THAT *JAY'S* HERE, WE'RE *READY.*

MY GOD, IT'S GOOD TO *SEE* YOU BOYS.

YOU TOO, JAY.

JAY, I KNOW I CAN TRUST *YOU* TO TAKE CARE OF *IRIS* UNTIL WE GET BACK.

AND WE *ARE* COMING BACK.

I'VE RUN HOLES IN MY BOOTS FROM *WATCHTOWER* TO *WATCHTOWER* UNTIL ONE BY ONE THEY FELL TO THE *ANTI-LIFE EQUATION.*

I SEARCHED THE COUNTRY *UPSIDE-DOWN* FOR JOAN AND LINDA AND THE KIDS AND I FOLLOWED *YOUR* TRAIL HERE, BARRY.

JUST TELL ME WHAT YOU NEED ME TO DO.

I KNOW YOU'LL FIND JOAN SOON.

WE'LL ALL BE REUNITED.

IF I CAN'T MAKE THIS WORK, WALLY, IT'S DOWN TO *YOU.*

THE BLACK RACER DIDN'T JUST *GIVE UP* CHASING ME.

HE WON'T STOP UNTIL HE *CATCHES* ME.

BARRY, I THINK I MET THIS GUY BEFORE WHEN HE WAS CALLED THE *BLACK FLASH.*

I *OUTRAN* HIM.

HEH.
I BET YOU DID.
PLACES, EVERYBODY! HERE *HE* *COMES.*
AND WE'RE GOING TO *USE* HIM.
DARKSEID IS SITTING AT THE CENTER OF A PERSONAL *SINGULARITY.*
NOTHING, NOT EVEN LIGHT CAN ESCAPE FROM HIS PRESENCE.
TO *GET* TO HIM WE'LL HAVE TO RUN FASTER THAN WE EVER HAVE BEFORE.
ON YOUR MARKS, WALLY.
GET SET...
...GODSPEED...

I WONDERED WHEN YOU WOULD SHOW YOURSELF.
STOP SKULKING IN THE SHADOWS.
ACCEPT THAT THE EQUATION HAS SOLVED THE HUMAN PROBLEM.
COME OUT.
EMBRACE ANTI-LIFE AND BE WHOLE.
DARKSEID.
YOU LOOK LIKE I FEEL.
YOU SHOULDN'T HAVE SHOT ORION.
IT WAS ORION'S DESTINY TO FALL IN "FINAL BATTLE."
SPLINTERED LIKE LIGHT THROUGH A PRISM IN AN INFINITE NUMBER OF DEATHS.
AND ON THE WAY HE WOUNDED YOU, BEYOND REPAIR, DIDN'T HE?
A ROTTEN CARCASS OF A GOD, CRAWLING INTO THE SEWER TO DIE.
I MADE A VERY SOLEMN VOW ABOUT FIREARMS.
BUT FOR YOU, I'M MAKING A ONCE-IN-A LIFETIME EXCEPTION.
A GUN AND A BULLET, DARKSEID.
IT WAS YOUR IDEA.

RADION. TOXIC TO YOUR KIND.
I SEALED THE BULLET THAT KILLED ORION IN MY BELT FOR INSPECTION.
BUT.
DO I MAKE MYSELF CLEAR?
LITTLE MAN.
CAN YOU OUTRACE THE OMEGA SANCTION?
THE DEATH THAT IS LIFE!
TRY ME.
RRRAAA!
HH.
GOTCHA.

HE'LL HEAR US, JIMMY.

WHEREVER HE IS, I KNOW HE'LL HEAR US.

INITIATE BLACK GAMBIT.

...DID YOU FEEL THAT?

I BROUGHT MY PEOPLE THROUGH FIRE AND TERROR; I SAVED THE BEST OF THEM.

BUT YOU, BEING HERE...

WE DIE IF WE'RE TOGETHER.

NO MATTER HOW FAR DOWN WE GO!

IT NEVER SEEMS TO GET CLOSER, HAL!

METRON, I CAN'T COORDINATE THIS!

IT'S ALL HAPPENING AT ONCE.

I KNOW I WAS EXILED IN THE DARKNESS WITH THESE GERM-PEOPLE FOR A REASON, BUT THIS...

RING POWER AT 19%

EVEN IF WE BURN OUT, EVEN IF WE DIE TRYING, KYLE.

RING POWER AT 19%

WE WILL NOT ABANDON OUR PEOPLE TO THAT!

EVERYTHING'S GONE SO QUIET.

IF ONLY BILLY WAS HERE.

IF ONLY HE COULD SEE US NOW.

WE WON'T GIVE IN.

WE CAN MAKE HIM PROUD, FREDDIE...

DON'T YOU UNDERSTAND?
I'D RATHER DIE AND BE REBORN IN A NEW LIFE.
MAYBE THEN YOU'LL LOVE ME AGAIN.
THAT'S NOT FAIR!
NIX UOTAN.
OBSERVE.
UNNH
HE'S POISONED THE ROOT.
HE'S BROKEN THE WORLD.
I NEED SOME HELP OVER HERE!
YOUR ARRIVAL INAUGURATES THE FIFTH WORLD.
THE AGE OF MEN AS GODS.
THESE NEW HUMANS FACE A GREATER MENACE THAN DARKSEID IF THEY BREACH THE BLEED WALL.
...WONDER WOMAN INFECTED THEM.
PEOPLE ARE LOSING THEIR POWERS AND DYING!
...I NEED TO GET BACK TO MY WIFE... PLEASE... I PROMISED...
BLACK GAMBIT IN PLAY.
LOOK!
UP IN THE SKY...
LOOK THERE!

KAL-EL?

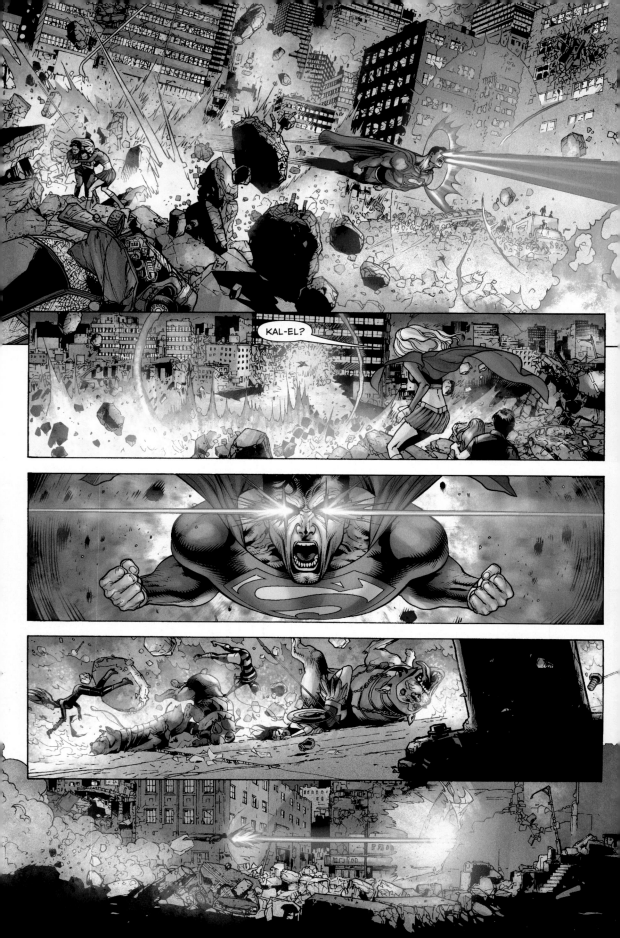

OH GOD, WHAT'S HAPPENING TO THE SKY?!
LOOK WHAT THEY'VE DONE TO THE SKY.
HOW CAN WE STOP THIS?!
NOBODY CAN STOP THIS.
WE'RE POWERLESS.
THIS IS THE END OF THE WORLD.
DAD?

YOU HAVE BEEN READING

HOW TO MURDER THE EARTH

GRANT MORRISON SCRIPT

JG JONES • CARLOS PACHECO • DOUG MAHNKE • MARCO RUDY • CHRISTIAN ALAMY • JESUS MERINO ART

JG JONES COVER   **ALEX SINCLAIR & PETE PANTAZIS** COLORS
ROB CLARK JR. LETTERING   **ADAM SCHLAGMAN** ASSOCIATE EDITOR   **EDDIE BERGANZA** EDITOR

THE END IS NIGH!

SIR. UPDATES ON THE *RED SKIES* CRISIS.

JUSTICE LEAGUE DATA HAS BEEN CONFIRMED BY *INDEPENDENT* SCIENCE REPORTS FROM THE *LHC.*

THE LATEST DISTURBANCES HAVE BEEN TRACED TO...AH...*GRAVITON* IMPACTS...

GRAVITONS ARE...

I ACTUALLY DO *KNOW* WHAT THEY ARE AND WHAT IT *MEANS*, COURTNEY, THANK YOU.

THANK YOU *ALL.*

NOW IF YOU'LL *EXCUSE ME*, LADIES AND GENTLEMEN.

MY DINNER WITH THE *ATLANTEAN FOREIGN SECRETARY* IS AT 6 P.M.

I'D APRECIATE SOME TIME *ALONE.*

BRAINIAC: VATHLO PRIME!

AFFIRMATIVE. MEGASONIC ALARM RECORDED AT 4:45 P.M.

I *HEARD* IT: *COVER* FOR ME: *ONE* HOUR.

AFFIRMATIVE.

I HAVE *BUSINESS* TO ATTEND TO...

...AT MY *OTHER* JOB.

THAT MUSIC!
GREAT KRYPTON, NUBIA!
THE ENTIRE UNIVERSE IS SHAKING!
WHAT IS THAT MUSIC?
LIKE I'VE KNOWN IT ALL MY LIFE: SO SAD, SO HOPEFUL, SO BRAVE...
THE MUSIC OF THE SPHERES.
THE SOUND OF THE TIDES OF THE INFINITE, BREAKING ON OUR MORTAL STRAND.

THE WONDER WOMEN OF AMAZONIA BRING ONLY ANTI-WAR TECHNOLOGY INTO THE WORLD.
BUT THE WONDER HORN WAS A GIFT FROM THE UNIVERSALS IN MYTHIC TIME BEFORE TIME.
TO BE USED ONLY ONCE, WHEN ALL ELSE HAS FAILED.
WHATEVER IT IS...
...SOMETHING'S RESPONDING!
AND BEARING A VESSEL.
SURGING ON A FOAM OF GRAVITONS, LIKE SOME NEW ARGO.
ITS CARGO NOT GODS.
NOT MONSTERS.
BUT HEROES.

...HEROES?

I DON'T %#$@%$# BELIEVE THIS.

A WHOLE %#$@%$ MULTIVERSE AND THEY ALL LOOK LIKE YOU GUYS?

MINUS THE SWEARING.

NAME'S CAPTAIN MARVEL: WE'RE HERE TO RECRUIT THE SUPERMEN OF THE MULTIVERSE ON A LIFE-OR-DEATH MISSION OF COSMIC PROPORTIONS!

I ENJOY SWEARING WHEN I FEEL THE SITUATION DEMANDS IT.

THE QUESTION.

GLOBAL PEACE AGENT.

THE WATCHTOWER.

WHEN SPACETIME FOLDED DOWN, THIS WAS *EVERYTHING* WE COULD SALVAGE.

BEYOND THESE WALLS, THERE'S NOTHING LEFT THAT ISN'T THE FOREVER PIT *DARKSEID* DRAGGED US ALL INTO.

A CRUMBLING SHARD FROM A *PARALLEL UNIVERSE* COLLIDED WITH US THIS MORNING... IF THE UNENDING *DARKNESS* CAN BE CALLED "MORNING" ANYMORE.

THIS ONE BROUGHT THE *METAL MEN* FROM *EARTH-44*, AND THEIR HUMAN LEADER "*DOC*" TORNADO.

WHEN OUR *MAGNETIC FIELD* SENT THEM *BERSERK*, THEY ATTEMPTED TO COMMIT "*TECHNOCIDE*" AND THE *TROPHY ROOM* WAS WRECKED.

IRREPLACEABLE MEMENTOES WERE LOST *FOREVER*.

SO WE ASSEMBLED WHAT *REMAINED* AND LOADED IT INTO THIS *ROCKET.*

MY NAME IS *LOIS LANE.*

THE *FINAL EDITION* OF THE *DAILY PLANET* ROLLED OFF THE PRESSES TODAY.

THE STORY OF THE *DEATH OF BATMAN.*

AND WHAT WE *STOOD* FOR.

AND HOW WE FOUGHT FOR WHAT WE *BELIEVED* IN, UNTIL THE *VERY END.*

I WROTE THE LAST STORY.

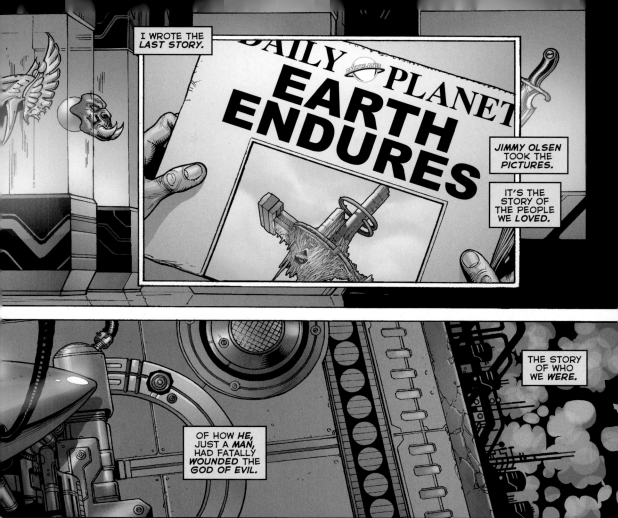

DAILY PLANET

EARTH ENDURES

JIMMY OLSEN TOOK THE *PICTURES.*

IT'S THE STORY OF THE PEOPLE WE *LOVED.*

THE STORY OF WHO WE *WERE.*

OF HOW *HE,* JUST A *MAN,* HAD FATALLY *WOUNDED* THE *GOD OF EVIL.*

CALL IT A MESSAGE IN A BOTTLE.

MAYBE *SOMEONE,* SOMEWHERE, WILL *FIND* IT.

AND READ THE STORY OF THE *FINAL CRISIS*.

DARKSEID.

YOU TURNED YOUR BACK AND I *WRECKED* YOUR WORLD.

I ROBBED YOUR PEOPLE OF THEIR *POWERS,* THEIR *HOPES,* THEIR *FUTURE,* *THEMSELVES.*

WHAT WILL YOU DO WHEN YOUR *FRIENDS,* YOUR *ENEMIES,* YOUR *LOVER,* ARE ALL DARKSEID?

WHEN THERE IS ONE *BODY.* ONE *MIND.*

ONE *WILL.*

ONE *LIFE* THAT IS DARKSEID.

WILL YOU BE THE ENEMY OF ALL EXISTENCE, THEN?

WHAT IRONY THAT WILL BE, SON OF KRYPTON.

HAHA HA HAHA!

MONSTER! WHAT HAVE YOU DONE!

KILL ME, SUPERMAN.

KILL THE FRAIL OLD MAN UPON WHOSE SOUL DARKSEID FED AND FATTENED!

HOW CAN YOU HURT A FOE MADE OF PEOPLE?

...I RECOGNIZE YOUR DNA.

...TURPIN? DAN TURPIN?..

OF ALL THE PEOPLE YOU COULD HAVE CHOSEN. BATMAN...

HE WOULD HAVE RESISTED LONGER THAN I WISHED!

TURPIN STRUGGLED JUST ENOUGH TO NURTURE ME BEFORE HIS SURRENDER!

KILL HIM.

AUUGH!

KILL ME AND YOU KILL EVERYTHING!

IT IS ALREADY OVER.
THE SUN HAS SET FOREVER.
THERE IS A BLACK HOLE WHERE MY HEART SHOULD BE.
NOW, SUPERMAN.
ARE YOU READY TO JOIN BATMAN IN OBLIVION?
CAN YOU OUTRACE THE OMEGA SANCTION?
MAYBE I WON'T HAVE TO.
YOU DIDN'T GET ALL OF US, DARKSEID.
IT'S NOT OVER YET.
AND THEN IT SEEMED AS IF THE SUN HAD RISEN IN THE WEST.
OBEY DARKSEID
AS IF THE DAWN WAS MADE OF LIGHTNING.
AND THE APPROACHING THUNDER BECAME THE ROAR OF A GUNSHOT YET TO BE.
OBEY DARKSEID
DEATH'S HOTONOURHEELS, BARRY!
HE'S GAINING ONUS!
MUSN'T LETHIMCATCH US!
NOT YET!

FROM HERE, WHERE HE NO LONGER EXISTS, ORION CANNOT SEE ME.
AS ALL TIME BECOMES ONE TIME, THE TIME HAS COME TO STRIKE.
TAKE AIM.
THOSE OMEGAFINDER BEAMSWILL FOLLOWUS UNTILTHEY CONNECT!
ATLIGHT SPEEDTIME STOPS!
FLASH FACT.
WE'RE APPROACHING ANEVERENDING INSTANT.
THEULTIMATE STOPSIGN!
HAVETOREACH SUPERLUMINAL VELOCITY!
SAVE YOURSELF, WALLY!
THINKI'DLEAVE YOUTODOTHISON YOUROWN?
TOGETHER, BARRY!
WE'REGOING INTOGETHERANDWE'RE COMINGBACKTOGETHER!
BARRY ALLEN?
THE TERMINAL MOMENT IS HERE.
NO.
NOT YOU.

I COME TO ALL!
EVEN YOU!
THIS IS THE STORY OF HOW THE FLASHES OUTRAN DEATH, THE BLACK RACER.
ON SEA-STORM!
THE STORY OF ARTHUR OF ATLANTIS, PROPHESIED TO RETURN IN HIS PEOPLE'S TIME OF GREATEST NEED.
AUUUHHH
THIS IS THE STORY OF THE LAST SUPERHEROES.
...IN US... IN ALL OF US...
AND THE MACHINE THEY MADE TO SAVE THE WORLD.

...SO WHAT IS IT?
WHAT ARE THEY BUILDING?
SOME KIND OF OMNI-COMPUTER.
SOMETHING THAT CAN CALCULATE THE LIFE EQUATION.
A SUPER-COMMUNICATIONS DEVICE--LIKE A CELLPHONE TO THE GODS, I HEARD.
SUPERGIRL THINKS SUPERMAN FOUND A WAY TO SHRINK AND BOTTLE THE WHOLE UNIVERSE FOR PROTECTION.
APPARENTLY IT'S A WEAPON.
THE WEAPON.
IN SUPERMAN WE TRUST.
A WILL-POWERED MACHINE THAT MAKES GL POWER RING TECH LOOK LIKE A SLIDESHOW PROJECTOR?
IF MY RING CAN HELP, HERE IT IS.
ÉL VA A ARRANCAR EL TIEMPO, ESTO ES LO QE ME HAN DICHO.
VIVIR EN EL MUNDO CON UN HOMBRE ASI.
OUTRAGEOUS.
TOO BAD WE'RE ONLY PERMITTED TO WORK ON SECTIONS, SIVANA.
THIS LOOKS TO ME LIKE SOMETHING CAPABLE OF REWRITING THE LAWS OF PHYSICS.
MEH.

THIS IS HOW CHECKMATE WENT DOWN FIGHTING.
PROFESSOR PALMER!
THE NANO-BEACON'S IN PLACE, BUT THE TUNNEL BETWEEN UNIVERSES CAN'T TAKE THESE STRESSES!
I CAN'T TAKE THESE STRESSES!
The Black Gambit is failing.
Inter-brane Escape Tunnel integrity is failing!
Emergency shutdown in progress!

..OXYGEN AT 10%. HEAT AT 5%...
OLLIE.
I THINK WE DID IT.
SATELLITE LIFE SUPPORT CRITICAL.
LOOK, OLLIE.
RAY MADE IT.
HE DID IT.
...WE RULE...
LET ME SHOW YOU WHAT MONEY UNLEASHED CAN DO!
THE TUNNEL'S COLLAPSING!
EVERYBODY OUT!
NOW!
LOLITA CANARY!
ONLY I CAN SAVE HER!
GET THE HELL OUT OF THERE!
THIS IS THE STORY OF ALL OUR STORIES.

AND THIS IS HOW IT ENDS.
...IMAGINE TWO WHOLE UNIVERSES SHEARING APART AS THE LIFELINE CONNECTING THEM WAS SNAPPED!
LORD EYE'S HAVING A BREAKDOWN AND CLOSING THE TUNNEL!
THOSE PEOPLE WILL DIE IF I DON'T STOP HIM, KENDRA!
What year is this?
Is it a test?
KEIGO!
DAMN YOU, CARTER!
YOU CAN'T DO THIS ALONE!
TIME!
SPACE!
I GOT HER! I GOT HER!
WHERE ARE YOU, LIGHTNING FLASH!
CATCH HER!!!
HOW DID IT GET SO COLD?
WHERE ARE MY OMACS?!
CAN'T SEEM TO RUN
FAST
ENOUGH
SHREDDING!
EVERYTHING IS SPLITTING UP!
SONIC LIGHTNING FLASH!
I LOVE YOU!
BUT I LOVE YOU.
HOW THE HELL DID WE GET HERE?
WHERE ARE WE?
WHAT JUST HAPPENE TO
BOOM

...AT THE EXACT MOMENT *EARTH-ZERO* FELL INTO THE *ABYSS*, MISTER MIRACLE'S *MOTHERBOXXX* SECURED A *BOOM TUBE* CONNECTION TO A *NEARBY* UNIVERSE AND THE *REST* OF US MADE THE *GREAT ESCAPE*.

...EVERY TIME I TALK ABOUT MY LIFE LATELY, I SOUND SCHIZOPHRENIC.

AFTER WE SAVE THE WORLD, I'M *OUT*, FOR SANITY'S SAKE.

IT WASN'T LIKE THIS WHEN I LEFT.

LOOKS LIKE *YOU* MISSED A HELL OF A PARTY, SONNY SUMO.

INCREDIBLE.

WE'VE LONG *SUSPECTED* THE EXISTENCE OF PARALLEL UNIVERSES, BUT *THIS*...

MULTIPLE SUPERMEN.

WELCOME TO A MIND-BENDING WORLD I STILL FEEL ILL-EQUIPPED TO DEAL WITH.

AND YET YOU VOLUNTEERED TO ACCOMPANY THE CHAMPIONS OF ALMOST 50 WORLDS ON A VOYAGE WITH PERHAPS NO RETURN.

NEIN!

I HAVE A LOT OF FRIENDS BACK ON EARTH... "EARTH-ZERO."

I WOULDN'T WANT TO LET 'EM DOWN.

OVERMAN, WHATEVER, I THINK I MET YOUR COUSIN AND...I'M SO SORRY, I...

JOHN STEWART *FOUND* THE BULLET YOU FIRED *BACKWARDS* IN TIME.

BATMAN USED IT TO MORTALLY *WOUND* YOU.

THIS WAS *SUICIDE*, DARKSEID.

NOT.

TALK TO ME. DARKSEID IS ORDER. DARKSEID IS *PEACE*.

DIANA? NO.

ON YOUR KNEES. SUBMIT. THE ARMIES OF *LIBRA* HAVE ARRIVED.

THE ODDS ARE *AGAINST* YOU, SUPERMAN.

AND HERE'S *ME* IN CHARGE OF AN ARMY OF MIND-CONTROLLED *SUPER-CRIMINALS*.

LIBRA? HEHH

SUPERMAN ALONE AGAINST THE WORLD'S GREATEST SUPER-VILLAINS!
HOW DO YOU THINK HE GOT OUT OF THAT?
WHEN WE'RE DONE, IT'S TIME FOR BED, CHILDREN.
BUT FIRST LET ME TELL YOU HOW I WAS INTRODUCED TO FRANKENSTEIN.
KNNF!
MORTICOCCUS, THE GOD-BACTERIUM DESIGNED TO STRIP EARTH'S HEROES OF THEIR POWERS, HAD NO EFFECT ON A LIVING DEAD MAN.
AND THE VILLAINS HAD BEEN INOCULATED.
NOT A SINGLE WORD, SUPERMAN.
WE'LL CALL THIS AN HISTORIC FIRST TEAM-UP OF THE FORCES OF "GOOD" AND THE FORCES OF "BAD."
AND I'LL TAKE THE CREDIT FOR A WIN.
WHATEVER YOU SAY, LEX.
WHATEVER YOU SAY.

...IT ALL SEEMS SO LONG AGO.
WHAT HAPPENED TO LUTHOR?
WHAT WAS ONCE TIME IS BROKEN NOW AND BLINDED.
WHAT USED TO BE MEANINGFUL AND SIGNIFICANT... IS LOSING IMPORTANCE...
THAT'S HOW IT SEEMS TO ME.
THE LAST SURVIVORS, PRESERVED ON TRAYS IN A FREEZER.
TIME FOR BED, CHILDREN.
I DON'T THINK I'VE EVER FELT ANYTHING SO STRANGE..LIKE IT'S ALL BROKEN UP FROM ONE MINUTE TO THE NEXT...
THERE HAS TO BE A WAY TO FIX THIS.
AND THE FIRST THING I HAVE TO DO IS FIND THOSE GUYS WHO WENT TO DEFEND THE EAST WALL!
I PROMISE I'LL RESTORE YOU ALL WHEN THIS IS OVER, LOIS.
BRAINIAC 5 ALLOWED ME TO LOOK AT THE MIRACLE MACHINE FOR NO MORE THAN A FEW SECONDS.
I TRIED TO MEMORIZE EVERY NUT AND BOLT AND CIRCUIT.
HEY.
I TRUST YOU.
AND YOU'LL GET THE BIG KISS WHEN I'M BACK FROM THE FRIDGE, SMALLVILLE.

IT WAS *WONDER WOMAN* WHO BOUND DARKSEID'S BODY.

WITH HER *LASSO OF TRUTH*, SHE CHAINED THE GOD OF EVIL.

AND NO ONE WAS HURT.

ALMOST *DONE.*

IT'S TAKEN ALL OUR RESOURCES, THE ACCUMULATED KNOWLEDGE AND EXPERTISE OF A WHOLE *CULTURE*, TO MAKE THE *MIRACLE MACHINE.*

ONE CHANCE, ONE *WISH.*

THE WALLS ARE COMING DOWN AROUND YOU.
IT IS OVER, SUPERMAN.
YOU'RE IN THE FINAL STAGES OF RADION POISONING, DARKSEID.
WE'RE ALMOST AT THE BOTTOM, WHERE IT ALL ENDS, WHERE THERE'S NO MORE FUTURE.
YOU'RE RIGHT ABOUT THAT.
YOU CONSTRUCTED A CARGO CULT MOTHER BOX CAPABLE OF A SINGLE OPERATION.
HOW COULD I ASK FOR A BETTER GIFT TO DESTROY YOU WITH?
MY WILL BE DONE.
THE WORLDS OF THE MULTIVERSE VIBRATE TOGETHER, DARKSEID, AND MAKE THIS...SOUND, LIKE AN ORCHESTRA.
EVERYTHING'S JUST FREQUENCIES, VIBRATIONS.
AND COUNTER-VIBRATIONS THAT CANCEL THEM OUT.
...DARKSEID...
...ALWAYS HATED MUSIC...

...SUPERMAN RECORDING... LOSING MY VOICE...
IT'S NOT OVER YET.
I SENSE A FAINT...HEARTBEAT... FROM WITHIN THE NEW GOD METRON'S ABANDONED MOBIUS CHAIR.
I'D NEVER HAVE HEARD IT.
BUT FOR THE ABSOLUTE SILENCE.
I THINK IT'S ELEMENT X.
FIRE OF THE GODS.
IT CAN TAKE...ANY SHAPE...BECOME THE LAST...LAST PART OF THE JIGSAW...
...HAVE TO... GIVE MY VOCAL CORDS A MOMENT TO HEAL...
A MOMENT'S SILENCE.
...TO PREPARE FOR COSMIC MIDNIGHT...
EXHAUSTED.
ISOLATED.
YOUR FATHER FAILED TO SAVE HIS WORLD.

NOW IT'S YOUR TURN, SUPERMAN.
THE DYING GOD LEFT YOUR UNIVERSE WOUNDED, BROKEN, DEFENSELESS AND ALONE IN THE ENDLESS DARK... WHERE MANDRAKK WAITS.
HERE AT THE END OF ALL STORIES.
COME CLOSER.
I NEED TO EAT YOU RAW!
SLLUBBBRR
AS I FED ON THESE "SERVANTS OF GOD" DEFENDERS OF THIS UNIVERSE.
DRAINED NOW.
MEANINGLESS.
THERE IS NO LIGHT, NO SPARK HERE TO POWER YOUR EMPTY WEAPON!
COME.
DIE SCREAMING AND WRITHING IN THE ARMS OF YOUR MASTER!
GOT TO SAY I'VE HAD BETTER OFFERS.
I'M A SOLAR BATTERY, MANDRAKK.
I STORE LIGHT IN MY CELLS.

I'LL USE IT ALL IF THAT'S WHAT IT TAKES TO ACTIVATE THE MIRACLE MACHINE.

...RINGS ARE *EXHAUSTED,* HAL.

BUT WHAT IN HELL ARE *THOSE* THINGS?

WHATEVER THEY ARE, THEY'RE OUR WAY ACROSS THE EVENT HORIZON!

LET'S HEAR IT!!

IN BRIGHTEST DAY, IN BLACKEST NIGHT, NO EVIL SHALL ESCAPE OUR SIGHT!

WHAT HAVE YOU DONE?

I RELIED ON *CAPTAIN MARVEL* OF *EARTH-5* TO COME THROUGH.

NOT SO EASY WHEN YOUR PREY *BITES BACK,* IS IT, MANDRAKK?

LOOK UP IN THE SKY.

READY, GENTLEMEN?

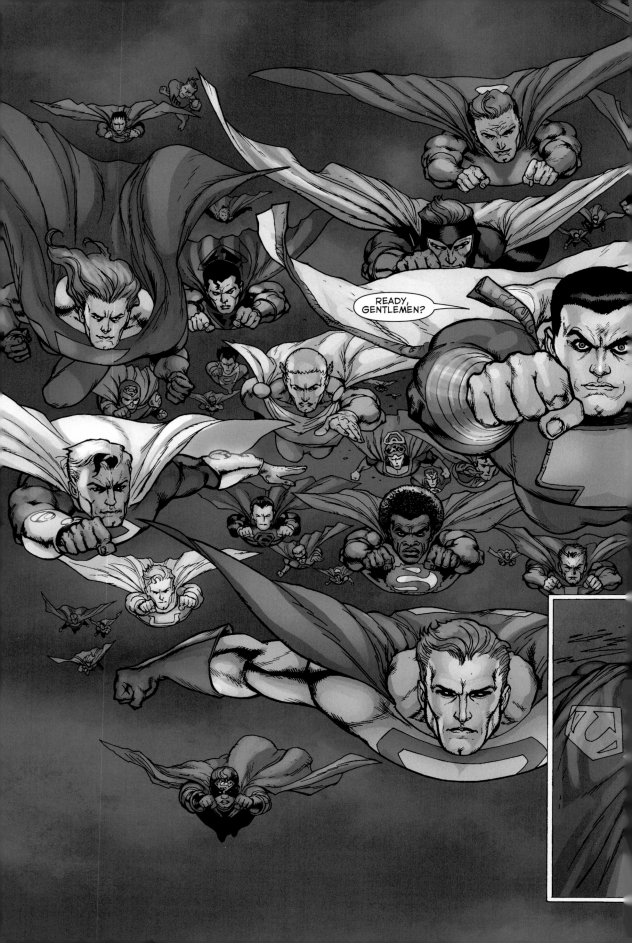

LET ME KILL THEM ALL, MASTER!
SHE CAN WAIT!
UNNHH...
LET THE SUN SHINE IN!
THANKS TO METRON'S INTERVENTION, I WAS NOW FREE TO ACT IN MY CAPACITY AS A MULTIVERSAL MONITOR.

I ARRIVED JUST IN TIME TO JOIN THE LAST STAND OF THESE INCREDIBLE CREATURES.
SUPERMAN.
YOUR SIGNAL HAS BEEN RECEIVED AND UNDERSTOOD.
THIS IS BETWEEN MONITORS NOW.
AND I SAW IN THEM THE GLORY METRON HAD SEEN.
MANDRAKK!
AT MY RIGHT HAND STANDS SUPERMAN HIMSELF.
AT HIS SIDE SOME EXILED EARTH-26 ANIMALS YOU OVERLOOKED...
BEHIND ME, THE VENGEFUL ANGELS OF THE PAX DEI DESCEND, THE ARMY OF GOD!
AND THE SUPERMEN OF THE MULTIVERSE: A TEAM OF SOLAR-POWERED HEROES SO INCREDIBLE IT CAN BE ASSEMBLED ONLY ONCE, AGAINST THE ABSOLUTE ENEMY!
DO YOU HEAR THAT CHANT GROWING STRONGER? "LET ALL WHO WORSHIP EVIL'S MIGHT..."
BEWARE MY POWER! GREEN LANTERNS' LIGHT!
NIX... UOTAN ?
...MY.... SON..?
TURN BACK.
CRAWL HOME TO YOUR TOMB WITH YOUR CARRION-SHADOWS.
DAWN IS ON ITS WAY.

HOW COULD I BE ANYTHING ELSE?
WITH THE WORD "TAARU," I SUMMON THE FOREVER PEOPLE OF THE 5TH WORLD FROM EARTH-51 EXILE!
WOW.
THERE IS NO LIMIT TO WHAT I CAN DO.
ULTRAMAN... KILL...YOU ALLLLLL
I SAW THE BOOK OF LIMBO.
THE END WAS ALL FLAMES AND SHADOWS!
RINGS CAN'T HANDLE THIS, JORDAN!
HOLY $%^& WHAT AM I LOOKING AT?
WE'RE ALL OUTTA JUICE, HAL.
OUR 24 HOURS IS UP!
SO GIMME ONE LAST EFFORT, TEAM.
ALL TOGETHER!
AND SPIKE THIS VAMPIRE!
THIS MULTIVERSE HAS NATURAL DEFENSES NONE OF YOU COULD HAVE IMAGINED.
NO ONE %$%$ WITH THE JUDGE OF ALL EVIL.

WE LIVED THROUGH *RAGNAROK* AND FOUGHT A *GOD.*

WE SURVIVED THE BITE OF A COSMIC *PARASITE.*

WE LOST GOOD *FRIENDS* AND SAW WHAT THE *WORST* IN US COULD DO IF WE LET IT LOOSE.

AND WE SAW THE *BEST* TOO.

THIS *WORLD,* THESE AMAZING *PEOPLE,* HAVE FACED ALIEN INVASIONS, NATURAL DISASTERS, QUAKES IN TIME.

AND ALWAYS WE *RECOVER...WE REBUILD...WE CONTINUE.*

EARTH *ENDURES.*

IT'S AS IF WE DON'T KNOW WHAT ELSE TO *DO.*

THE DAMAGE CAUSED TO THE *ORRERY OF WORLDS* BY DARKSEID'S *FALL* IS UNDER *REPAIR.*

AS IT WAS EVER DONE, SO SHALL IT BE DONE AGAIN... WITH *APOLOGIES* TO *MONITOR NIX UOTAN.*

WE MUST ALSO DISCUSS *REPLACEMENTS* FOR *ZILLO VALLA* AND *ROX OGAMA.*

EARTH *DESIGNATES-43* AND *31* ARE CURRENTLY *UNMONITORED.*

THE GERM-CREATURES *THEMSELVES* REESTABLISHED THE SYMMETRY OF THE *ORRERY,* THE "*MULTIVERSE*" AS THEY CALL IT.

I'VE NEVER *WITNESSED* SUCH INDUSTRY, SUCH *INTELLIGENCE.*

AND THE WHITE-HOT *PASSIONS* THAT DRIVE THEM...

PASSIONS POWERFUL ENOUGH TO TRIGGER CATASTROPHIC *CHANGES* IN BEINGS MADE OF PURE THOUGHT, LIKE *US.*

FOR THIS REASON, I ADVISE IMMEDIATE *WITHDRAWAL* OF CONTACT WITH THE GERM WORLDS.

AND NO FURTHER *EXPLOITATION.*

YOUR CONCERNS ARE *NOTED.*

PLEASE JUST *CONTINUE* WITH YOUR REPORT, SPARING NO DETAILS.

WELL...NOW WE KNOW WHY THERE'S A *BLACK HOLE* AT THE BASE OF *CREATION.*

IT'S WHERE *DARKSEID* FELL THROUGH *EXISTENCE* TO HIS *DOOM.*

LEAVING HELL *DESERTED.*

AND THERE, IN *HIS* ABSENCE, THE FIRST *FLOWER* GREW.

SO *BEGINS* THE MYTH OF A *NEW* CREATION.

APOKOLIPS REBORN AS *NEW GENESIS.*

THE *NEW GODS* RETURNED TO GUIDE THE DESTINY OF A *NEW WORLD.*

AND *HERE:* THE *PLAN* I USED TO *RECONSTRUCT* EARTH DESIGNATE-51, DESTROYED BY *OGAMA'S* TREACHERY.

I SAW THE WORLD *REMADE* WITH MY OWN EYES.

WITH PIECES OF OTHER TIMES, *OTHER* PLACES.

ALL IN A VISION THAT CAME TO *ME* IN *COMMAND-D.*

DESIGNATE-51 LIVES ANEW.

REPAIRS WERE ACCOMPLISHED, TIME ANOMALIES CORRECTED, *COHERENCE* AND HARMONY RESTORED.

THIS ALL BUT *CONCLUDES* MY REPORT AS I PREPARE TO *RETURN* TO MY DUTIES.

...OUR STORY HAS BECOME TOXIC...

...OUT OF CONTROL...

...WE MUST END IT...

FORGIVE *MONITOR TAHOTEH* HIS ENCROACHING SENILITY.

YOUR EXILE IS *OVER,* UOTAN.

YOU ARE INVITED TO *REJOIN* THE *CIRCLE OF MONITORS* WITH FULL HONORS.

PRIME MONITOR HERMUZ.

IF I MAY *DECLINE* ANY SUCH HONORS AS ESSENTIALLY *MEANINGLESS,* THERE ARE MORE CRITICAL MATTERS TO ATTEND TO.

WE ALMOST *DESTROYED* THIS BEAUTIFUL LIVING THING IN OUR MIDST.

THIS MULTIVERSE OF LIFE DESERVES ITS *FREEDOM* FROM OUR INTERFERENCE.

MAKE YOUR PEACE.

ALL THE LOVELY CLOCKWORK IS *ERASED* FROM THE SKY.

THE SEARING *EMPTINESS* OF THE OVERVOID DRAWS EVER CLOSER.

THE HOUR GROWS *LATE,* NIX UOTAN.

THEY COULDN'T MAKE ME *FORGET* YOU.

YOU BROUGHT ME BACK, WEEJA DELL.

YOU WERE MY *DREAM GIRL* FROM A WORLD I THOUGHT I COULD NEVER *REACH.*

YOU SOUND... DIFFERENT.

I LIVED AMONG THEM.
I SAW THE DAMAGE WE WERE DOING TO THEM AND WHAT WE'D HAVE TO SACRIFICE TO SAVE THEM.
I WON'T FORGET YOU.
THEN THIS REALLY IS THE LAST DAY.
I THINK SO.
THE FINAL CRISIS IS OURS.
WEEJA DELL.
IT WAS GOOD TO HAVE A FACE AND TO LOVE AND BE LOVED.
TELL ME ONE LAST THING BEFORE WE PART, NIX UOTAN.
WHAT WAS SUPERMAN'S WISH ON THE MIRACLE MACHINE?
HE'S SUPERMAN.
HE WISHED ONLY THE BEST FOR ALL OF US.
CLOSE YOUR EYES.
HE WISHED FOR A HAPPY ENDING, WEEJA DELL.

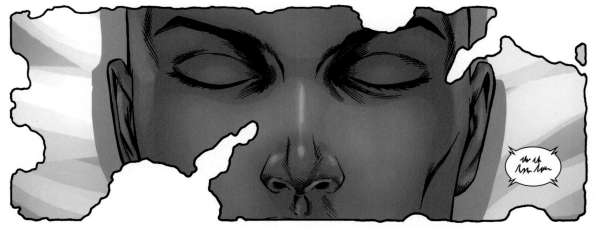

...YOU'VE JUST JOINED *WGBS* ON A *BEAUTIFUL* DAY IN *METROPOLIS!*

WITH MORE ON THOSE NEWLY DISCOVERED *PARALLEL WORLDS* AND HOW THEY COULD CHANGE OUR LIVES *FOREVER!*

THIS IS ONE STORY THAT'S ONLY JUST *BEGINNING.*

YOU HAVE BEEN READING

NEW HEAVEN, NEW EARTH

GRANT MORRISON • SCRIPT   **DOUG MAHNKE** • PENCILS

TOM NGUYEN, DREW GERACI, CHRISTIAN ALAMY, NORM RAPMUND, RODNEY RAMOS, DOUG MAHNKE & WALDEN WONG • INKS

JG JONES COVER   **ALEX SINCLAIR** w/**TONY AVINA** & **PETE PANTAZIS** COLORS
TRAVIS LANHAM LETTERING   **ADAM SCHLAGMAN** ASSOCIATE EDITOR   **EDDIE BERGANZA** EDITOR

SOME TIME LATER, WHEN OLD MAN HAS FINISHED REFRESHING THE STORIES ONE FINAL TIME AT THE HOLY GROUND...

...HE COMES TO REST.

HE THINKS OF THE SHINING ONE AND THE BURNING BUSH IN THE LONG-AGO NOW.

OLD MAN HAS CARRIED THE STRONG FIRE FROM PLACE TO PLACE, LEARNING ALL ITS URGENT LESSONS.

HE HAS MADE WITH HIS HANDS THINGS FIRST SEEN IN ITS SWIFT AND SUBTLE HEART.

WHERE NEW THOUGHTS ARE BORN IN A FURNACE.

HIS SKULL IS FILLED ONE LAST TIME WITH BRILLIANT FLAME.

AND THEN...

...IN A HALO OF BLAZING LIGHT THAT SEEMS TO COMPLETE EVERYTHING...

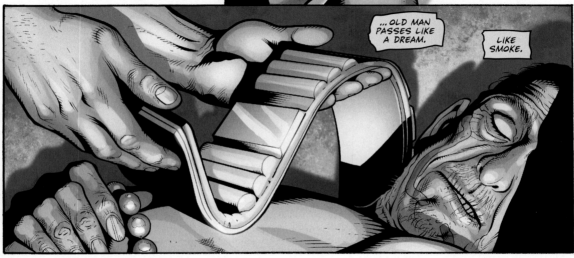

...OLD MAN PASSES LIKE A DREAM.

LIKE SMOKE.

BUT THE FIRE BURNS FOREVER.

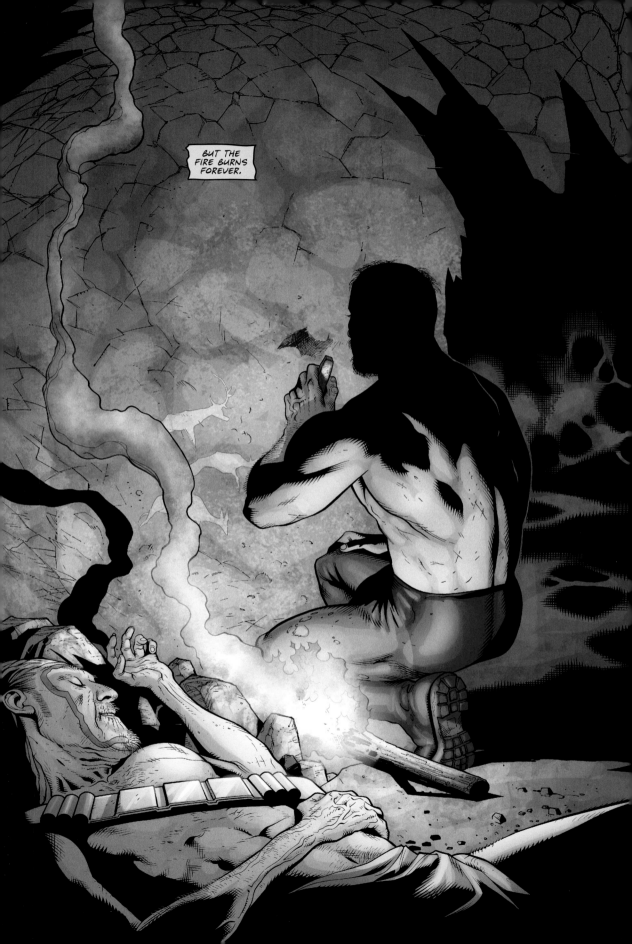

BATMAN: THE RETURN OF BRUCE WAYNE № 1
cover by Andy Kubert and Brad Anderson

WHAT'S IT *OF?*

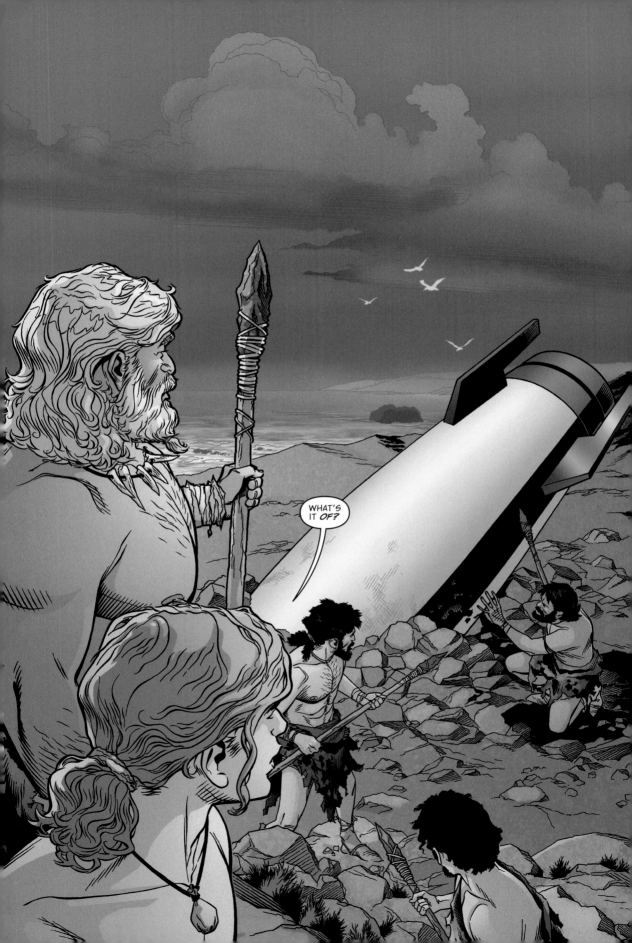

HOW IS IT SO HARD TO *LOOK* AT?

DA-MAN.

≥SHUSH≤ OLD MAN SAID IT'S *HOLY*.

THINGS *HAPPEN* HERE THAT *CAN'T* HAPPEN OTHER WHERES.

THERE'S HOLY AND THERE'S *HAUNTED*...

IT'S A *SHINING-CART*.

SAME AS BROUGHT DOWN THE *FIRE*, IN *OLD MAN'S* STORY.

"MADE WITHOUT STITCH OR SEAM."

SO WHAT'S IT MADE OF? *SKY*?

LIKE A FLAKE OFF *SKIN* OR *FLINT*?

IT'S THE SAME BLUE *SKY* IS.

SKY'S *DIFFERENT* BLUE. MORE *LIGHTNESS* IN IT.

AH, BUT SKY'S *ALL* DIFFERENT.

STAY.

THIS IS WHAT BLUE IT WAS WHEN IT FIRST *FELL*.

WE'RE TOO FAR FROM *DEER PEOPLE COUNTRY*.

BLOOD MOB BOUNDARY'S OVER *THAT RISE*.

IT'S NOT *SAFE* HERE.

EVEN THE *BLOOD CHIEF FEARS* WHAT'S HOLY.

HE'S A *DEVIL*.

HE KNOWS IF HE COMES *HERE*, IT'S *BAD LUCK* FOR HIS KIND.

BAD LUCK IF HE MEETS *ME*.

BAD LUCK FOR *US*, TOO.

HAS NOBODY SEEN *THIS* HERE?

WHAT MADE TRACKS LIKE THESE?

THEY SAY WHEN SHINING ONES COME AGAIN, IT'S THE *ALL-OVER.*

SHINING ONES?

WHO SAYS?

WHAT'S THE *ALL-OVER?*

GIANT?

NEVER YOU MIND SURLY'S TALK.

YOU'RE HERE TO LEARN THE SECRET OF BEING A *MAN* AND NOT A *BOY.*

HERE'S THE FIRST SECRET: MEN DON'T *SCARE* EASY.

WHAT'S THERE?

SHOW YOURSELF.

?

BATMAN: THE RETURN OF BRUCE WAYNE PART ONE
SHADOW ON STONE
GRANT MORRISON WRITER
CHRIS SPROUSE PENCILLER
KARL STORY INKS
GUY MAJOR COLORIST
JARED K. FLETCHER LETTERS
ANDY KUBERT COVER
JANELLE SIEGEL ASSISTANT EDITOR
MIKE MARTS EDITOR

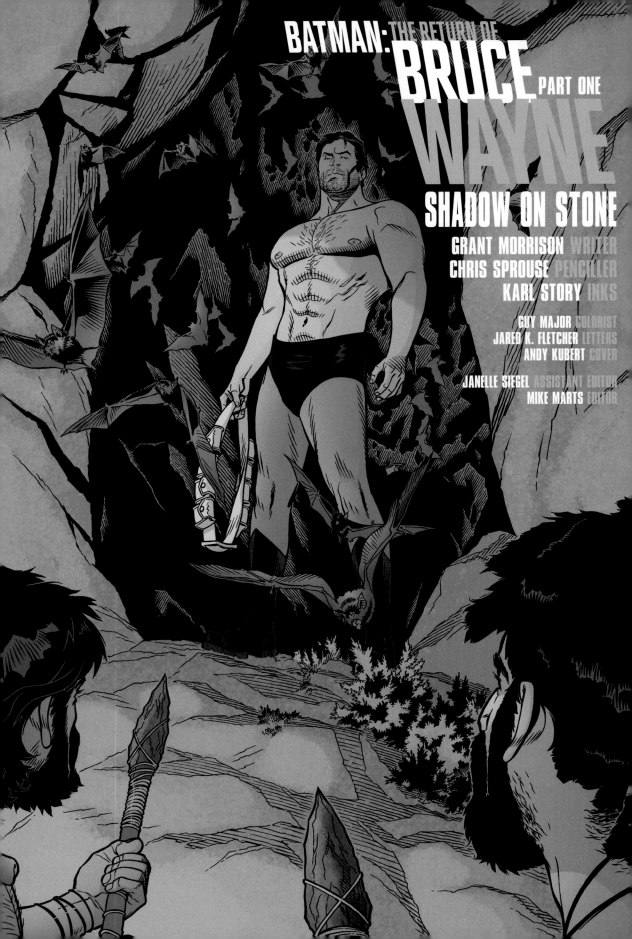

I WARNED YOU!
SURLY.
SHUSH.
WHERE'S YOUR TRIBE AT?
WAYRAMEYE
WODDIZDIZPLAZE
GIANT.
YOU TELL HIM WHO WE ALL ARE.
GO ON.

THIS HERE'S MAN, OLD MAN'S SON.
AND HIS SON, BOY.
HERE TO LEARN TO BE YOUNG MAN.
SURLY.
SERIOUS!
I'M GIANT.
JOKER.
HAHA HAH
RRRR
JOKER.
UH-UH.
≥ULP≤

NOW HE'S SEEN HIS SKY-CART.

HH.

THAYAWLMANNSTED

UMSARRY

MADNESS.

HIS CART *DID* COME DOWN A *BUMP.*

MAYBE HIS HEAD GOT *SCRAMBLED.*

...HAHAHA...

JOKER!

...IT *DID* MAKE A HARD FALL, EH?

DA? WHERE'S *OLD MAN?*

I SMELL *DEATH.*

STAY, BOY.

AM I LEARNING TO BE A MAN NOW?

DA?

OLD MAN?

ARE YOU *THERE?*

I HEAR HIM NOW.

DA?
IS IT...
OLD MAN.
HE HAD A SMILE AND THIS...
...THIS WAS IN HIS HAND.
IT WAS WHITE FAWN'S.
MA WORE THIS WHEN THEY WERE YOUNG.
HE HAD IT HELD WHERE HIS HEART IS.
THIS STAYS WITH US, MAN TO BOY, UNTIL THE ALL-OVER.
IT NEVER LEAVES.
NOT EVER.

...WE CAN'T JUST IGNORE HIM.
WHY DOESN'T HE TELL US SOME GREAT SECRET OR SHOW US A NEW TOOL OR A WEAPON SAME AS SHINING ONES ARE SUPPOSED TO?
WHEN HE SPEAKS IT'S LIKE A FLOWING RIVER.
NOT WORDS AT ALL.
I SAY WE CALL HIM MAN OF BATS.
...IF OLD MAN'S DEAD, WHO'LL TEACH ME THE SONGS?
HOW WILL I EVER BE A MAN?
THIS MAKES EVERYTHING DIFFERENT, BOY.
TAKE HIS BELT, SEE IF HE FOLLOWS.
WE'LL FIND OUT IF SHINING ONES GET HUNGRY.
...WELL, AT LEAST HE EATS LIKE A MAN.
OR A PIG!
AHAHAHAH
I SAY HE IS A MAN.
FROM ACROSS THE OCEAN, I SAY.
SHH!
THERE'S EYES, I CAN FEEL THEM ALL OVER.
IT'S ONLY NIGHT ON HOLY GROUND, THAT'S ALL.
DAWN COMES, I'LL TELL YOU EVERYTHING OLD MAN TOLD ME WHEN I WAS YOU.
THERE'S NOT MUCH TO BEING A MAN AFTER...
LOKKA!

BLOOD MOB!
GNNF!
STRANGER...
SAVE MY SON!
DAAAAAA!

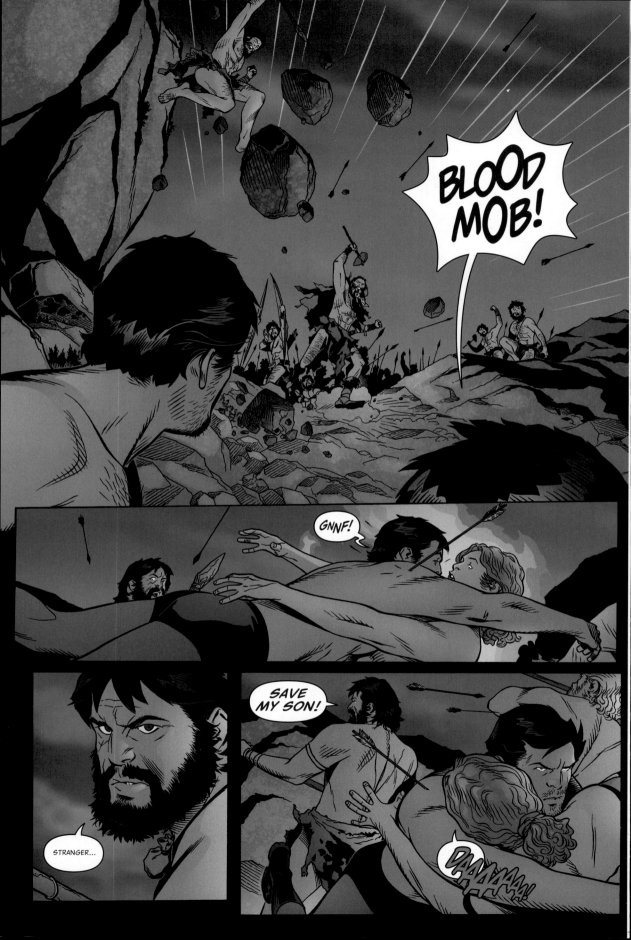

TK

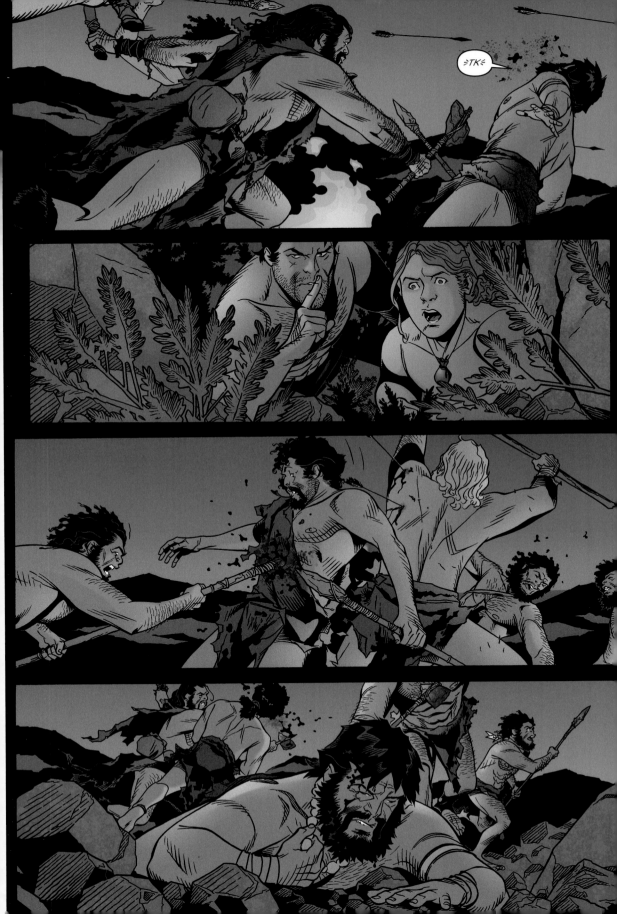

OUFF!

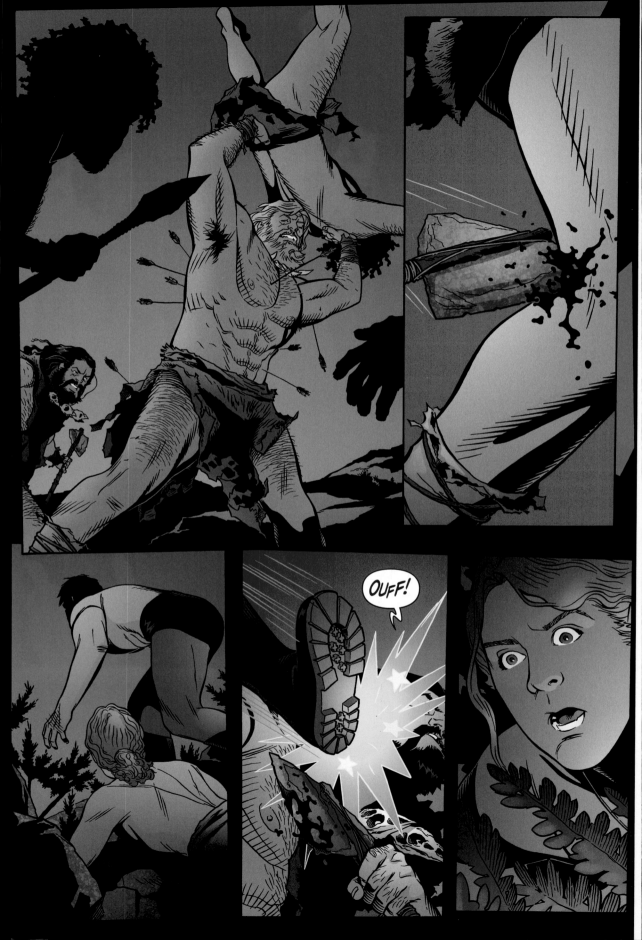

TCHKK!
NNN
HOLD HIM!
MAN-GOD...
GG!
I'LL TAKE THIS.
THE REST RETURNS WITH US!
TO CAMP!

A SKY-CART OF THE BRIGHT ONES!

FOUR SCALPS OF *DEER* WARRIORS!

AND A *MAN-GOD* WHO CAME FROM ABOVE TO CHALLENGE *ME.*

THE CHIEF WHO SCARES DEATH HAS RETURNED!
CONQUERING CHIEF SAVAGE BRINGS GIFTS FROM THE FORBIDDEN LAND!
LIKE THE BAT-BEAST BEFORE HIM...
...THIS WAS HIS REWARD...

WE WAIT UNTIL THE GREAT SUN RISES!
I WANT THE SUN TO WATCH ME EAT HIM ALIVE!
UNNH
CHIEF SAVAGE WILL MAKE BLOOD PEOPLE STRONGEST OF ALL!
UNTIL THEN, LET HIM SUFFER.
HURRNN

FIGHT HIM NOW.
BREAK HIS BACK.
I SAID NOT NOW.
I PREFER AN ADVANTAGE AGAINST A SKY MAN.
NOTHING KILLS CHIEF SAVAGE.
BECAUSE SAVAGE IS CUNNING AS WELL AS STRONG.
SICKNESS COMES IN THROUGH THE SKY-MAN'S WOUNDS.
BY SUN'S RISE, HE'LL BE WEAK.
I'LL TEAR THIS MAN-GOD'S BRAIN FROM HIS SKULL AND EAT IT RAW.
THEN I'LL LEAD A WAR PARTY AGAINST THE DEER PEOPLE.
NAIL HIM OUT.

UHHN
UFF
NN
HUFF
RR
UHHHH

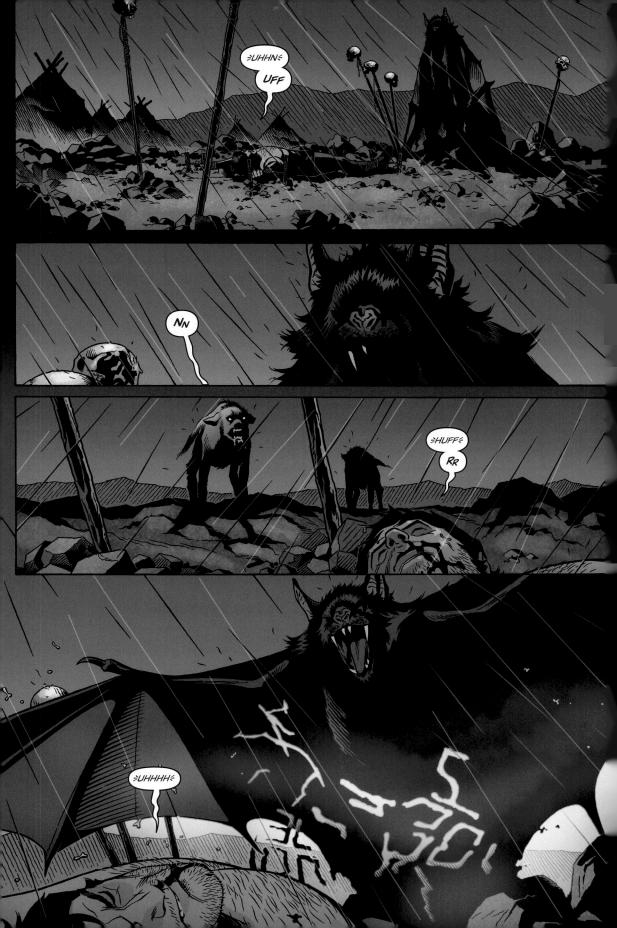

NIGHT.
TERROR.
SUPERSTITIOUS.
OMEN.
CREATURE.
BLACK.
TERRIBLE.
BAT.
DISGUISE.
MAN.
BAT.
MAN OF BATS!

MAN OF BATS.
I FOLLOWED YOU.
THERE.

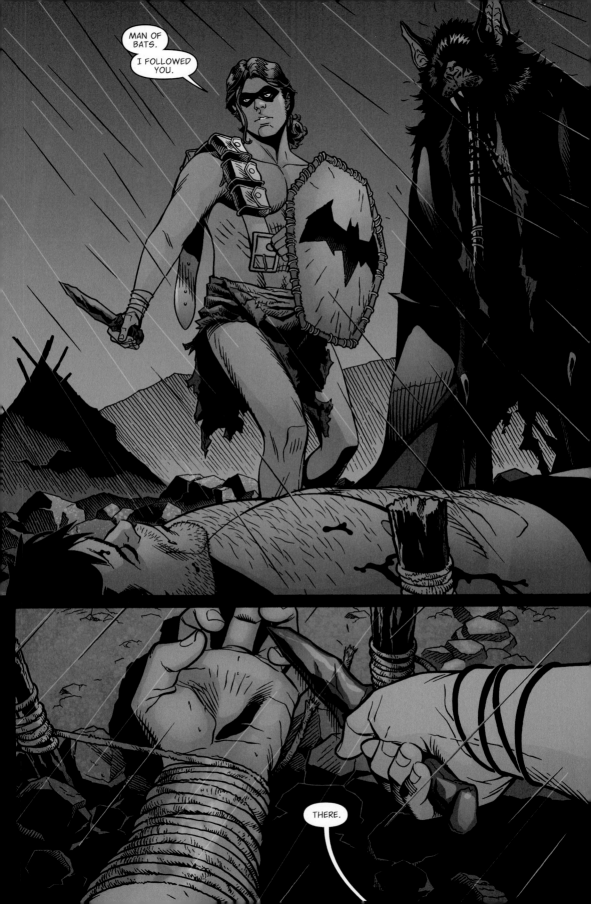

I BROUGHT *THIS.*
AUHHH
WE HAVE TO *LEAVE* NOW.
WARN THE DEER PEOPLE THAT *SAVAGE* IS COMING...
SNURRR

WHO WANTS TO SEE ME KILL A GOD? AND EAT HIS HEART!

FOLLOW ME!

CHIEF SAVAGE!

THE DOGS, THE MEN...

...L-L-LOOK...

WHERE IS MY MAN-GOD?

SHOW YOURSELF, COWARD!

RRRAAAUUU
GRRK
DON'T JUST STAND THERE GAWPING!
MUST I DO EVERYTHING?

WHAT *ARE* YOU?

YAAAA!

≥GNN≤

NOT SO FAST! A SORCERER, TOO!

GGRRAAA

GTT!

YOU FIGHT LIKE NO LIVING MAN.

BACK! IT'S NOT DEER PEOPLE YOU FACE NOW!

THE BAT PEOPLE ARE HERE!

COME THEN!

SAVAGE AND HIS SPEAR...

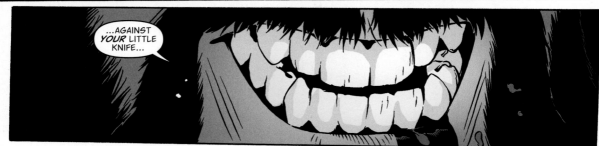

...AGAINST *YOUR* LITTLE KNIFE...

AUGH!

GRNNAAA

*

THEY'RE AFRAID.

CHIEF SAVAGE HAS ANGERED THE SUN!

≥HH≤

...THE SUN...

...AREN'T YOU SCARED?

GAW!

...NO,
I CAN'T...
I...

AAAAAA!

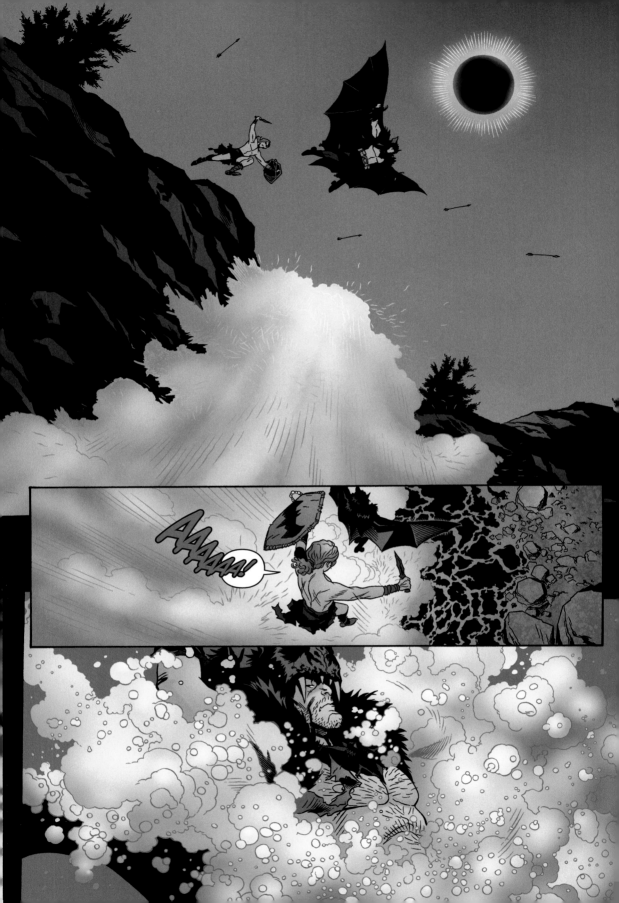

AUFF!
MAN OF BATS?

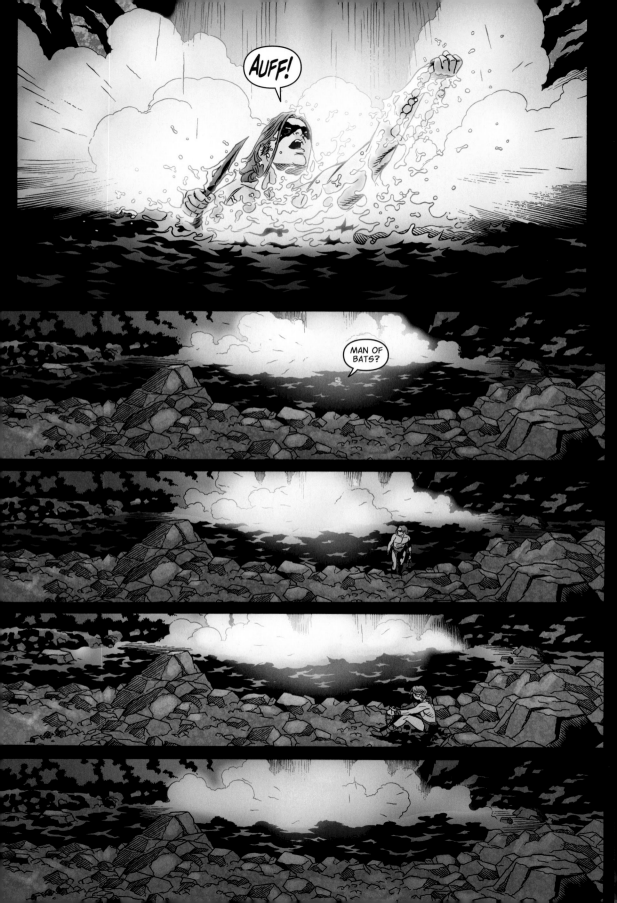

YOU MADE THE SUN GO AWAY!
NEVER COME BACK!
GO!
FOOLS!
I COULD HAVE MADE YOU INTO THE GREATEST WARRIORS EVER KNOWN!
INSTEAD YOU REJECT ME!
CURSE YOUR KIND!
CURSE YOU ALL!

GONE.
BY THE TIME WE TRACKED THE OMEGA RADIATION, HE WAS GONE.
THERE'S NO SIGN OF HIM IN THIS TIME ERA.
I CAN HEAR EVERY HEARTBEAT ON THE PLANET AND BATMAN'S ISN'T AMONG THEM.
BUT WE SAW THE PAINTINGS IN THE CAVE.
WE KNOW HE WAS HERE.
AND WE HAVE TO FIND HIM.
BATMAN HAS NO MEMORY OF WHO HE IS. HE HAS NO IDEA WHAT'S HAPPENING TO HIM.
WHAT CHANCE DOES HE HAVE?
EVEN HE CAN'T MAKE IT.
YOU ARE JOKING, RIGHT?
HE CAN SURVIVE ANYWHERE.
ANYTIME.
SURVIVING IS WHAT HE DOES.
BUT IF HE SURVIVES THIS, IF HE DOES THE IMPOSSIBLE AGAIN...
...IF BATMAN MAKES IT BACK TO THE 21ST CENTURY ON HIS OWN...
...EVERYONE DIES.

...OUT!
AFF!
WHAT IS THIS?
WHERE'S THE *BOY?*
MY GOD.
MASTER DEMON.
WHATEVER YOU ARE.
WHAT HORSE IS THIS YOU RODE IN ON?

BATMAN Nº 38
cover by Greg Capullo, Danny Miki and FCO Plascencia

This block is called Foundry Square.

It sits in the center of the oldest section of Gotham, the Lower East Side, the neighborhood where the city began.

Where the first Dutch settlers overcame the Miagani, where the British overcame them.

BATMAN: PART ENDGAME FOUR

WRITER **SCOTT SNYDER** PENCILLER **GREG CAPULLO**

INKER **DANNY MIKI** COLORIST **FCO PLASCENCIA**

LETTERERS **STEVE WANDS** AND **JARED K. FLETCHER**

COVER **CAPULLO, MIKI** AND **PLASCENCIA**

ASSISTANT EDITOR **MATT HUMPHREYS**

EDITOR **MARK DOYLE**

It's always been a place of change. Blood and violence and fire. Torn down and built up a dozen times. Barely anything older than fifty years remains standing anymore.

Except for this block. Foundry Square.

For some reason, through the years, the residents here banded together to **protect** these modest homes from the forces of the day. Every building is more than two hundred years old.

It's why **Jim Gordon** chose an apartment here. It's history, unchanged. Steady. Judicious...

...until today.
HOLD ON, DUKE! I HAVE YOU.
BATMAN!
BUT WE LOVE YOU, BAT--
JIM!

JIM!
HERE...
YOU... ⊰KOFF⊱ YOU SHOULD SEE THE OTHER GUY.
JIM. DON'T TALK. IT'S GOING TO BE ALL RIGHT.
I...GOT HIM, BATMAN. IT DOESN'T MAKE SENSE. *Heh.* MUST BE A ***JOKE...*** BECAUSE HE GOT UP ⊰KOFF⊱ HE GOT UP JUST FINE, BUT THAT SHOT, IT WAS A ⊰KOFF⊱ CLOWN KILLER. I--
PLEASE, JUST REST.
DUKE, BATHROOM. THERE'S A FIRST AID KIT.
...
DUKE!

I JUST... MY PARENTS. I JUST REALIZED, THEY...
I KNOW. BUT THEY'RE GOING TO BE ALL RIGHT. I PROMISE YOU I'LL DO EVERYTHING I CAN TO MAKE IT HAPPEN. BUT I NEED YOU TO CALM DOWN. AND I NEED SOME HELP.
CAN YOU DO THAT? CAN YOU BE A FRIEND, DUKE?
DON'T DO IT...KIIIID.
HE'S A BAAAAD FRIEND! HAHAHA!

AND HE NEEDS TO--

THUNK THUNK

Unh!

I KNOW, I KNOW. BUT I'M JUST NOT A BLOODY *CAVE* PERSON.

I MEANT WHAT I SAID. THE CAVE IS LESS SECURE WITH YOU HERE.

THAT'S "THANK YOU" IN AMERICAN, NO? ALSO, I HAVE NEWS THAT MADE IT SEEM MORE IMPORTANT TO BE *HERE*.

WE DID FURTHER TESTING ON THE *VIRUS*. WHATEVER CHEMICAL IS MAKING THE STRAIN RESISTANT...IT ALSO CAUSES A KIND OF "CELLULAR ROT."

SO IT'S *DEADLY*. HOW LONG?

I DON'T KNOW, YET. BUT I CAN FIND OUT.

HEY. DAD SAID THINGS GOT BAD HERE SOMETIMES. BUT HUMOR ME, YEAH? THIS ISN'T JUST A TUESDAY.

NO. IT'S UGLY, JULIA.

YOU'LL DO IT.

I KNOW YOU CAN. YOU'LL SAVE THEM. MY PARENTS. ALL OF THEM. JUST LIKE YOU ALWAYS DO.
FAMILY FIRST AID KIT GOTHAM MEDI CROSS
KRREEEAK
TAKE DUKE TO THE BASE. SEE WHAT YOU CAN FIND ABOUT THE VIRUS' LETHALITY. AND STAY LOW AND QUIET.
I'D GIVE YOU THE GLIDER, BUT THERE ARE SIMPLY TOO MANY OF THEM WITH GUNS NOW. THEY NEARLY SHOT US OUT OF THE SKY.
LOW AND QUIET. WE ARE GOTHAM CHURCHMICE. YOU?
I'LL SECURE JIM, THEN I'M GOING AFTER THE SOURCE OF THIS THING.
"TO MAKE SOMETHING THIS BAD..."

"...HE'D NEED HELP."
MR. MALONE. I LEAVE GOTHAM FOR FIVE MINUTES AND THIS IS WHAT HAPPENS.
DID YOU GET THE BLOOD SAMPLE I SENT, BIRDWATCHER?
I DID. AND THERE *IS* SOMETHING REGENERATIVE IN IT. AND THERE ARE SIMILARITIES TO LAZARUS, AS YOU SUSPECTED, BUT IT'S NOT LAZARUS.
FOR ONE, I CHECKED THE PITS GLOBALLY. NO TAMPERING. AND FOR TWO, THIS STUFF, IT'S ***STRONGER.*** LIKE SCARY STRONG.
PLEASE, JUST TELL ME THE SAMPLE... IT ISN'T FROM HIM, IS IT?
JIM TOOK A SHOT AT HIM, AND THE SPRAY PATTERN, IT WAS ARTERIAL. HE SHOULDN'T HAVE COME BACK FROM IT. HE ***WANTED*** US TO SEE.
LORD... YOU'RE NOT SAFE THERE.
NONE OF US ARE.
NO...
...I MEAN NOW, BENEATH YOU. ***MOVE!***
THIS IS ABOUT THE VIRUS. DON'T WORRY ABOUT ME.
YEAH, WELL. APOLOGIES. OLD HABITS.

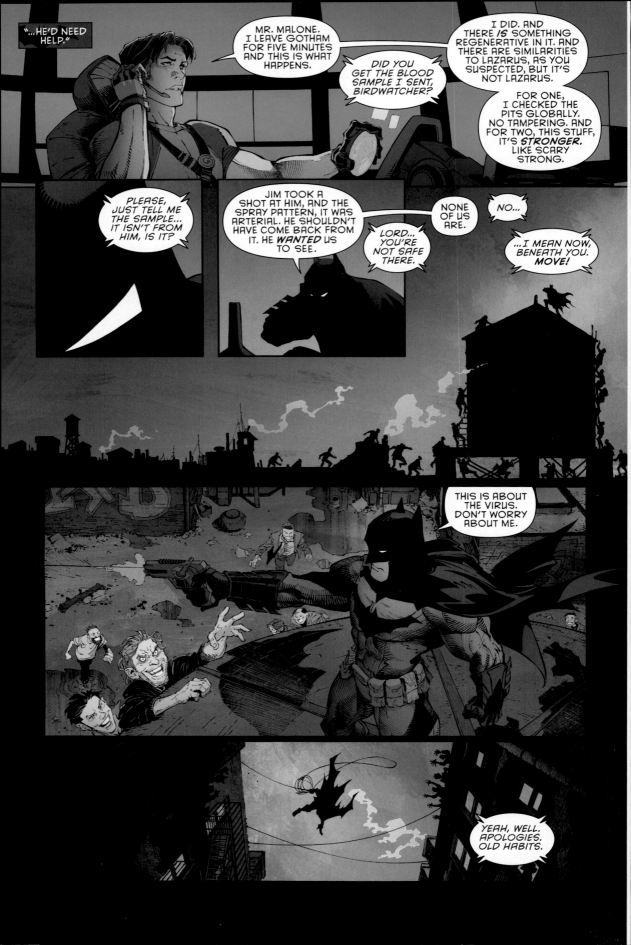

PULL SOMETHING UP FOR ME. THE VIRUS' STRUCTURE, BRING IT UP NEXT TO THE BLOOD SAMPLE I SENT.
...I'M LOOKING. IN THE VIRUS, THERE'S A KIND OF DECAY HAPPENING IN--
I KNOW, DAMMIT. LOOK AT THE DECAY FACTOR OF THE VIRUS *AGAINST* THE REGENERATIVE FACTOR IN HIS BLOOD.
Huh. EUREKA.
THEY'RE *INVERSES,* AREN'T THEY? WHATEVER HE'S TAKING, WHATEVER THE HELL IS IN HIS BLOOD THAT'S GIVEN HIM THIS ABILITY TO HEAL...
...THE VIRUS CONTAINS AN INVERSE STRAIN.
THEY'RE *OPPOSITES.* IT'S A GAME HE'S PLAYING. LIFE AND DEATH. COMEDY AND TRAGEDY. LOVE AND HATE.
HEY. THERE'S SOMETHING UP AHEAD. YOU NEED TO--
NO. WHAT I NEED IS FOR YOU TO HELP ME FIGURE OUT A *CURE...*
...BECAUSE IF I CAN'T DO IT, AND DO IT *FAST,* IT ALL GOES...

...BOOM.

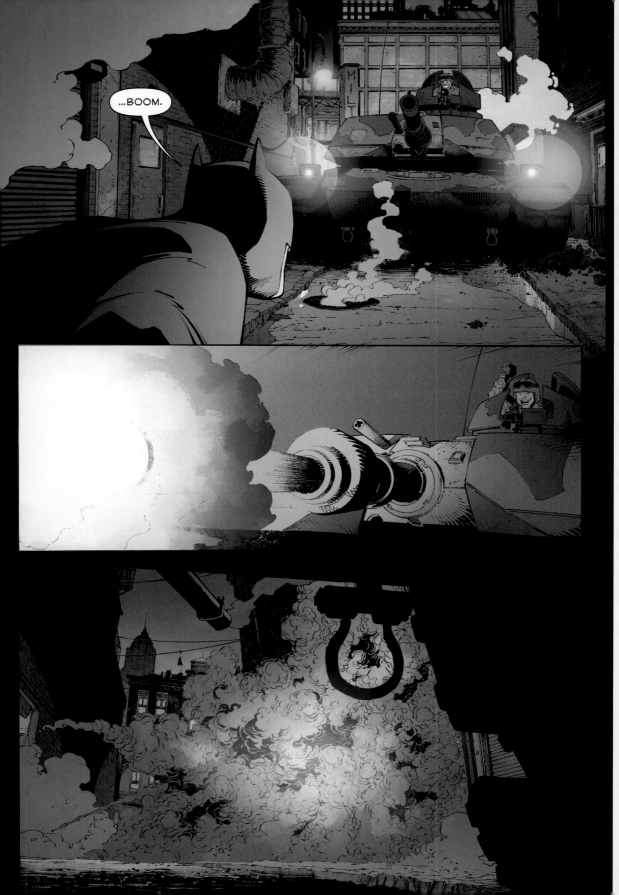

HEEHEE! SSSSSSPIT ON THE GRAVE NOW.
MR. MALONE! THEY'RE GOING TO--
SHUT UP. JUST LISTEN. UNH
ARKHAM. IT HAS TO BE THE KEY. IT'S PART OF WHY HE WAS THERE. SOMEONE IN THERE HELPED HIM.
"I CAN ONLY THINK OF THREE SCIENTISTS CAPABLE OF CREATING SOMETHING AS POWERFULLY REGENERATIVE AS WHATEVER JOKER'S TAKING."
HAHAHA! SPIT!
"ALL THREE WERE PART OF THE SAME BIO INITIATIVE SET UP BY MY UNCLE WHEN HE RAN WAYNE ENTERPRISES. HEADED BY DR. KARL HELFERN."
THERE! COME ON!
HELFERN. DR. DEATH.
UNH
BLAST FROM THE PAST. I KNOW.

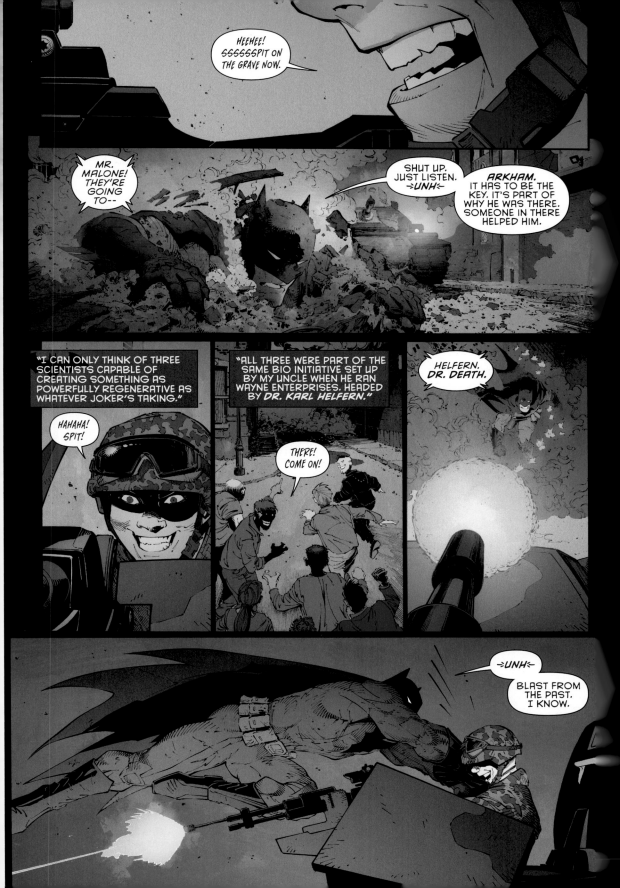

HELFERN WORKED IN ONE. HUGO STRANGE IN REGENERATING EURAL MATTER. AND THERE WAS ALSO DR. PAUL DEKKER, WHO WORKED IN SOFT TISSUE."
"BONE, BRAIN AND BODY. PHILLIP CALLED THEM THE DOCTORS THREE."
"HUH. PAUL DEKKER? AKA--"
"YES. HELFERN IS DEAD. STRANGE HASN'T BEEN IN GOTHAM FOR YEARS. WHICH LEAVES DEKKER."
WHERRRRE? WHERE'D HE GO?
"AAAND LISTEN TO THIS. PAUL DEKKER. CONFINED TO ARKHAM UNTIL JUST A YEAR AND A HALF AGO. RELEASED TO A REHABILITATIVE FACILITY ON ORDERS BY--"
ERIC BORDER."
BINGOOOO!
HE'SSSS IN THE TANK!
ALL RIGHT. I'VE GOT WHAT I NEED. BUT LISTEN, THERE'S SOMETHING YOU NEED TO KNOW...
...JOKER KNOWS WHO I AM.
"...WHAT DO YOU MEAN HE KNOWS WHO YOU--"
"HE KNOWS."
"IT'S OVER, THEN.
HA HA AHA HA AHA!
"I MEAN...OVER.

"I REFUSE TO BELIEVE THAT."
"AND HE KNOWS WHO YOU ARE...
PEEEKABOOO...
"I DON'T SEE A WAY OUT OF THIS ONE."
"LOOK, I'M THE ETERNAL OPTIMIST HERE, BUT YOU HAVE TO SEE IT FOR WHAT IT IS.
"THE VIRUS IS DEADLY. IT'S OVERTAKEN THE CITY.
"JOKER CAN'T BE TAKEN DOWN.
"THERE'S ALWAYS A WAY OUT."
"WELL LET US HELP YOU. BATGIRL'S THERE. RED HOOD, RED ROBIN. I CAN BE THERE IN SIX HOURS."
"NO. YOU ALL NEED TO STAY SAFE WHERE YOU ARE FOR NOW."
"DON'T SHUT US OUT OF YOUR PLAN. YOU REMEMBER WHAT HAPPENED LAST--"
I'M NOT, BIRDWATCHER. THE FACT IS...
...I DON'T HAVE A PLAN YET.

"...I DON'T KNOW WHAT TO DO.

"THESE ARE UNCHARTED WATERS."

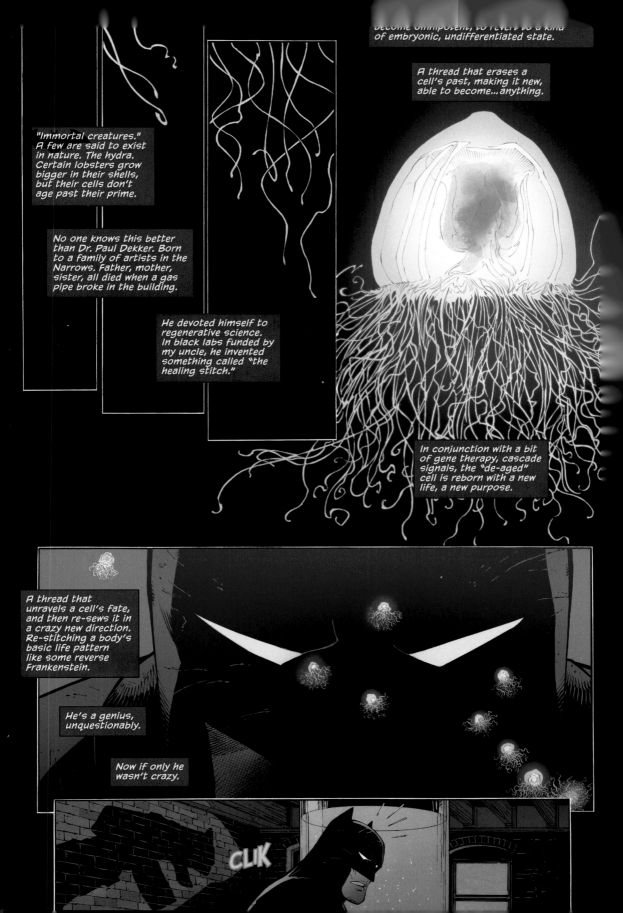

become omnipotent, to revert to a kind of embryonic, undifferentiated state.

A thread that erases a cell's past, making it new, able to become...anything.

"Immortal creatures." A few are said to exist in nature. The hydra. Certain lobsters grow bigger in their shells, but their cells don't age past their prime.

No one knows this better than Dr. Paul Dekker. Born to a family of artists in the Narrows. Father, mother, sister, all died when a gas pipe broke in the building.

He devoted himself to regenerative science. In black labs funded by my uncle, he invented something called "the healing stitch."

In conjunction with a bit of gene therapy, cascade signals, the "de-aged" cell is reborn with a new life, a new purpose.

A thread that unravels a cell's fate, and then re-sews it in a crazy new direction. Re-stitching a body's basic life pattern like some reverse Frankenstein.

He's a genius, unquestionably.

Now if only he wasn't crazy.

CLIK

YOU LIKE MY JELLYFISH, BATMAN?
TURRITOPSIS DOHRNII. ONE OF THE ONLY ANIMALS THAT CAN ACTUALLY AGE BACKWARDS WHEN IT SO DESIRES, REVERT FROM MEDUSA TO POLYP.
IT EXISTS OUTSIDE THE NATURAL LIFE CYCLE.
JUST LIKE HIM.
I'M ONLY HERE ABOUT THE VIRUS, DEKKER. I KNOW YOU HELPED HIM MAKE IT. NOW WHAT THE HELL DID YOU CONCOCT TO--
CONCOCT?!
THE MATERIAL AT THE CORE OF THAT VIRUS ISN'T ANYTHING I COULD MAKE IN A LAB.
IT'S SOMETHING MUCH OLDER, SOMETHING I'VE BEEN LOOKING FOR ALL MY LIFE. SOMETHING JOKER SHOWED ME...
THE CITY IS TEARING ITSELF APART! MILLIONS OF PEOPLE WILL DIE IF YOU DON'T TELL ME THE TRUTH! WHATEVER STORY HE TOLD YOU ABOUT HIMSELF, ABOUT HIS PAST--
AH! STORIES ABOUT THE PAST!

SEE, BATMAN, RESEARCHERS IN MY FIELD, WE JUST LOVE STORIES FROM THE PAST! AFTER ALL, IN ANCIENT TIMES, SO MANY TALES FEATURE HUMAN BODIES DOING PRETTY MUCH EXACTLY WHAT *WE'RE* TRYING TO GET THEM TO DO!

HEAL MIRACULOUSLY. ENDURE FOR CENTURIES. WITHSTAND DEATH...

...FUNNY THING, THE MECHANISM IN THE OLD STORIES IS ALMOST ALWAYS THE SAME. SAID BODY ENCOUNTERS SOMETHING IN THE NATURAL WORLD, SOME SPECIAL SUBSTANCE IN THE SOIL OR VEGETATION OR WATER, AND IS...*TRANSFORMED.*

THE WATERS OF GILGAMESH'S TIME WERE SAID TO BEAR PLANTS THAT GRANTED RENEWED LIFE. THE RIVER STYX BESTOWED EPIDERMAL INVINCIBILITY.

HERODOTUS WROTE OF MACROBIA IN 400 BC, A TOWN WHERE A HIDDEN SPRING OFFERED *ETERNAL* HEALTH.

SO MANY *STORIES* ACROSS SO MANY CULTURES, BATMAN. TOO MANY TO IGNORE.

DEKKER. OUTSIDE THAT WINDOW, PEOPLE ARE DYING! YOU'RE TALKING TO ME ABOUT DAMN LEGENDS AND--

NOT LEGENDS, BATMAN! *CLUES* TO SOMETHING *REAL!*

A CHEMICAL COMPOUND THAT EXISTED IN NATURE LONG AGO, SOMETHING VERY RARE, BUT PRESENT IN CERTAIN PLACES. SOMETHING THAT COULD ACTIVATE JUST THE RIGHT GENES...

...THE SAME ONES WE TINKER WITH ENDLESSLY. LIN28. AMPK...THE MATRIX THAT CONTROLS HOW OUR BODIES REPAIR THEMSELVES.

I NAMED IT, BATMAN. I CALL IT *DIONESIUM.* A LITTLE SCIENTIST HUMOR, SEE? AFTER DIONYSUS, THE GREEK GOD ASSOCIATED WITH REBIRTH. HEARTS SEWN INTO THIGHS.

HELFERN AND STRANGE THOUGHT IT CAME FROM *METEORS.*

BUT I THINK IT'S *INDIGENOUS* TO OUR PLANET.

Heh. DOESN'T FEEL LIKE A BATMAN STORY ANYMORE, DOES IT?

"THAT'S BECAUSE IT ISN'T. IT'S ABOUT **THEM**. THE CARRIERS. AND **GOTHAM**.

"PEOPLE WHO ENCOUNTERED THE CHEMICAL LONG AGO AND STILL WALK AMONG US. HERE IN GOTHAM, I'VE HEARD STORIES OF A FEW.

"THERE'S THE **SAVAGE** WHO WAS AMONG THE OLDEST MEN ALIVE. HE ENCOUNTERED IT IN ITS RAWEST FORM.

"AND THERE'S THE MAN LIKE A **DEMON** WHO KEEPS POOLS OF THE CHEMICAL IN SECRET PITS AROUND THE WORLD. A CORRUPTED VERSION, BUT EFFECTIVE IN ITS WAY.

"AND **HIM**. THE LINK BACK TO GOTHAM. THE PALE MAN. THE ONE WHO LAUGHS AT US. WHO ENCOUNTERED IT SOME-TIME BEFORE GOTHAM ROSE."

YOU WANT TO KNOW A SECRET, BATMAN?

FOR A LONG TIME, I THOUGHT *YOU* WERE ONE. OLDER THAN GOTHAM, A BARBATOS. IT'S WHY I DID THE TERRIBLE THINGS I DID. QUILTING LIFE ABNORMALLY...JUST TO MEET YOU!

BUT THEN I DID MEET YOU, AND I REALIZED...YOU WERE JUST... FLESH AND BLOOD!

BUDDA BUDDA BUDDA

Huh? WHERE--

AAAAAAAGH!
YOU SYNTHESIZED IT. THIS "DIONESIUM." YOU GAVE IT TO THAT MANIAC, AND THEN YOU CREATED A DAMN INVERSE FOR THE VIRUS! WHERE ARE YOU KEEPING IT?!
WHERE?!
YOU HAVE IT ALL WRONG! I'VE CREATED MOMENTARY HEALERS, FLASHES, BUT THAT'S IT! I'VE NEVER BEEN ABLE TO MAKE ANYTHING CLOSE TO IT IN POTENCY.
THE SUBSTANCE IN THE VIRUS, IT'S FROM HIM. I GOT IT FROM THE JOKER'S BODY... FROM HIS SPINE.
I'VE SAMPLED AND TESTED HIS BLOOD DOZENS OF TIMES!
IT ONLY EXPRESSES IN CASES OF CATASTROPHIC DAMAGE! IT'S INVISIBLE OTHERWISE!
SO IF YOU DIDN'T GIVE IT TO HIM, WHERE DID HE GET IT?
TELL ME!
FOR A BAT YOU DON'T LISTEN WELL, DO YOU? IT'S GONE, EXTINCT FOR HUNDREDS OF YEARS! BUT IT'S IN HIM. BECAUSE HE'S ONE OF THEM. HE'S GOTHAM'S OWN DIONYSIAN MAN.
AFTER ALL, DIONYSUS WAS ALSO THE GOD OF MADNESS. TRAGEDY, TOO. HELL, THE VERY WORD TRAGEDY MEANS "GOAT SONG" IN ANCIENT GREEK, FOR ALL THE GOATS SLAUGHTERED TO HIM! AND DON'T YOU SEE? GOTHAM IS THE GREAT SACRIFICE!
SO WELCOME, BATMAN, TO THE LAST BACCHANAL!

THERE'S NO STOPPING IT! BUT AT LEAST YOU HAVE A FRONT ROW SEAT, RIGHT? *HAHA!*

BATMAN?

STICK AROUND.

BATMAN? *HEY!*

PENNY-TWO. WHAT DID YOU FIND?

IT'S BAD, BATMAN. THE VIRUS. THE STRAIN IN IT IS MORE POWERFUL THAN THEY THOUGHT.

HOW LONG?

...

HOW LONG?!

TWENTY-FOUR HOURS. MAYBE LESS. IT'S NOT A MATTER OF DAYS. *IT'S A MATTER OF HOURS.*

ALSO... I DID A FACIAL RECOG FOR *JOKER* THROUGHOUT GOTHAM HISTORY. TRAGEDIES. JUST TO DEBUNK HIS CHARADE. BUT...HE'S ALL OVER.

IT'S VERY POSSIBLE IT'S A TRICK, BUT IF SO, THE PHOTOS ARE THE BEST DOCTORING JOB I'VE SEEN. I MEAN--
IT'S A TRICK. IT HAS TO BE.
HE'S ONE OF THEM, BATMAN! AND SOON, I WILL BE, TOO!
WHAT...
DEKKER, DON'T.
WHATEVER HE GAVE YOU, IT'S NOT WHAT YOU THINK IT IS. HE WOULDN'T RISK IT!
YOU'RE WRONG, BATMAN! I'LL FINALLY BE ONE OF THEM.
MAYBE I'LL BE GOTHAM'S BATMAN. THE REAL ONE, HAHA!
SCREEEEEEE
EEEEEEEE...

BATMAN... BATMAN, ARE YOU THERE?
BATMAN?
THIS CAN'T BE REAL. IT CAN'T END THIS WAY. IT CAN'T.
WHAT ARE YOU GOING TO DO?
...
SOMETHING I NEVER THOUGHT I WOULD.

ALL RIGHT.
LET'S TALK ABOUT HISTORY.

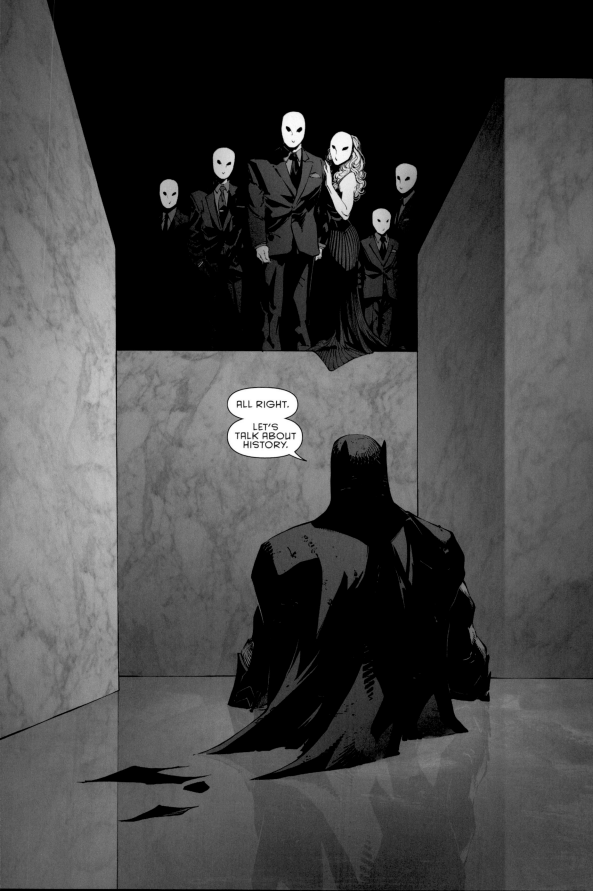

TMAN Nº 39

r by Greg Capullo, Danny Miki and FCO Plascencia

GOTHAM CITY, NOW.

My enemies have a *secret pact.*

They think I don't know about it, but I do.

The pact is, on the day I die, they will shine the Bat-signal over the city.

It was Joker's idea. A light in the sky to commemorate me. A bat, hanging *upside down*, at rest.

Seeing it now, I can't shake the feeling I'm dead already. Narrating my funeral...

BATMAN: ENDGAME
PART FIVE

WRITER
SCOTT SNYDER

PENCILLER
GREG CAPULLO

INKER
DANNY MIKI

COLORIST
FCO PLASCENCIA

LETTERER
STEVE WANDS

COVER
CAPULLO, MIKI & PLASCENCIA

ASSISTANT EDITOR
MATT HUMPHREYS

EDITOR
MARK DOYLE

...from deep in the underworld.

WELL, WELL. LOOK WHAT WE HAVE HERE.

OH, LET HIM SEE! WE'RE GROWING, AND HE CAN'T STOP US.

YOU MIGHT WANT TO GET THAT *LEAK* FIXED BEFORE YOU START BRAGGING. OH RIGHT, YOU *CAN'T.*

YOU GROW AS MUCH AS I *LET* YOU.

YOU REALLY BELIEVE THAT, DON'T YOU? YOU HAVEN'T EVEN NOTICED WHAT WE'VE DONE YET. THE SERRATIONS, ALL AROUND THE--

ENOUGH. I CAME HERE BECAUSE THE VIRUS THE JOKER SET LOOSE UP THERE, THE CHEMICAL AT ITS CORE IS SOMETHING I CAN'T OVERCOME.

"I NEED TO FIND IT. AND THE DOCTOR WHO DESIGNED THE VIRUS SPOKE OF A MINING PROJECT HUNDREDS OF YEARS AGO, AN ATTEMPT TO FIND THIS SUBSTANCE BENEATH GOTHAM."

"THERE'S ONLY ONE ORGANIZATION THAT HAD THE MEANS AND THE WILL TO UNDERTAKE SOMETHING LIKE THAT."

YOU.

YOU HAVE IT, DON'T YOU, THIS *DIONESIUM.* IT'S IN THE ELECTRUM YOU USE TO BRING BACK THE TALONS.

WE DID SEARCH, YES. BUT WHAT WE FOUND WAS A *CORRUPTED* VERSION.

IT'S IN OUR ELECTRUM. AND IT SERVES OUR *PURPOSE,* NOW THAT WE HAVE THE CATALYST. BUT IT'S NOTHING AS PURE AS WHATEVER'S IN *THAT* CLOWN'S BLOOD.

THAT CLOWN IS BURNING THIS CITY TO THE GROUND.
YOU DON'T TELL ME THE TRUTH ABOUT WHERE HE MIGHT HAVE GOTTEN THAT CHEMICAL, ALL OF US, ME, YOU, EVERYONE... THE CITY WILL DIE. IT WILL--
WE ALWAYS BUILD THEM HANGING PSIDE DOWN, THEN TURN ND PLACE THEM, BATMAN. WE DO IT TO REMIND OURSELVES THAT WE'RE BENEATH GOTHAM, THAT IT'S SOMETHING ABOVE US, ALWAYS.
WE SHAPE IT, BEND IT TO OUR WILL, BUT IT'S GREATER THAN ANY ONE OF US.
SO LET THE CLOWN BURN IT AND MOVE ON TO SOME OTHER PLACE. IT'S WHAT CLOWNS DO. THE CITY WILL RISE AGAIN. PURE AND CLEANSED AND WE'LL HELP IT ALONG. A NEW G--

COME ON...
...I KNOW YOU'RE HERE.

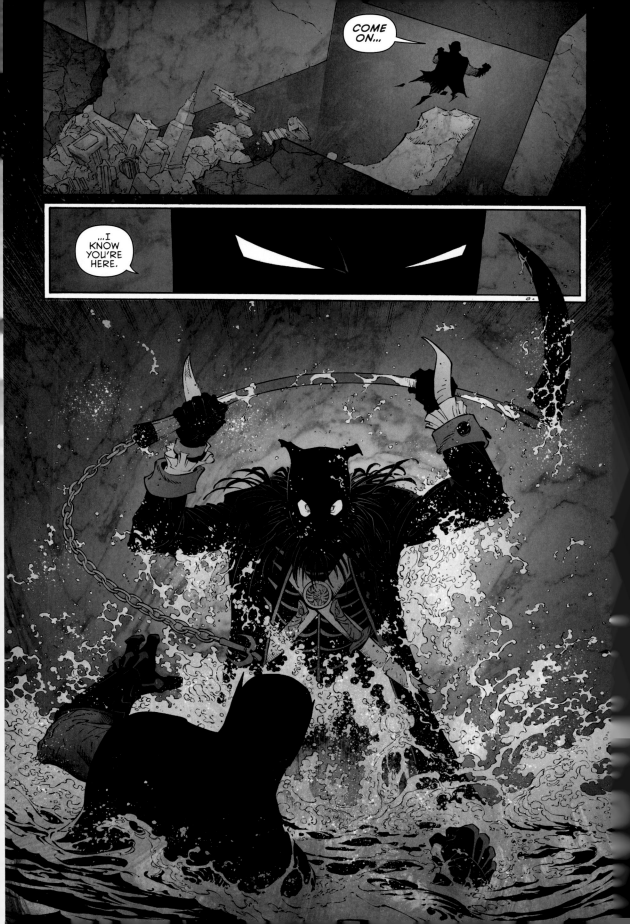

BATMAN...
...THE COURT OF OWLS...
Unh!
...HAS SENTENCED YOU...
...TO DIE!

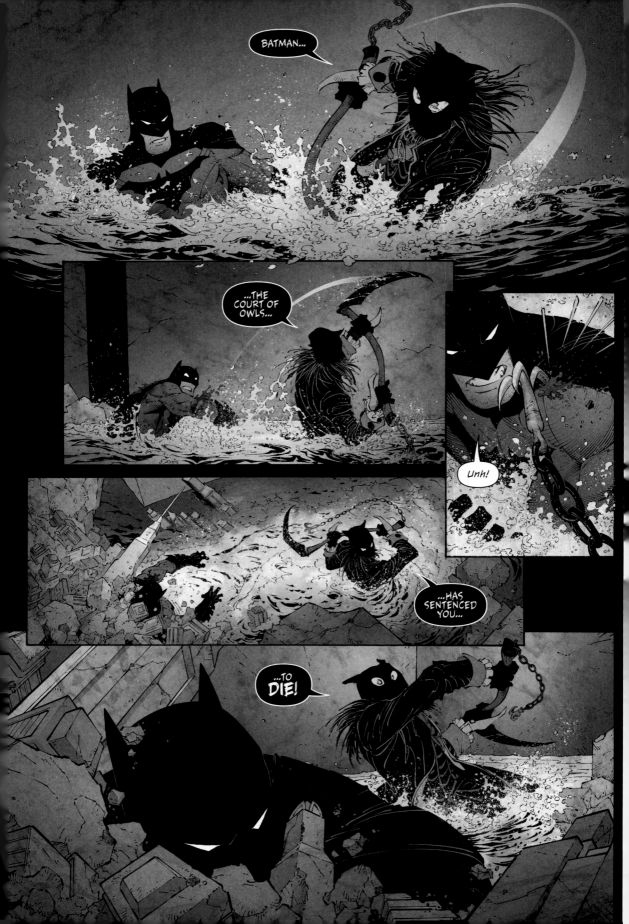

YES, I WILL DIE! MAYBE EVEN BY THEIR HAND! BUT NOT HERE! -unh- AND NOT NOW!
ARRGH!
YOU'RE ONE OF THE FIRST TALONS, URIAH! YOU'RE FROM BEFORE ALL THIS! THE SKYSCRAPERS! FROM WHEN THE CITY WAS BRICK AND WOOD! URIAH BOONE!
...
I AM A TALON. I AM FROM HERE, ALWAYS. YOU...
...ARE JUST A NAME SCRATCHED ON THE WALL!
Unh! JUST TELL ME ONE THING! WAS HE AROUND THEN?
WHO? SAY IT! WHO?
WAS HE AROUND, WHEN YOU WERE ACTIVE 400 YEARS AGO? THE JOKER? THE PALE MAN?
WAS HE?!

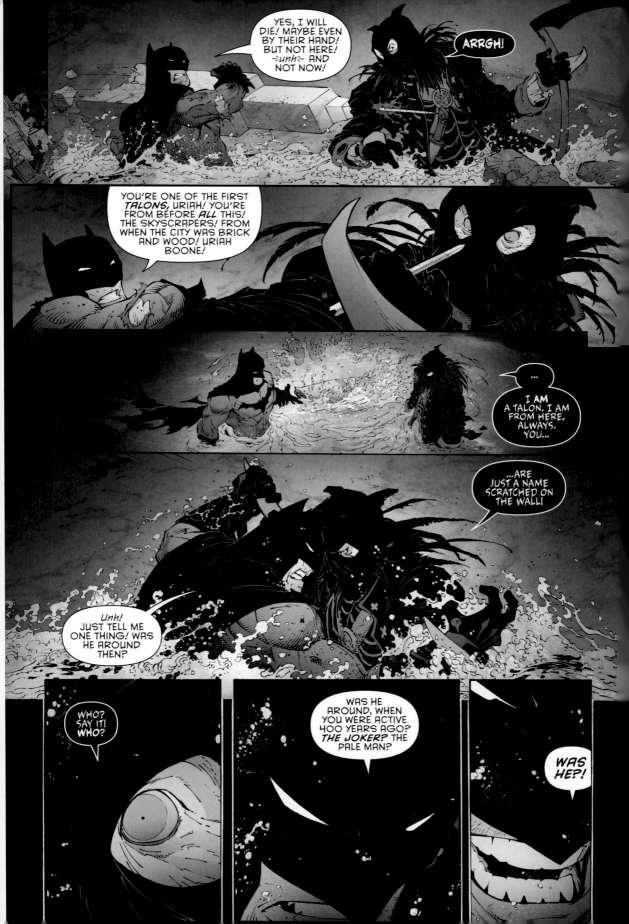

ad my share
r-death
ences.
he was Robin, Dick used
oke that it wasn't a real
kend unless my heart had
pped at least twice. He'd
me if I remembered to say
o some long-dead actress
him this time around.
Then next weekend.
death. Not to believe in it. That was the first, most important precursor to becoming Batman.
The last time I remember believing--really believing--I was going to die, I was ten years old, looking down the barrel of a gun.
He kept shifting targets as he spoke. I remember watching that tiny black hole as it moved from my father to my mother, to me, and then back to my father and the realization hit me--and hit me hard.
Bruce, you're going to die today.
All of you. Your mother, your father, and you, too.
And scary as that was, there was comfort in it. We would go down together, as a family.

GOTHAM CITY, THREE HOURS AGO.
Then the gun fired.
Once...
Twice...
...nothing.
And then I was afraid like I've never been afraid before. Because I was alone, and none of this made sense.
It was just me, by myself, in the dark.
PENNY-TWO ~koff~...COME IN.
Greg
Jamie
BATMAN! DID YOU FIND THE DIONESIUM?
~Unh~ NO.
WHAT IS IT? I HEAR IT IN YOUR VOICE. SOMETHING HAPPENED.
I...I TRIED TO REACH YOU... BATMAN.
IT'S BLOODY AWFUL AND I--
KIDSSSS... WHERE ARE YOU?!
IT'S ALL "BLOODY AWFUL," PENNY-TWO...

"...AND IT JUST KEEPS GETTING WORSE."
AND THIS DAY JUST KEEPS GETTING BETTER AND BETTER!

AW, YOU KEPT IT.
BLAM
YOU ARE NOT WELCOME HERE!
HEE...AH, ALFIE. THE FAITHFUL RIGHT HAND MAN...
...I'VE BEEN READING UP ON YOU SINCE OUR LAST PLAYDATE, YOU KNOW...
YOU WERE A THESSSPIAN IN PICADILLYDILLYDILLY. I WATCHED RECORDINGS...
YOU CAN'T SCARE ME, JOKER. YOU MIGHT HAVE GOTTEN THROUGH THE CAVE'S DEFENSES WITH JUST A FEW SCRATCHES ON YOUR FACE, BUT YOU WON'T GET THROUGH ME!
...AND MY FAVORITE PERFORMANCE OF YOURS WAS EEEEASILY THE FOOL IN LEAR! YOU WERE FANTASTIC!
AND I KNOW FOOLS! HAHAHAHA!

SO NATURAL, JEEVES...THE THING MOST PEOPLE MISSSS ABOUT THAT FOOL IS THAT DEEP DOWN, HE'S A BIG PHONEY, AM I RIGHT?
I MEAN, HE SEEMS SO LOYAL, BUT THEN...AS SOON AS THINGS GET ROUGH FOR OLD LEAR, HE DISAPPEARS! GONE BY SCENE SIX OF ACT THREE! WHOOSHHHH!
SHUT YOUR FILTHY MOUTH!
HIDING OFF-STAGE SOMEWHERE...TUCKED AWAY, ALWAYS SO SSSSSAFE. YOU TELL ME. BUT TO MY MIND, THAT FOOL'S NOT MUCH OF A RIGHT HAND MAN TO ANYONE BUT HIMSELF...
...IS HE?!
THEN AGAIN, WHAT THE HELL DO I KNOW ABOUT THEATER?!
I MEAN LET'S FACE IT...
...I'VE ALWAYS BEEN MORE OF AN IMPROV MAN MYSELF! HAHAHAHAHA!
"BATMAN?"

...
...BATMAN, ARE YOU THERE?
...PENNY-ONE, IS HE...?
HE CRAWLED INTO THE ARMORY TO GET SOMETHING TO ATTACK THAT MANIAC AGAIN...
...AND LUCKILY, I WAS ABLE TO BRING THE DAMN DOORS DOWN ON HIM REMOTELY. HE'S STABLE AND SAFE FOR NOW.
-SIGH- YOU'RE SURE.
YES. BUT WHAT I DON'T UNDERSTAND IS WHY JOKER WOULD BREAK IN ANYWAY.
THE WEAPONS AND VEHICLES ALL HAVE SELF-DESTRUCT FAIL-SAFES IF THEY'RE REMOVED FROM THE CAVE. HE JUST TOOK TROPHIES. DISPLAY--
LOOK!
WHAT THE... BATMAN, SOMETHING IS COMING OVER THE SCREENS. A BROADCAST. SOME KIND OF IMAGE, BUT THERE'S SOUND TOO, IT SOUNDS LIKE--
MUSIC.
WHAT IN GOD'S NAME IS THAT?
"PEOPLE OF GOTHAM! I HAVE ONE QUESTION FOR YOU..."

I MEAN, WHY NOT?! HELL, IN LOTS OF PLACES AROUND THE WORLD DEATH IS FOLLOWED BY CELEBRATION!
IT MAKES SENSSSSE, AM I RIGHT? WE STRUGGLE AND STRUGGLE IN LIFE...
...TRYING NOT TO LOOK AT THE END, TO LOOK AT THE NOW AND FIND MEANING, TO FIND PURPOSE...
...ALL FOR NAUGHT. NOTHING. ZZZZIP.
BUT AHHHH! THE DIRT NAP. TO REST YOUR FEET! SWEET RELIEF! SO LET'S DO IT! LET'S LOOK TOGETHER! LOOK IT IN THE FACE...

...WHO'S IN THE MOOD TO PARTY?!
...AND SMILE!
ONE LAST LUMBERING DANCE TO JUST THE RIGHT CHORDS. HAHAHAHA!
BATMAN. ARE YOU SEE--
I SEE. IT'S WORDPLAY. LUMBER, LUMBAR. CHORD... HE'S TAUNTING ME. DARING ME TO COME GET THE DIONESIUM FROM HIS SPINE.
WELL, WHAT DO WE DO?

GOTHAM CITY, NOW.

"I HAVE A PLAN."

COME ON, BATMAN!

STOP BEING SO DAMN LAZY AND LET'S DO THIS.

BLUEBIRD, GIGGLER ON YOUR RIGHT.

GOT HIM. MERCY BUCKETS, BATGIRL.

"WAIT, WAIT..."

GOTHAM CITY, ONE HOUR EARLIER.
...THAT CAN'T BE THE PLAN.
WE WON'T MAKE IT A BLOCK IN THAT MAW.
NO, WE WON'T.
BUT THE MATERIAL I NEED TO SYNTHESIZE A CURE IS IN JOKER'S SPINE. I HOPED WE COULD FIND IT ELSEWHERE, BUT I HAVEN'T BEEN ABLE TO. I NEED THAT CHEMICAL, OR...
I NEED IT.
SO IT'S MASKS, AND US?
WHAT KIND OF PLAN--
THAT'S NOT THE WHOLE PLAN.
ACE
Um... BATMAN? IF THERE ARE ONLY FIVE OF US ON TEAM SAVE-THE-CITY-FROM-A-HORRIFYING-DEATH, WHY ARE THERE SO MANY MASKS?
FUNNY YOU SHOULD ASK...

Like I said, my enemies have a pact. Shine an upside down bat-signal and mourn me...
...Here, *together*, at Ace Chemical where it all began.
WE WERE WONDERING THE SAME THING.
OH, I GET IT. WITH THE CITY BURNING, WHY NOT MAKE TIME FOR ONE LAST MATCH *eh?*
Heh. OR SNACK.
I'LL START WITH ***VEGAS*** HERE. NICE SUIT, KID.

SHUT UP, ALL OF YOU!
LISTEN TO ME. THE VIRUS WORKS BY CHANGING A VICTIM'S *NEUROLOGY.* MAKING THEM GO AFTER ANYTHING THEY HAVE *AFFECTION* FOR.
MY ALLIES AND I, WE CAN USE THE TUNNELS *BENEATH* ACE TO GET AS CLOSE TO THE *PARADE* AS POSSIBLE, WITHIN A BLOCK, EVEN, BUT, ONCE WE'RE UP ON THE STREET, WE'LL BE *MOBBED.*
YOU WANT TO USE US AS HUMAN SHIELDING?!
I TAKE IT BACK. I LOVE THIS PLAN.
DO YOU NOW?
HERE'S THE FACTS.
I NEED TO GET UP ON THAT *FLOAT,* GET A SYRINGE INTO JOKER'S SPINE--HIS *SPINE.*
THEN I NEED TO MAKE IT OUT OF THERE ALIVE, *AND* GET THE SAMPLE TO MY BASE, WHERE I HAVE SOMEONE STANDING BY, READY TO SYNTHESIZE A CURE AND DISSEMINATE IT.
SO YES, IT'S A BAD PLAN. ANYONE HAS A BETTER ONE, I'M ALL EARS.
NO? THEN THE BOTTOM LINE IS THIS: IT'S *OUR* CITY. ALL OF OURS. AND WE NEED TO TAKE IT BACK FROM HIM, *NOW, TOGETHER,* OR IT'S OVER. *FOR ALL OF US. FOREVER.*
SO TELL ME...

GOTHAM CITY, NOW.
"...WHO'S IN?!"
HEE-HEE!
PERFECT.
AND NOW, FRIENDS, FOR MY BEST TRICK OF ALL...

NIGHTWING Nº 17
cover by Javier Fernandez and Chris Sotomayor

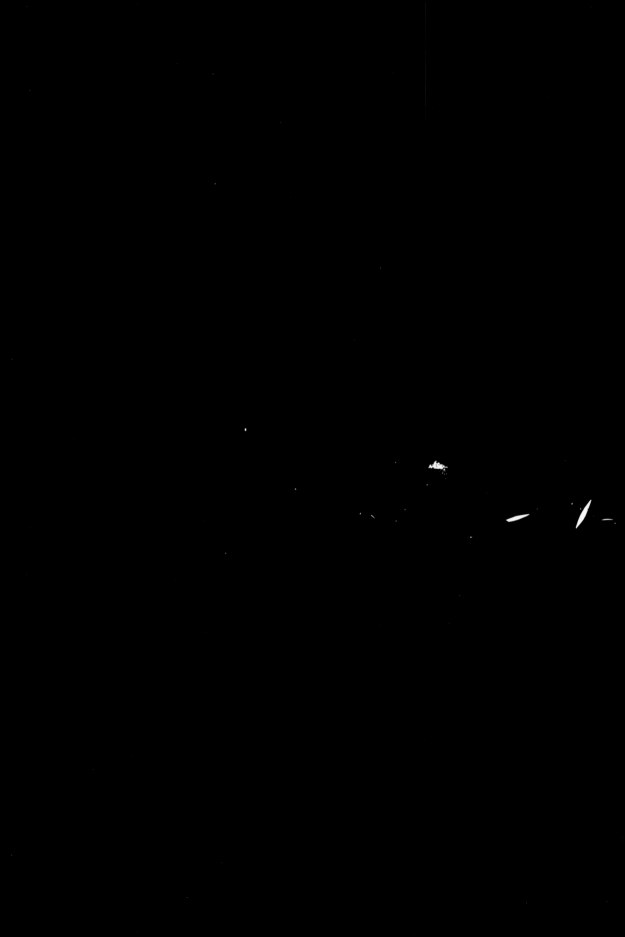

"IT WAS ONE OF MY MORE EMBARRASSING PREDICAMENTS TO BE SURE.

"I HAD BEEN CAPTURED BY THE JOKER TO BE USED AS BAIT IN HIS BATTLE WITH MY FATHER'S LATEST ARCHENEMY, *DR. SIMON HURT.*

"*YOU* WERE DRESSED AS *BATMAN.*

"*I* WAS TIED UP, DUMPED INTO A COFFIN THAT SMELLED OF ROTTED, DRIED FLESH, AND WORST OF ALL...

"...I WAS DRESSED AS A CLOWN.

AND YET, DESPITE EVERY-THING, I CAN SAY WITH SOME AMOUNT OF CONVICTION, THE HOURS INSIDE THAT ROTTING

...WERE PREFERABLE TO THE THIRTEEN HOURS STUCK IN THIS BATMOBILE WITH YOU.

YOU WANTED TO STRETCH?

YES. THIS AGAIN. IT IS CLEAR YOUR RELOCATION TO BLÜDHAVEN IS A MEANS TO STEP AROUND THE LINE. TO GO AROUND THE NATURAL PROGRESSION.

TO SET UP YOUR OWN "FRANCHISE."

A "FRANCHISE"?!

IS THAT WHAT YOU THINK I'M DOING WITH SHAWN? BREEDING BABY ROBINS?!

CONSIDER THE EVIDENCE, GRAYSON, AS YOU WERE TAUGHT. YOU ABRUPTLY LEFT GOTHAM. YOU BEGAN ACTING AS A NEW CITY'S DEFENDER.

YOU HAVE BILLBOARDS, ESSENTIALLY DECLARING YOU THE "BATMAN OF BLÜDHAVEN".

SO LET'S STRETCH.
I've been driving across endless miles of ocean in a borrowed Batmobile following a cryptic clue.
And my copilot--Damian Wayne, Robin--isn't making me feel any better.
Especially since he won't let me kick his petulant butt.
YOU'VE LEARNED SOME NEW MOVES SINCE LAST TIME WE SPARRED.
CONSTANTLY IMPROVING ONESELF IS WHAT BATMAN DOES. IT'S WHY I'LL INHERIT THE LEGACY, NOT YOU.
THIS AGAIN.
EVERY CLUE POINTS TO YOU BEING THREATENED BY MY VERY EXISTENCE.
THAT YOU'RE BUILDING A FOUNDATION TO TAKE THE MANTLE OF BATMAN FROM ME DESPITE THE FACT THAT YOU HAVE ALREADY HAD YOUR TURN.
AFTER ALL THESE YEARS, ALL OUR TIME WORKING TOGETHER...THAT'S WHAT YOU THINK OF ME?!
THAT I CARE ABOUT BEING BATMAN?!
MY GIRLFRIEND IS MISSING AND SHE MIGHT BE PREGNANT! I'M NOT EVEN SURE I WANT TO BE NIGHTWING!

QUOI?

AUTOPILOT DISENGAGED.

I CAN BARELY KEEP MY LIFE TOGETHER AS IT IS! HAVING THE RESPONSIBILITY OF A *CHILD* WHILE TRYING TO PROTECT A CITY, BEING PART OF THE FAMILY, RUNNING THE TITANS...

...I DON'T THINK I CAN MANAGE IT ALL!

AND DO YOU KNOW HOW I KNOW THAT? WHAT MY CLUES ARE? ALL I HAVE TO DO IS LOOK AT *YOUR DAD.*

MY FATHER IS A GREAT MAN.

HE'S NOT JUST *ONE MAN.* HE HAS TO BE BRUCE WAYNE, BATMAN, A MEMBER OF THE JUSTICE LEAGUE AND A FATHER TO A BUNCH OF BATKIDS.

AND THE ONE WHO I THINK SUFFERS THE MOST? YOU, DAMIAN. HIS ONE *REAL SON.*

-tt-

YOU ARE A FOOL, GRAYSON. I SHOULD LET YOU GO ALONE.

YOU DEMANDED TO COME ALONG. BUT YOU CAN LEAVE RIGHT NOW, MAN. I'LL DO THIS WITH OR WITHOUT YOU.

LET US JUST FIND YOUR WOMAN QUICKLY.

SNNN

THE FASTER WE END THIS NONSENSE, THE FASTER YOU CAN HANG UP YOUR MASK, AND LEAVE ME TO MY LEGACY.

The coordinates written in a copy of the **Adventures of Robin Hood** book I loaned Shawn are for **Fontevraud-l'Abbaye** in Western France.
The Abbey has a long history, first as a monastery, later as a prison, now as a tourist attraction.
I've wanted to visit since I was a kid.
Whoever brought me here wants me to know that this is personal.
That they know my dreams. What I read as a kid. What I read now to escape into a comfortable world of nostalgia. Who my heroes are.
And they know my nightmares. They know my fear that being a "hero" will hurt someone I love.
GRAYSON.

The tomb of Richard I.

He's the real-life king who has cameos in a lot of the Robin Hood stories. His fictionalized moustache-twirling brother was Robin Hood's archenemy.

The thing is, all that's here is the tomb. Most of Richard's actual body was lost during the French Revolution.

The tomb is empty.

MY THERMO-GRAPHIC LENSES SAY THERE IS...

...SOMEONE INSIDE.

Oh god. It's Shawn. Someone put her in a tomb.

GRAYSON. DON'T. PLEASE. WAIT.

WHAT THE HELL ARE YOU TALKING ABOUT?!

GET OUT OF THE WAY! THIS IS NO TIME FOR YOUR EGO GAMES!

PLEASE. RICHARD. IT'S FOR YOUR OWN GOOD.

NO! NO, SHE CAN'T BE--

THE TEMPERATURE VARIATIONS. WHO-EVER IS IN THAT TOMB...

...HAS NO FACE!

I HAVE A FACE.

THE FACE OF DICK GRAYSON. THE FACE OF
DEATHWING.
He has my mask. My old uniform.
And worst of all. He has my voice.
YOU CAME. I KNEW YOU WOULD. YOU DO WHAT I WOULD DO. JUST NOT AS WELL.
But it's twisted. Cruel. Angry.
HNH!
LET HIM GO!
ARE YOU SURE? YOU MAY BE AN INFERIOR COPY, BUT YOU FEEL THE WAY I DO.
WHICH MEANS SOME-TIMES...

...YOU JUST WANT TO HIT HIM.
HNF!
Who the hell is he?
He has my moves. My speed. But none of the restraint.
Which means the only way I can save Damian from his grip is to play as hard as he does.
KRAK
Because, if I can't save Damian, how can I save Shawn?
How could I be a good father?
STAY BACK, ROBIN!
DON'T BE STUPID. HE'S ONE MAN.
NO, HE THINKS HE'S ME, WHICH MEANS HE'S DANGEROUS AS HELL. THIS IS NO TIME FOR YOUR LITTLE HARDHEAD ROUTINE!
HARDHEAD?!
THAT DIDN'T HURT. I KNOW PAIN.
I'VE BEEN TORMENTED MY WHOLE LIFE.
HUNG OUT BY BATMAN ON A HOOK. A BRIGHTLY COLORED BULLET MAGNET.
SLSH
UNF!
WHAT HURT WAS WHEN BATMAN KICKED ME ASIDE, LIKE A BROKEN TOY.
NO!

WHEN HE MADE ROOM FOR *YOU*, DAMIAN.

GHK!

He knows Damian. It's like he has my memories. All the feelings I had but was ashamed of.

WOK

KRAK

THAT'S WHY I HAD TO BECOME LIKE BATMAN.

BATMAN IS ABOUT CONTROL. BEING THE ONE WHO *DECIDES* WHO HURTS.

WHEN I BECAME BATMAN, I FELL IN LOVE WITH WHAT IT DID TO ME. I BECAME A PERFECT FORM.

NGH!

He's my dark side given very ugly physical form.

IT WAS THERE ALL THE TIME, BUT WAITING FOR THE SCULPTOR TO BRING IT FROM THE MARBLE.

DAMIAN!

REMEMBER WHEN YOU WERE BURIED, ROBIN?

WHO ARE YOU?! WHO MADE YOU THINK YOU'RE ME?!
WHERE THE HELL IS SHAWN?!
CRSH
KRK
YOU THINK THIS IS ABOUT SHAWN? SHAWN IS *NOTHING* TO ME.
ALL SHE WAS IS THE LAST THING STANDING IN THE WAY...
WOK
...OF *YOU* BECOMING *ME.*
OF BECOMING WHAT YOU *NEED TO BE.*

RRAGH!

NO LEVERAGE. NAILED SHUT. NOT ENOUGH DISTANCE. FISTS TOO SMALL.

DAMN YOU, GRAYSON! YOU INSULTED ME, CODDLED ME LIKE A CHILD, CALLED ME *HARDHEADED* AND NOW...

Hmn. HARDHEADED.

TELL ME!

YOU'RE DELUSIONAL. *PROGRAMMED.* TELL ME WHERE SHAWN IS AND I'LL HELP YOU.

I CAN'T *TELL* YOU...

...YOU NEED TO SEE WHAT WAS SHOWN TO ME. YOU NEED TO SEE WHAT'S COMING.
SLSH
The blade glints black. Like it's made out of night.
The cut doesn't hurt. Not exactly. But it feels like something is spilling out. My mind maybe.
HNGH.
GIVE IN TO THE BLOOD.
A drop of blood hangs for an eternity before my eyes.
And then it drops.
And I go with it.
All the way down.
GIVE IN...
AH.

I'm at the bottom, looking up.
All around me, paths branching off.
I can't remember which one of me I am. Am I the hero or the villain?
Is this a dream? Or a **nightmare?**

SH-SHAWN. W-WHERE...
SHAWN HAD TO GO. SHE KEPT THE SCULPTURE TRAPPED IN THE BLOCK.
SHE OFFERS YOU STABILITY AND COMPLACENCY WHEN YOU HAVE TO SHED THIS LIFE AND BE REBORN.
TO BE THE MAN I'VE BECOME, YOU HAVE TO SUFFER LOSS. YOU HAVE TO FALL FAR...
...FARTHER THAN THE GROUND.
FARTHER THAN *HELL*.
NO!

KRAK
NOT WHILE ROBIN LIVES.

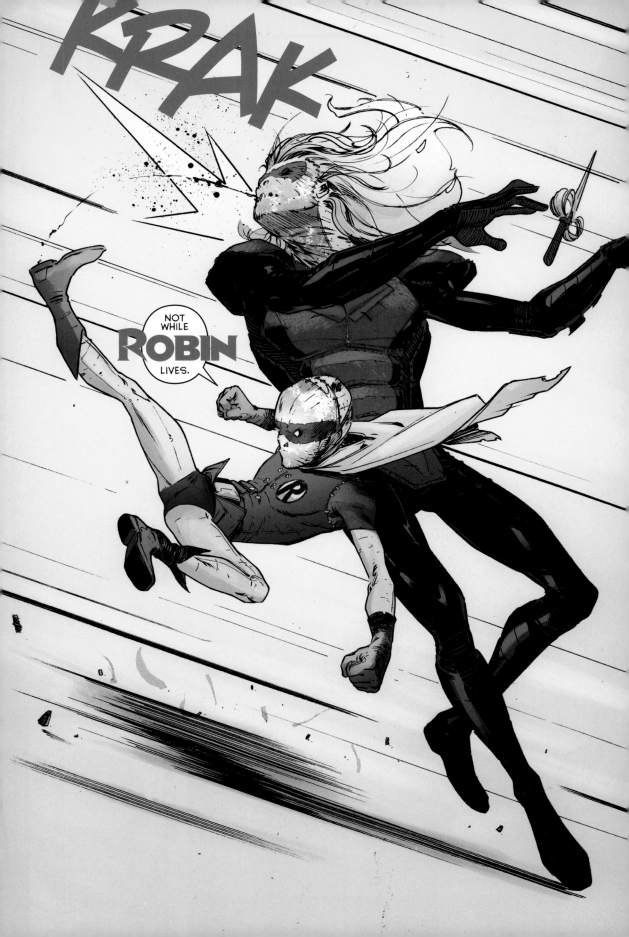

NIGHTWING! THE FOOL MAY HAVE NAILED THE LID DOWN, BUT HE COMPROMISED ITS STRUCTURAL INTEGRITY.
THE SAME THING CANNOT BE SAID OF MY FOREHEAD--
WHO?
IT'S ME, YOU FOOL! DAMIAN.
WHERE... WHERE HAVE YOU GONE?
YOU. YOU'RE A MISTAKE. EVEN HE SAID SO. YOU DON'T HAVE MY BLOOD.
NO.
SHING
BUT I WILL.

AN OCEAN OF WORLDS... NO SHORE... NO SHAWN.

REMEMBER WHO YOU ARE, YOU WEAK-WILLED SOT! REMEMBER ME!

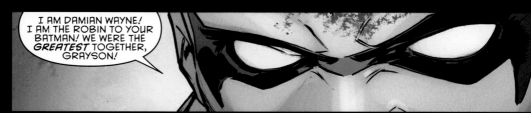

I AM DAMIAN WAYNE! I AM THE ROBIN TO YOUR BATMAN! WE WERE THE *GREATEST* TOGETHER, GRAYSON!

WE *WERE*. BUT IT'S DIFFERENT NOW. YOU'RE...YOU'RE GONE.

FINDING NEW LIFE. CONSIDERING HAVING A CHILD TO REPLACE ME. I DON'T KNOW WHAT I WILL BE...ALONE.

I NEED YOU HERE, RICHARD.

DAMIAN?

DAMIAN. WHERE? WHAT HAPPENED?
NOTHING. NOTHING HAPPENED...
...BUT THIS IS INSANITY.
Another Robin?!
For a second I think I'm still in the ocean of worlds.
But this is my world. My story. I'm the hero.
And this is most definitely the villain.
KRAK
PUT DOWN THOSE WEAPONS, AND JUST TELL US WHO YOU ARE, OKAY?
THERE'S NO NEED TO FIGHT.
THAT'S MORE LIKE IT.
N-NO. OF COURSE NOT. YOU WOULD SIMPLY LOSE...I AM THE GREATEST.

MY NAME IS... DA--*DANESH?* MY FATHER IS A TRUCK DRIVER...

NO. MY NAME...IS *DAMIAN WAYNE.* MY FATHER IS *BATMAN.*

The stitches. The pale, melted skin. The faint antiseptic smell.

YOU'RE *WHAT?* I'LL--

ROBIN! LOOK AT HIS FACE. AT DEATHWING'S.

OH. GOD.

ROBIN. YOU CAN HELP US FIND SHAWN, RIGHT? YOU KNOW WHERE SHE IS.

YES. DEATHWING WAS TO DELIVER MS. TSANG TO OUR CREATOR.

THEN OUR CREATOR SAW HER ART. HE BECAME ENAMORED WITH IT.

HE BELIEVED SHE COULD BE GREAT IF SHE LET HIM UNLEASH HER TRUE POTENTIAL. LIKE ELIZA DOOLITTLE, HE SAID.

Her "potential." The "Dollotron" copies of Damian and me. It's worse than I imagined.

Shawn was kidnapped by one of the sickest minds Damian and I ever encountered...

...Professor Pyg.

IT'S SO NICE TO WORK WITH A FELLOW ARTIST FOR ONCE, MS. TSANG.

YOU PUT SO MUCH OF WHAT'S *INSIDE* YOU INTO YOUR OWN WORK.

NIGHTWING
MUST DIE!
PART TWO

TIM SEELEY
WRITER

JAVIER FERNANDEZ
ARTIST

CHRIS SOTOMAYOR
COLORIST

CARLOS M. MANGUAL
LETTERER

JAVIER FERNANDEZ & CHRIS SOTOMAYOR
COVER ARTIST

DAVE WIELGOSZ
ASST. EDITOR

REBECCA TAYLOR
EDITOR

MARK DOYLE
GROUP EDITOR

AND NOW I'LL PUT WHAT'S INSIDE YOU INTO *MINE*.

EDDY BARROWS
+
Eber Ferreira

DETECTIVE COMICS Nº 950
cover by Eddy Barrows, Eber Ferreira and Adriano Lucas

MONTHS AGO.
THE BIG PICTURE
JAMES TYNION IV Writer
EDDY BARROWS Pencils
EBER FERREIRA Inks
ADRIANO LUCAS Colors
MARILYN PATRIZIO Letters
ALFRED, YOU WERE RIGHT. ITS *TEETH* WERE REINFORCED.
SEND THE CAR TO THE ALLEY BETWEEN 119 AND 120, ON AVE. R., TRICORNER.
I TOLD ALFRED HE COULD HEAD UP EARLY TONIGHT, ACTUALLY.
SCREEECH

WHOOPS... LOOKS LIKE MY REDBIRD DRIVING'S GOTTEN A LITTLE RUSTY.
RED ROBIN?
YOU AND I NEED TO HAVE A TALK.
TIM... IS THERE SOMETHING WRONG AT THE BELFRY?
OH, NO. THINGS ARE JUST PEACHY. SEE FOR YOURSELF.
"STEPH'S REALLY COMING INTO HER OWN, ISN'T SHE? BATWOMAN'S WORKING US TO THE BONE, BUT THAT'S NO SURPRISE. STILL NO WORD ON OUR MILITARY FRIENDS."
I DON'T EVEN WANT TO KNOW WHAT BIT YOU, DO I?
I WAS JUST STARTING TO NETWORK THE BELFRY INTO THE BAT-COMPUTER WHEN IT FINALLY HIT ME. I HONESTLY FEEL A LITTLE STUPID THAT I DIDN'T SEE IT BEFORE.
I THINK I NEEDED TO SEE IT FROM THE TOP DOWN.
...
WHAT ARE YOU TALKING ABOUT?

MY *ROBIN'S NEST* IS A FARADAY CAGE. *NOTHING* WILL GET IN OR OUT. THERE'S NOBODY LISTENING, EXCEPT FOR ME.

NOT EVEN ALFRED. SO I WANT YOU TO BE *HONEST* WITH ME.

DICK'S WALKING A FINE LINE, ISN'T HE? BACK IN THE NIGHTWING COSTUME, CAUGHT BETWEEN THE MOST POWERFUL INTELLIGENCE AGENCY AND THE MOST FAR-REACHING CRIMINAL EMPIRE ON THE PLANET.

SUDDENLY, BATMAN HAS *EYES* IN *TWO* PLACES HE NEVER HAD EYES BEFORE. FIGHTING TWO SIDES OF THE DANGEROUS SECRET WARS THAT COULD SHAPE OUR WORLD.

AND THEN THERE'S *JASON.* SEEMS LIKE THAT ASSASSINATION ATTEMPT WASN'T ALL IT SEEMED TO BE, *WAS* IT, BRUCE? AND NOW YOU HAVE A ROBIN KEEPING AN EYE ON THE ENTIRE CRIMINAL UNDERWORLD OF GOTHAM.

I DON'T KNOW WHAT YOU'RE GETTING AT.

YES, YOU *DO.*

I'VE BEEN LETTING MY TITANS DUTIES *SLIP* THE MOMENT I STARTED BUILDING THE BELFRY. I'M GUESSING YOU'VE PROBABLY HAD A LITTLE CONVERSATION WITH *DAMIAN,* PLANTING THE SEED THAT HE SHOULD FIND SOME COMMUNITY HIS OWN AGE.

YOU'RE NOT TRAINING *DUKE* TO BE YOUR PARTNER, YOU'RE TRAINING HIM TO BE SOMETHING *ELSE.*

AND THIS NEW TEAM AT THE BELFRY...IT'S THE MOST OBVIOUS IN THE LOT, BRUCE. YOU'VE STARTED PREPARING PEOPLE FOR A NEW KIND OF BATTLE, THEY JUST DON'T KNOW IT.

AND WHAT'S *NEXT?* YOUR OWN PRIVATE *JUSTICE LEAGUE?*

BUT THAT'S WHAT IT ALL IS. ALL THE PIECES TOGETHER. YOU'RE SHORING THINGS UP, MAKING ABSOLUTELY CERTAIN THAT EACH OF THE ARENAS YOU OPERATE IN IS THOROUGHLY PROTECTED IN A WAY THAT YOU *NEVER* HAVE BEFORE.

TIM...
BRUCE, I NEED TO ASK THIS BLUNTLY.
WHY ARE YOU PREPARING FOR WAR?

THE MAP OF TH

THE MULTIVERSAL VIBRATIONAL REALMS

SOURCE WALL

Here is the Limit even to Thought. Beyond lies only Monitor-mind, The Source and the Unknowable.

MONITOR SPHERE

Dwelling place of the mighty Monitor race — once countless in number, the 52 Monitors that remained after the CRISIS event were each tasked with the preservation and study of a separate universe.

LIMBO

Home of the Lost and Forgotten of the Orrery, Limbo is the furthest edge of the manifest DC universe. This is where matter and memory break down.

SPHERE OF THE GODS

From the heights of the Skyland Pantheons to the prison depths of the Underworld, this is the great realm of Archetypal Powers and Intelligences inhabited by Gods and New Gods, Demons, Angels and the Endless.

DREAM

On the borderlands is the magical realm of Morpheus the Dream-King, incorporating the Halls of The Endless, the Courts of Faerie and the Twelve Houses of Gemworld. Home to Oberon, Titania, Amethyst, Santa Claus and the Easter Bunny.

HEAVEN

The Silver City. The Word of the Voice. Home of the Spectre, Zauriel and the Guardian Angel Hosts of the Pax Dei — The Bull Host, The Eagle Host, The Lion Host and the Host of Adam.

NEW GENESIS

Sunlit lordly New Genesis is the proud home of the New Gods and the young Forever People. The floating city of Supertown is the dwelling place of Highfather, Orion, Lightray, Avia, Big Barda, Scott Free and others.

SKYLAND

Home of the Shining Ones, the Old Gods of Thunder and Lightning, Love and War and Death. Here is Asgard, Olympus, and the Throne of Zeus. The Pantheons of Celts, Mayans, the Divine Bureaucracies of China, and the Gods of Oceania, Mesopotamia and Egypt, the Loa and the Elohim are all gathered here, each with a peak of its own.

NIGHTMARE

The creepy-crawly Shadow Side of Morpheus's domain. Here is the Goblin Market where nothing is real. The Land of Nightshades. Home to the Bogeyman and the Corinthian, haunt of Witches, Yeth Hounds and Bad Dreams.

HELL

Known to some as Sheol, or Jigoku, the burning iron Place of Torment is home to Neron, Belial, Trigon, Azazel, Abnegazar, Rath, Ghast and the Demon Etrigan — high on a list of a legion of fiends. Here are the Djinns and the Fallen Angels, and the Haters of Humanity, waiting...

APOKOLIPS

The fiery planetasm ruled with the iron fist of the ultimate tyrant, Darkseid of the New Gods, and his cruel acolytes — Desaad the Torture God, Granny Goodness, Glorious Godfrey, Kalibak and many, many others.

UNDERWORLD

Here is Hades, Annwn, the realm of Pluto and the Throne of Erishkagal, the Land of No Return. Known also as The Phantom Zone, this gloomy prison of shades and formless shadows plays host to the criminals of the planet Krypton — General Zod, Ursa the She-Devil, Xadu the Phantom King and many others.

WONDERWORLD

Orbiting Creation itself at unimaginable velocities, Wonderworld is the "Worldquarters" of the long-lost Theocracy, a team of stupendous primal superheroes.

SPEED FORCE WALL

The Speed Force Wall is otherwise known to the denizens of the Orrery as the Speed of Light. It is only a limit to matter.

THE FREQUENCIES OF KWYZZ

Radio universe, home to KRAKKL the Defender.

ORRERY OF WORLDS

52 'brane universes vibrating in the same space, all at different frequencies, within the all-enclosing Bulk, otherwise known as Bleedspace. Four Bleed Siphons have been drilled in from the Monitor Sphere to the Orrery, to permit harvest of the miracle Ultramenstruum fluid.

GODS
THE
OF
SPHERE
MONITOR SPHERE
SOURCE WALL
LIMBO
UNDERWORLD
APOKOLIPS
THE PIT
HELL
THE BLEED
SPEED FORCE WALL
48
4
9
50
45
35
41
39
6
7
44
37
15
40
38
43
3
10
19
13

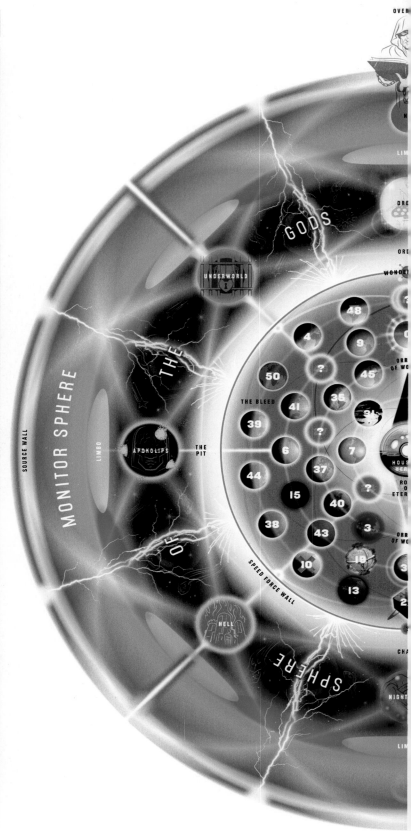

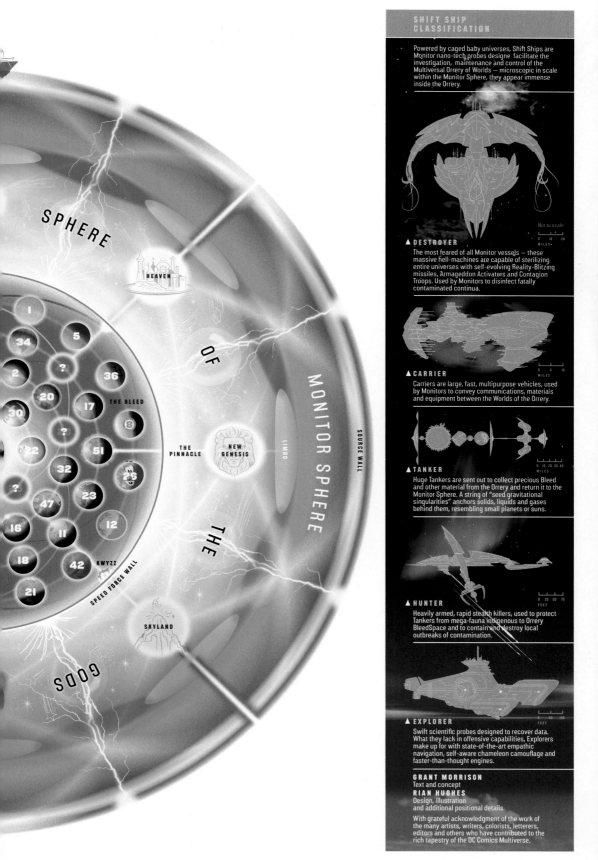

E MULTIVERSE

SPHERE OF THE GODS
HEAVEN
NEW GENESIS
THE PINNACLE
SKYLAND
LIMBO
MONITOR SPHERE
SOURCE WALL
THE BLEED
KWYZZ
SPEED FORCE WALL
1
34
5
?
2
36
20
17
30
8
?
22
51
32
26
?
23
47
12
16
11
18
42
21

SHIFT SHIP CLASSIFICATION

Powered by caged baby universes, Shift Ships are Monitor nano-tech probes designe facilitate the investigation, maintenance and control of the Multiversal Orrery of Worlds – microscopic in scale within the Monitor Sphere, they appear immense inside the Orrery.

Not to scale
0 10 20
MILES

▲ DESTROYER

The most feared of all Monitor vessels – these massive hell-machines are capable of sterilizing entire universes with self-evolving Reality-Blitzing missiles, Armageddon Activators and Contagion Troops. Used by Monitors to disinfect fatally contaminated continua.

0 5 10
MILES

▲ CARRIER

Carriers are large, fast, multipurpose vehicles, used by Monitors to convey communications, materials and equipment between the Worlds of the Orrery.

0 10 20 30 40
MILES

▲ TANKER

Huge Tankers are sent out to collect precious Bleed and other material from the Orrery and return it to the Monitor Sphere. A string of "seed gravitational singularities" anchors solids, liquids and gases behind them, resembling small planets or suns.

0 25 50 75
FEET

▲ HUNTER

Heavily armed, rapid stealth killers, used to protect Tankers from mega-fauna indigenous to Orrery BleedSpace and to contain and destroy local outbreaks of contamination.

0 50 100
FEET

▲ EXPLORER

Swift scientific probes designed to recover data. What they lack in offensive capabilities, Explorers make up for with state-of-the-art empathic navigation, self-aware chameleon camouflage and faster-than-thought engines.

GRANT MORRISON
Text and concept

RIAN HUGHES
Design, illustration
and additional positional details

With grateful acknowledgment of the work of the many artists, writers, colorists, letterers, editors and others who have contributed to the rich tapestry of the DC Comics Multiverse.

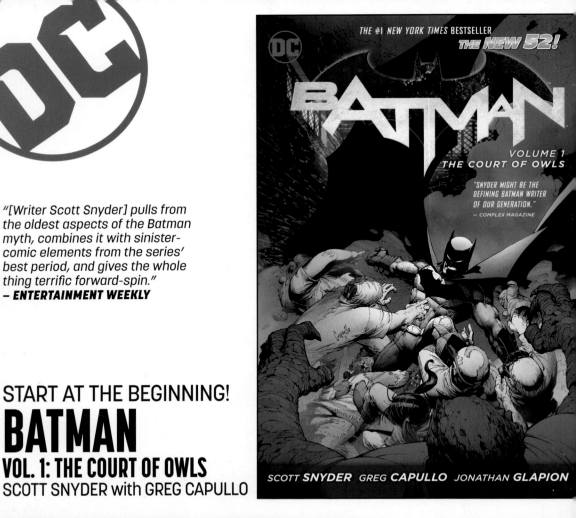
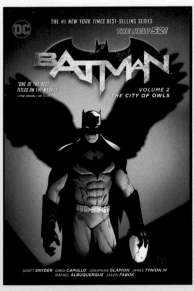
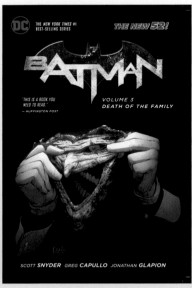

salute
to a sufferer

LESLIE D. WEATHERHEAD

salute
to a sufferer

an attempt to offer the
plain man a Christian
philosophy of suffering

ABINGDON PRESS   new york   nashville

SALUTE TO A SUFFERER

Library of Congress Catalog Card Number: 63-8669

Scripture quotations unless otherwise noted are from the Revised Standard Version, copyrighted 1946 and 1952 by the Division of Christian Education, National Council of Churches, and are used by permission.

SET UP, PRINTED, AND BOUND BY THE PARTHENON PRESS, AT NASHVILLE, TENNESSEE, UNITED STATES OF AMERICA

This book is dedicated to my friends
Norman and Hansie French
as a small token of my appreciation and
gratitude for all that they have done to
make a yoke easy and a burden light

This book is dedicated to my friends

Norman and Hanna French

as a small token of my appreciation and
gratitude for all that they have done to
make a yoke easy and a burden light.

Preface

FIRST OF ALL I MUST ACKNOWLEDGE THE GREAT HONOR IN BEING invited to deliver one of the Peake Memorial Lectures. My predecessors in this lectureship have all been scholars. I have no claim whatever to be a scholar. I have been a working minister ever since I was ordained. In this capacity I have tried to bring the truths which scholarship uncovers and by which men live, and set them in simple language before needy men and women.

This I think would appeal to Dr. Peake. A great scholar, a devout saint, and a great student and lover of the Bible, he was nevertheless a modern in the best sense of the word. He was far too eager-minded to be imprisoned in theories of verbal inspiration and dead formulas. For him revelation was progressive both within the Bible and after its completion. Truth is unchanging, but man's appreciation of truth widens with his increasing insight and understanding, and man must be free to break out of every verbal prison, however venerable and sacred, when the light of the Holy Spirit, pledged to guide us into all truth, shines upon him. He who is unwilling to move cannot be guided anywhere.

I hope nothing in this book will upset the reader. I think there is nothing contrary to the teaching of Christ and its implications, and therefore I think that Dr. Peake, whom I came so deeply to admire and love, would not disapprove.

What I have tried to do is to imagine that I am writing this book for a Christian friend of ordinary education and outlook

7

who has suddenly fallen seriously ill, perhaps incurably ill, or whose wife or child has done so.

I imagine that his mind is in a whirl of confusion about it. He has never given much thought to the problems inherent in the mystery of suffering. How can his mind find peace? He knows there are many questions which no one can answer. But is there a philosophy of suffering which can give to his troubled mind a place where it can find rest? How can he fit this terrible verdict of his doctors into the teaching he has accepted throughout the whole of his Christian life—that God is both utterly good and all-powerful? Why should this event befall *him?* Is it the will of God to be placidly accepted? Is it fate? Is is accident? Is it bad luck? Is it a punishment for some sin of long ago? Should he rely on doctors or should he seek help from so-called faith healers? Should he ask his fellow Christians to pray for him, and if so, what should he expect to happen? Are prayer and faith likely to succeed where medicine fails? What should be his mental attitude if all that he can do fails to avert death?

These, in my experience, are the questions men ask when suffering of body or mind—either their own or that of a dear one—descends upon them. I have no glib, easy, final answers. The element of mystery remains. The demand on faith remains. Trying to answer mental problems does little to make pain easier to bear. If all were explained, suffering remains to be faced and borne, and intellectual answers do not supply courage and faith. These are of far greater importance and far greater value than understanding. I can only hope to banish a few false ideas which make the problem darker than it need be and with which many sufferers mentally torture themselves.

Let us then go into this dim cathedral called human pain. It is a sacred place. Many who have served the world best have suffered most. Many, with even less light than we have, have been quite unbroken by their suffering. Their faith has triumphed. There are many windows in the cathedral, so that we do not walk in black darkness. And under the eastern window, beyond which the sun of understanding rises ever higher in the sky, is a cross which whispers its eternal message that God himself in Christ came right down into our pain and shared it. He understands how we feel. He promises that one day we shall understand too.

In 1755 when John Wesley wrote his famous *Notes on the New Testament,* he said in the Preface:

I write chiefly for plain, unlettered men who understand only their mother-tongue and love the Word of God and have a desire to save their souls. . . . I have used all such methods of reasoning and modes of expression as people in common life are acquainted with.

It is also recorded that when he had completed the writing of a sermon he would frequently read it over to the kitchen maid so as to discover any word or phrase that was beyond her understanding. If he did discover one he would substitute a simpler. I have long had the ambition to speak and write so that anyone of fifteen years and upwards could understand.

So, in ten brief chapters, written as simply as I can, I have tried to shed on this dark mystery a tiny bit of light which I have gathered during my forty-five years' ministry. The chapter headings indicate the line of argument followed.

I feel that I must express my gratitude to my wife, who always

9

takes such a helpful interest in anything I write and has once
more helped me to correct the proofs, and to my friend, Miss
Elsie B. Thompson, who has given me invaluable help in
preparing this little book for the press.

—LESLIE D. WEATHERHEAD

Contents

Contents

Chapter 1

Does God want me to be ill?

My answer to that is an emphatic no! My evidence is the nature of God as Jesus revealed him. Jesus kept on telling men that one of the best clues to the nature of God they could find anywhere is the nature of man at his best. He said to them, "If ye then, being evil"—or grudging, as I am told the Greek word means—"know how to give good gifts unto your children, how much more shall your Father which is in heaven give good things to them that ask him?" (Matt. 7:11 K.J.V.) Truly, as every father knows, there are some gifts a father must not give at all, and others which he must not give until certain conditions are fulfilled, and others again, the gift of which would express favoritism. But who has met a father who did not want all his sons and daughters to have good health?

The temporary pain that warns that something is wrong is a good thing, and a father would desire it. The cut finger and the burned hand warn the child, and we hardly need so eminent an authority as Sir Russell Brain to tell us that "insensitivity to pain can be far more dangerous than the actual suffering of it." [1] But chronic, long-continued pain and disease cannot represent the will of God in any intelligent use of the word "will."

God's ideal intention for all his sons and daughters is perfect health of body, mind, and spirit. The whole healing ministry of Jesus proves, both by deed and word, that this is so. When

[1] Sir Russell Brain, now Lord Brain, past president of the Royal College of Physicians, lecturing on "Pain" to the annual professional nurses' and midwives' conference in London. (*The Times* [London], October 17, 1961.)

13

a poor woman who had been ill for eighteen years was brought to Jesus, he healed her. So far from leaving her ill and telling her that her illness was the "will of God," he referred to her in no uncertain way as "this woman whom *Satan* hath bound . . . these eighteen years" (Luke 13:16 K.J.V.).[2] Whether we regard "Satan" as a powerful evil intelligence or as a useful "type-name" for the evil that befalls us from the mass ignorance, folly, and sin of mankind, does not affect the question. Any pain worth calling "suffering" is evil. It is something that ought not to be. It is something we must endlessly labor to remove. Let us never look upon some human form, stricken with disease, and say, "This is the will of God." On the morning when all the newspapers announce that yet another disease is conquered and banished let us then say, "Thy will be done."

God may be thought of not only as Father but as the great Artist, an artist who has not yet completed his work but still labors at his task. As Jesus said, "My Father *has never yet ceased his work,* and I am working too." (John 5:17 N.E.B.)[3] God is hindered in that ceaseless task because he has chosen, in so many situations, to work in co-operation with man. When he makes a sunset he does it alone, but when he makes human health he puts up with man's interference, is hindered by man's ignorance, folly and sin, and waits for man's co-operation. But this does not alter his *desire,* or deny that his *will* is perfect health. What artist would *desire* or *will* any imperfection in any part of his creation? What musician, poet, or sculptor would *desire* a flaw anywhere in his work?

Further, it is when we have perfect health at every point of our being that we can offer to God a maximum usefulness. In

[2] Italics mine.
[3] Italics mine.

14

this study we shall look at the Cross again and again and see what Christ attained through his suffering and what we can still attain through ours, but as he moved through Galilee, Jesus would have been of *less* use to God if he had been lame, or blind, or crippled, or diabetic, or rheumatic.

No one denies that immense good has been achieved in the world by the suffering saints, but it was not the suffering that made them saints. It was their reaction to suffering. It was such a splendid reaction that they accomplished far more good than most people accomplish with their health. The suffering awakened them spiritually and they reacted nobly. But *if they had been equally awakened* without the challenge of illness and pain, as their Master was, they could have been of even more use to him because they could have offered him in their bodies a *perfect* instrument for his will. God does not *need* any kind of evil—and suffering is evil—to accomplish his good, although he endlessly seeks to bring his good out of man's evil.

The notion that pain, in itself, makes people saintly should be put to a relentless test by the one who asserts this error. Next time he has a severe toothache, or drops a heavy stone on his foot, he should tell himself that he is at once nobler for the pain involved, and we should make sure to ask those who live with him whether they agree with him!

I find it hard to understand how anyone who loves and thinks can contemplate a human being racked with pain and say in his heart, "This is the will of God," "This is what God wanted to happen." Think of a lovely teen-age girl reveling in life, delighting, as she should, in the health of her body which allows her to swim, to dance, to play tennis, to climb the hills, suddenly stricken down with poliomyelitis, lying with twisted limbs and paralyzed back, with all her dreams of career or marriage and

15

motherhood broken. If it is the *will* of anyone that this should happen, he must be a fiend from hell; and to say, "This is the will of God," when Jesus said it was Satan, seems to me a far worse blasphemy than any other theological denial could be.

Let us not label as "the will of God" a situation for which, if he could accomplish it, a man would be lodged in a criminal lunatic asylum or sent for a long period to jail.

I am hoping in this book to bring comfort to people who are ill, and the very first thing I want to say to them is that God does not want them to be ill. He wants them to be well. He must not do for his human family what it must learn to do for itself. He must not, as it were, do our homework for us, or have individual favorites, but he is not just sympathizing with the individual sufferer. He is sharing the suffering.

Further, God is ever fighting, in all the ways that perfect love and holiness and power make justifiable, to get his will done; that is, to make us perfectly well in body, mind, and spirit.

God can be *temporarily* defeated—and we shall study this point —for if he were not, man's freedom would be a farce. Even if we do not recover in the way we wish, God is not finally defeated, as we shall see. In the meantime, let us hold on to the thought that so far from being God's will, our suffering is something he is actively trying to overcome. God is actively at work, outside us, in the activities of those who are treating us, and within us, seeking to remove everything which delays recovery and to quicken everything that speeds it.

Chapter 2

But surely it is God who allows my suffering?

THE ANSWER TO THAT QUESTION MUST BE, "YES, HE DOES." LET US clear our minds at once by the thought that, like a human parent, God allows what he does not will. He *allows* human sin, or man would have no real free will. He does not will or intend sin. God is responsible for its possibility, not for its actuality.

If your little boy is learning to walk in the living room where there is a soft carpet, you *allow* him to stumble and even fall. You don't *intend* him to fall or you would push him over. And you make sure of the conditions in which he is learning. The living room is all right, where there's a thick carpet, but a busy intersection is not, nor is a room where he could do himself lasting harm; where there could arise a situation which would do more harm than good; where your purpose would be defeated.

So, in the case of suffering, which so often comes to the individual through the ignorance or folly or sin of the human family to which a man belongs rather than through any fault of his own, God *allows* the suffering because he wants the human family to learn, to substitute knowledge for its ignorance, wisdom for its folly, and holiness for its sin; and these three exchanges cannot be imposed on human nature. They have to be achieved by the hard way of learning.

But God would not *allow* a situation to befall us which would defeat his purpose ultimately, any more than you would with your child. So the very fact that he *allows* it to happen has a

17

hidden treasure for us which is worth picking up. If he *allows* it, it means he can use it for our good. So far from its defeating his purpose, he can use it as you use a fall to teach your child to walk. If this is true, the measure of any present calamity must be the measure of our faith, since both are less than the measure of his loving purposefulness and desire to use the evil he did not will.

Let us turn to the best illustration of all, the cross of Christ. It must be stated fearlessly that the cross was not the will of God in the sense of being God's intention. Jesus did not come into the world to be murdered. He came to be followed. Any opposite view involves the deduction that Judas, Pilate, and the evil, crafty priests were pawns in a divine game and carrying out a divine plan. This is impossible logic. It was wicked men who put Christ to death. Peter stated this clearly on the occasion of his very first sermon. He spoke of Jesus and said, "[Whom] you crucified and killed by the hands of lawless men." (Acts 2:23.)[1] Wicked men do not do the will of God; they do the opposite.

When Jesus was in the garden of Gethsemane he could easily have run away. The disciples did. But he was in a dilemma. He must either run away or be crucified. *In those circumstances imposed on him by evil men,* we can say that it was God's will that he should be crucified, and so we hear him say, "Nevertheless, not as I will, but as thou wilt," but it was only what I have called in another book, God's circumstantial will.[2] It is incredible that God's ideal intention was that his dear Son should be murdered and that men should commit sin to do God's will.

So, if you like, you can say of your illness, that *in the circum-*

---

[1] God's foreknowledge we shall look at later.
[2] See *The Will of God* (Nashville: Abingdon Press, 1944).

stances of evil imposed on the human family by ignorance, folly, or sin, it is God's will that you should be ill rather than be a favorite, magically immune or delivered from what others have to face. But do keep the thought clearly in mind that God's ideal intention, what he *wants,* is health.

Similarly, a man might want his son to be an architect. This might be his ideal intention and he might help the boy to train for this profession, but if war came, then *in the circumstances imposed on the community by the evil called war,* the father might want his son to do his bit in the army, navy, or air force. But how wrong it would be to suppose that fighting was the father's will for his boy. Architecture was the father's will.

But the story of the Cross takes us further and is very relevant to the whole problem of suffering. Christ did not just passively endure it while God looked on. He took such an attitude to it, accepting it in such a positive and trusting spirit, that he wrested from it triumph and victory. He did not just meet the evil that men did to him as one might meet the debit account in a ledger with a credit amount that canceled it out. He used the evil. He turned the debit into a credit, so that Good Friday is not a sad story with a happy ending on Easter Day. Both are days of triumph as we look back on them.

Good Friday was terrible for Jesus beyond our power to compute. The Cross felt like defeat. It looked like defeat. It was called defeat. It seemed as if evil had triumphed and his cause was lost. He felt deserted even by his Father. But that suffering love which would not run away revealed itself to be the greatest redemptive force the world has ever known. As H. H. Farmer once pointed out, "You cannot defeat defeat." Men could only "look on him whom they had pierced" and break down at the

19

wonder and grandeur and power of such a revelation of the nature of God.[3]

Present illness can be very depressing. We too can feel lonely and even deserted by God. I know that when I was ill in a hospital for many weeks some years ago, I felt very lonely, perplexed, and miserable. But suffering can be what businessmen call a "frozen asset." We cannot realize on it yet, and while suffering continues we may be unable to see anything remotely like an asset about it; but gradually, especially as we look back on it, we can take such an attitude to it that we can do what Jesus did: offer it to God and in so doing help him turn it into a victory for our own souls and of use to others whom he is trying to help.

To me one of the most wonderful truths in religion is that God can use evil in his overall plan as powerfully as he can use good; not indeed for our happiness but for our final well-being and the establishment of his kingdom. This, of course, does not enable us to say that if evil is done "it doesn't much matter because God will use it." Evil costs crucifixion. It hurts God and often man, and is always a temporary hindrance.

But the whole meaning of omnipotence is not that everything that happens is God's will. Clearly, in a world where there is free will, where men learn slowly and make mistakes, where men act foolishly, blindly, uncomprehendingly, and sometimes sinfully; in a world where we are so closely bound together that we make one another suffer—in such a world a million things can happen which are not the will of God. Many are the opposite. Omnipotence means that nothing that is allowed to happen has within itself the power finally and ultimately to defeat God.

[3] I have tried to work out the meaning of the Cross for us today in a book entitled, *A Plain Man Looks at the Cross* (Nashville: Abingdon Press, 1945).

As the psalmist said in a moment of amazing insight, "Surely the wrath of men shall praise thee." (Ps. 76:10.)

Not *in spite of* the Cross but *through* the Cross, the ultimate aim of God in Christ was achieved as completely as it would have been had men followed Christ from the first instead of murdering him. That is why we place the Cross in the very center of what we call God's plan of redemption.

So, in the case of human suffering, God does not will it or desire it, but finally it will not defeat him in his plan for the individual sufferer—and he has such a plan for each one of us. The fact that the suffering is allowed at all carries the guarantee that God, so far from being defeated by it finally, can weave it into a pattern as wonderful as one which left it out. God can bring us, not in spite of our suffering, but because of it and his use of it, and our reaction to it, to the same place as we should have reached if suffering had never come our way and with final gain instead of loss.

Indeed, I feel that the teaching of the Bible is that suffering is an asset almost to be coveted. After all, our heroes are not those for whom life has always been prosperous and painless. We all want to be healthy, happy, and to possess enough money to allow life to run smoothly and easily. Yet the pulpit illustrations held up before us are rarely drawn from such people. Now that I am at the receiving end of sermons I notice how all the illustrations —and my own were the same—are drawn from the lives of those who suffered in body, mind, estate, or in their planning, and who yet turned loss into asset and dross into gold. Without desiring to suffer we all agree that "the mark of rank in nature is capacity for pain," and certainly suffering which is gladly undertaken for the sake of others can hardly be listed as evil at all, since it ennobles the one who bears it, the one who benefits by it, and all who see it or hear of it.

Commenting on the idea of suffering, Harry Emerson Fosdick puts the matter well.[4]

Far from being an occasion of shame, in the writer's eyes, the church's sufferings [i.e., the sufferings of church members endured] were a cause of hope, since their explanation lay not behind in past sin but ahead in future good consequence—"All chastening seemeth for the present to be not joyous but grievous; yet afterward it yieldeth peaceable fruit. . . ." This conviction that an untroubled life is uneducated, that to deal with tragedy is to handle reality and to deal well with it is a great gain, that no softly cushioned life can ever be wise or strong or good, runs throughout the Testament. Not sporadic and occasional, but constant and fundamental is this treatment of affliction as opportunity, not disgrace, an indispensable implement for building faith and character, rather than a means for their destruction.

In the light of all this, two sayings may well be true. First, that what happens to us eventually matters little, but our reaction to what happens to us matters much. Second, a French saying which roughly translated runs, "To suffer passes. To have suffered, never passes." The pain of body and mind will cease one day. But what we learn in these dark experiences is our treasure forever. It is a treasure no one can take from us.

---

[4] *A Guide to Understanding the Bible* (New York: Harper & Row, 1938), p. 185. Italics mine.

Chapter 3

Didn't God know that suffering would fall upon me?

THE ANSWER AGAIN IS "YES." BUT LET US LOOK AT WHAT LIES behind the question. Probably there are two doubts in the sufferer's mind. He might well say to me, "You say that most suffering falls on men from the world's (if not the individual's) ignorance, folly, and sin. But God *knew* from the beginning that men would be ignorant, foolish, and sinful. He made them that way. So, if those three things bring suffering, he willed that suffering. Secondly, if he *knew* it would happen, it *had* to happen."

Let us look at the second point first. The fact that God knows beforehand what is going to happen does not make it happen. If I go to the door beyond which is a starving dog, and if I open it and hold out a lovely, meaty bone, I *know* that the dog will move toward the bone. But it is not my knowing that makes the dog move. It is his hunger. I *know* that after a service in church the bulk of the congregation will get up and walk out, but it is not my knowing that moves them.

The truth probably is that the future stands to God in the same relation as the past does. Men speak of "an eternal present" to cover past, present, and future. Now even we, who know the past, do not look back and say, "It was my present knowing of the past that made past events happen." The truth is that the events determined the knowledge. Why then should we suppose that a *present* knowing of the future makes future events happen?

23

It is not God's foreknowledge of events that makes them happen. It is their happening—and he can see the future as we see the past—that determines his knowledge. In regard to our illnesses he knows all the long chain of events that leads up to illness, but it is not his knowing that is the determining factor.

The first part of the doubt in the questioner's mind must be answered honestly. God must have known and decreed that men should learn slowly and have freedom to be foolish and to commit sin. That is why in the last chapter I emphasized the difference between what God wills and what God allows.

He *allows* ignorance and folly and sin. Can we imagine a world in which men were magically supplied with all the knowledge they would need to avoid suffering, all the wisdom they would need to have had magically implanted so that no foolish act would ever be committed? And what would holiness be if it were mechanical, if man were not *free* to sin? God himself cannot take two naturally contradictory paths of action at the same time. He cannot endow "holiness" with any value and at the same time make impossible man's freedom to sin.

We must admit then that God is responsible for the possibility, nay the probability, of suffering, but he ever seeks to implant the opposite of its causes, that is, knowledge instead of ignorance, wisdom instead of folly, and holiness instead of sin. Further, he knows that where those opposites cannot be established he can still make evil serve his purposes, and this is the justification of its possibility.

The Bible often speaks of suffering as fire, and the very use of the word is a compliment to human nature. It implies gold. "Wood, hay, and stubble" are *destroyed* by fire. Gold is purified by it. If our reaction is right, God can use the suffering that falls upon us from the ignorance, folly, and sin in the world—our own

24

and other people's—as fire is used upon gold. Unbearable and intolerable as we often feel suffering to be, it is a sign that God cares enough to bother with us. Wouldn't it be much easier if he either blotted us out altogether or was content to use his power merely to achieve our happiness instead of bothering with our characters? The refiner of gold goes on using fire until he can see his own image reflected in the gold. God seems to do the same with men, using the fire *he* did not make to serve his purposes (I Cor. 3:12-15; I Pet. 1:7).

C. S. Lewis made much of this point in his book *The Problem of Pain*,[1] and I am indebted to him here. Think of the number of people who are fond of dogs. A trained dog who is a household pet lives longer, is far happier, and is more highly cultured —one might say, is nicer to know—than the wild, untrained animal of the prairie or the pariah dog that haunts an Eastern city. A man who loves his dog washes it when it doesn't want to be washed. He housebreaks it, refusing to allow it to befoul his house. He may strike it to stop it from stealing. It is a matter of great importance to the man that the dog should not be repulsive in its habits. He takes infinite pains with it. Why? Because through discipline there is more than a chance that the man can bring the dog into a communion with himself higher and deeper than would otherwise be possible. If the dog could think and talk to other dogs, no doubt the experience he underwent at the hands of the man would lead him to confide to other dogs that his master could not possibly love him since he suffered so much. His doggy dignity would often be lowered and his happiness temporarily destroyed. But the sufferings of the dog and the trouble of the man are a compliment to the dog. After

[1] (New York: The Macmillan Company, 1944.)

all, a man does not go to the same trouble with a rat or a frog. Presumably they are incapable of being brought into such a high communion with man.

Look at the relationship between God and man in a similar way, save that *God uses a whip already provided by the effects of man's ignorance, folly, and sin,* whereas the man in relation to the dog introduces the whip from outside the situation. But God uses the whip of human suffering for the same purpose—namely, to bring man into communion with him.

We may see the thought of the compliment in a different illustration. A child brings his autograph album to a great composer who, to please the child, scribbles a few bars in the book and the child is contented about it. But look at the trouble that composer takes with his great masterpiece, writing, rubbing out, rewriting, introducing this harmony, varying that melody, as Beethoven did with his sonatas. It doesn't require a wild flight to try to imagine that the composition is itself sentient. It might complain and say: "I wish he would not keep rubbing me out and rewriting. I was all right as I was." We know that the truth is that the pains the composer takes are a compliment to the composition. It is just because it is a masterpiece that it merits so much more care than the hastily scribbled bars which please the child.

We could find another illustration in the attitude of the great poet to his poem. Those who have seen the original of Tennyson's *In Memoriam* say that he hardly left a line unaltered. He wrote it, then scratched it out, and then altered the arrangement of the verses, when one might imagine the poem saying, "My lines rhymed before. Why can't he let me alone?" But to be left alone would mean that the poet was content with something less than the best, less than something that the poem might become.

Herein is illustrated in part our attitude to God.[2] When trouble assails us we cry out to God and say, "We wish you would leave us alone. All we want is to be happy." But the trouble the Artist takes to use every kind of discipline that evil brings into life as a means of purifying our character, though intolerable to us at the time, is a tremendous compliment; and when we cry out to be left alone we are asking for less care, not more care; for less love, not more love. We are like a dog, unwashed, filthy, and with stinking habits, saying, "I only want to be left alone." But the God who left us alone as we are now would not be God. Therefore God will use any means, including the suffering he does not will, to shape us and alter us and improve us and win us from our wild, filthy, foul, and unclean habits, so that at last we may be made ready to enter into a communion with him, the depths of which have never been plumbed.

Let me lighten our thought by recalling a Sunday-school treat to which with great delight I went as a child. We had a benevolent superintendent who greatly desired that we should all have a happy day. Those who ran in the races and won got a prize, but those who came in last got a surreptitious sweet. At the end of the day "a good time had been had by all." But the attitude of the superintendent was kindness rather than love. Love has in it a stern note, something stronger than mere benevolence. Kindness makes us happy, but it has no power in it to make us improve. Love has.

In the City Temple we have what is called an adoption scheme. Poor and underprivileged families are adopted by individuals or groups of individuals, and Miss Jones from the City Temple goes

---

[2] I say "in part" because in the above illustrations the imperfection is the fault of the composer and poet. In our relationship to God, the fault of imperfection lies with us.

27

to visit her adopted family and showers pennies and sweets on the children. She doesn't bother much if they are filthy or foul-mouthed or have runny noses. But their *mother* is much more concerned about these things because she loves them with a love that is greater than mere benevolence and kindness. We cannot imagine a true father saying about his son: "I don't care if he is filthy and a liar and a knave and a cheat so long as he is happy." Happiness is not a true end. It is always a by-product. Character is the end, for our character development contributes to the glory of God which is the end of all human existence.

Now look from these illustrations at God's relationship with us. We ask him to be kind. There is a true sense in which God is not kind. His relationship with us is bigger and grander and closer. Kindness is often a love substitute which we offer to people whom we may not love, cannot love, or cannot be bothered to love, and kindness is too poor a thing to express God's relationship to us. We keep on pleading with him to be kind because we want to be happy. His attitude is higher and deeper. He *loves* us because he wants to bring us into communion with him and he knows that we cannot be really deeply, completely, and permanently happy until we have been brought into communion with him. Whereas if he is merely kind, we shall make happiness our goal and be content with something less than the best, with something less than we may yet become, something less than God can make us, and when we ask God to be kind to us that we may be happy, we are asking for less love, not more; we are being content to remain wild dogs, we are being content to be the rapidly scribbled half-dozen bars of music instead of the master-piece, we are being content to be the rhyme instead of the poem.

When I think about God I realize that, in weak moments of self-indulgence, I should like to live in a world where "a good

28

time was had by all," where God was kind and everybody was happy. But in better moments I realize that it would be asking for a love substitute, kindness. It would be being content with happiness instead of character. If we could see deeper into the nature of reality, including the things that are unseen, we should realize that the things we want which are not his will, ultimately bring only more suffering and misery however innocent they seem, however badly we want them, however passionately we insist on having them, however accompanied they may be by brilliant planning, and however marked they may be by what the world calls success. Our truest happiness is a by-product of our quest for blessedness, and blessedness is the complete identity of our will with God's and the fullest realization of our communion with him.

Paul puts it like this: "Our light affliction, which is but for a moment, worketh for us a far more exceeding and eternal weight of glory; while we look not at the things which are seen, but at the things which are not seen: for the things which are seen are temporal; but the things which are not seen are eternal." (II Cor. 4: 17-18 K.J.V.) There is possible to us the glory of sons caught up into the Father's fellowship, honored by the Father's love, brought into communion by his endless patience and the suffering which both he and we endure. This thought can stay us in the hour of our anguish and nerve us in the day of our distress. I only have to look into my own heart to be certain of this: that if God were content with me as I am, it could only mean that he had stopped caring and had given me up as a bad job.

Chapter 4

Why should this happen to me?

THIS IS THE VERY NATURAL QUESTION WITH WHICH WE ALL lash ourselves when our own suffering or that of a dear one comes to upset our lives. A woman who wrote to me when her husband died, leaving her with three little children, allows me to quote from her letter: "I have tortured myself thinking of all the human failings I have had in the past in our lives together and how I could have been a much better wife. I keep telling myself that I must have done something *awful* to deserve this."

All through my ministry the same problem has pressed upon my mind. In one's church it sometimes seemed as if the most valuable members were stricken down. Some others, from whose nagging and criticism one would have enjoyed a brief holiday, boasted about the truth that they had "never had a day's illness." Why does suffering come to one who certainly does not deserve it and pass by another who, in our judgment, does?

Let us honestly try to think out a Christian answer to the question, "Why should this happen to me?" remembering two preliminary ideas. (1) Many non-Christians in Eastern lands have their answer ready and it is mentally satisfying to them. They say that we have lived before in an earlier incarnation and that the cause of present suffering runs back into earlier lives, and the effect of our life now, including our reaction to present pain, will be harvested in future lives. I do not find this answer convincing, though I do not feel that there is anything contrary to Christ's teaching in it. Indeed, there is evidence that it was held to be orthodox in the Christian church for the first few centuries and that, although never of vital importance, it was part of the mental background of the Gospels.[1] We read, for instance, that the disciples asked Jesus about one man, "Rabbi, who sinned, this man or his parents, that he was born blind?" (John 9:2.) Clearly, if the patient's own sin had brought blindness from *birth*, the sin must have been committed in an earlier life. Jesus did not rebuke this as if it were erroneous thinking. His reply was significant, and to get its truth we must rearrange the punctuation which in Greek is absent altogether. Jesus' answer should not be misunderstood to mean that the man was born blind in order that he might provide an occasion for Christ to show his miraculous power. The passage should read: "It was not that this man sinned, or his parents." (Note the full stop.) "But that the works of God might be made manifest in him we must work the works of him who sent me, while it is day." Christ seemed unready to theorize about why the man was blind, save to deny that sin had caused his blindness. He seemed eager first to make the patient see. That was the priority in the situation.

A second preliminary thought we should honestly hold in mind is that we only ask, "Why should this happen to me?" when *trouble* befalls us. When some lovely girl consents to become our wife, when a perfect baby is born into our home, or when we are given some coveted position in our trade or profession, we rarely ask, "Why should this happen to me?"

The truth is that only rarely can we put our finger on the cause of our suffering. One's own folly, ignorance, or sin *may* have brought one's troubles on oneself. In these days we realize that faulty emotions long harbored deep in the mind can touch

[1] I have worked out this idea in a pamphlet called, *The Case for Reincarnation*, obtainable from Mrs. Peto, 16 Kingswood Rd., Tadworth, Surrey, England, or from the City Temple, London, E.C.1.

31

off, or even cause, disease and nervous breakdown. Such emotions as worry, terror, and prolonged anxiety appear to be able to set off troubles like gastric or duodenal ulcers and asthma; while resentment, bitterness, and jealousy sometimes appear to lie behind some forms of arthritis. Repressed hatred seems even to lead to outbursts resembling epilepsy, and guilt is suspected to be behind some forms of skin and digestive troubles. But it is very dangerous to suppose that this is *always* so, and often such a conclusion is quite inaccurate, and also unfair and unkind.

It is healthy enough that we should examine ourselves about this; but more frequently no causal connection can be established, and it is morbid continually to lash one's memory by endlessly asking, "Why did this happen to me?"

The truth is that in regard to human suffering we are all in it together. No one, even if he could prove that a particular experience of suffering was *not* his own fault, could really feel exonerated from *a* contribution to the total of human suffering. In his fine book *A Doctor's Casebook in the Light of the Bible,* Dr. Paul Tournier truly says:

I realized that it is absolutely impossible by intellectual processes to separate that of which we are the victims from that for which we are to blame. . . . The Cross is at one and the same time forgiveness where we are guilty, and true relief where we are the victims.[2]

In many ways it seems to me that life is like a game of hockey. In the clash of bodies driven by opposing wills, someone is going to get hurt. If we are playing we might ask, "Why *not* me?" In such a game the goalkeeper may never have to save a shot. In another game he may get a dislocated shoulder. But he does not

[2] (New York: Harper & Row, 1960.)

say either about immunity or accident, "Why did this happen to me?" He is a member of the team and is more concerned with whether his side wins or loses. He says, "*We* lost," or, "*We* won," and if you ask him about the shoulder he will say, "Oh! that's just one of those things—the breaks of the game." He knows that in a game like hockey one must take the risk of personal injury, and he doesn't think of it as personal. It's all in the game.

I think in the game of life, in which there is such a clash of purposes and wills, in which we are all very ignorant, in which we all make mistakes and do foolish and sinful things, and in which we are so bound up together that what I do and know and say affects other lives, someone is bound to get hurt without there being any answer to the question, "Why should this happen to *me?*" save to say that you were in the team. Your disaster is your share of the team's adventure. Often it is the thrill of health and happiness. Sometimes it is the burden of ill health and unhappiness. But the Christian believes that in the game of life the *team* will win and he finds a measure of comfort in that fact. The Captain has assured him that the team cannot lose. Thomas Carlyle has a word for the individual sufferer here: "For us was thy back bent, for us were thy straight limbs and fingers so deformed; thou wert our conscript on whom the lot fell, and fighting our battles wast so marred."

So part of the answer to the question at the beginning of this chapter must be, "Because you belong to the human family." Your suffering is part of the price the team pays in its great struggle toward perfection. We will cope later with the retort, "But that is unfair to me."

This matter of the suffering that comes to us because we belong to the human family is important enough to demand further explanation.

33

Even God could not arrange human life on two bases which are mutually contradictory *or give men the benefits which derive from both*. Two possibilities lay before him. He could arrange life on the individual basis or on the family basis. He chose to arrange life on the family basis, and by "family" I mean the great human family.

We can see how wise this basis is if we imagine life arranged on the basis of the individual instead of the family. Had God chosen the former method, then nothing would have come to us through the misdeeds or ignorance or folly of others, but, also, nothing would have come to us through the wisdom, courage, and nobility of others. We should not have to carry the burden of others; but neither should we ever be carried by the wings of others. Nothing undeserved, whether an asset or a liability, would ever have come to us. We should live an individual life. The innocent would never suffer.

To sit down and let the mind imaginatively conceive an existence where everything was cut off from us that did not come to us through our own merit, is to feel a tremendous relief that the government of the world is in the hands of a God who saw far enough ahead to plan the world on the family basis and save us from the curse of individualism. Take one example. Suppose you fell ill through your own fault. No wisdom could be at your disposal save your own; no kindly sympathy or nursing; no knowledge in other men's brains; no skill in other men's fingers. What happens today? You are whirled to a hospital in a car which, in itself, represents the brains of a thousand men through a long period of years. At the hospital you are tended by the patient skill and nursing of others. Inventions and discoveries of brilliant men of all nations and all ages are at your disposal through the training the doctor has had. In a word, the brains and the skill of the family are at your beck and call. As an individualist you would have died like a dog in a ditch.

Nor is it only in emergency that we gain from belonging to the family. As has often been said, "When I rise and go to my bath a cake of soap is handed me by a Frenchman, a sponge is handed me by a Pacific Islander, a towel by a Turk, my underclothes by one Englishman, my outer garments by another. I come down to breakfast. My tea is poured out by an Indian or a Chinese. My porridge is served by a Scottish farmer, or my corn flakes by Mr. Kellogg and his friends. My toast I accept at the hands of an English farmer who has joined hands with a baker. My marmalade is passed to me by a Spaniard, my banana by a West Indian. I am indebted to half the world before I have finished breakfast." The secret of half my happiness is that I belong to a world family.

To imagine life on the individual basis leads us to a situation which it is amusing to contemplate but would be no fun to realize. No clothes would be available save those we could make for ourselves, presumably from the skins of beasts, since, if we are not to have the fruits of other men's labors, nothing woven for us is available. We should sally out to try to procure breakfast with no weapon save that which we ourselves could fashion.

As I sit at my desk I realize that any good I can do through writing these words is a good only possible through the co-operation, literally, of hundreds of my brothers. I think of the pen with which I write, the electric light, the warmth of the fire, the friendly books on the shelves which line the room, the subsequent co-operation of publishers, printers, proofreaders, retailers, and travelers and a score of other helpers, without whom sending out this message would be impossible.

Shall we, then, receiving such untold benefit from our membership of the family, deem it unfair when we are asked to bear the consequences of the family ignorance, the family folly, the family sin? Shall I cry to God and say, "Why did you make a world like this?" when I have just decided that this is the best choice that lay before God himself, and that my best judgment confirms his choice?

These may seem hard words to some lonely sufferer, and in truth there is a greater word for him, as we shall see; but there is light for many in the thought that God was faced with a real alternative in making the basis of life that of the family or the unit, that the latter choice would have brought far more pain to the individual, and that selfishness would have been a greater evil than suffering. There would never be any happiness for a worthy individual in a private escape from suffering to which others were exposed. Solitary comforts are poor things. The very essence of our best self is love, and love wants to share not only pleasures but pain. Love would refuse an emancipation from pain which only included the self, just as love rejects the thought of salvation which is not available for every son of man. The thought which, for the noblest men and women on earth, would make life intolerable if carried into effect, is that they should be excluded totally from the pain of others.

Dr. Crichton-Miller, in his book *The New Psychology and the Preacher*,[3] gives an illustration which I have permission to reproduce here. An important express was about to leave a London terminus. An agitated lady assailed the stationmaster and begged him to postpone the departure of the train. He told her he had no power to do so, and that the only man who could was the general manager. She rushed to his office and repeated her request.

[3] (London: Jarrolds), p. 209.

"We have just heard," she said, "that our boy has met with a serious accident and is not expected to live. My husband is on his way, but he cannot possibly arrive until fifteen minutes after the hour of departure. If you keep the train waiting you will be giving him the only chance of seeing the boy alive. Surely if you have any spark of human sympathy you will not refuse!"

The general manager said, "Madam, I am very sorry for you and for your husband, but I cannot do it."

"You mean you won't do it," she said crossly. "You know very well that you could hold the train up if you wished to do so."

"Madam," he said, "the train makes more than one important connection which would be lost if I delayed it. There may be others in the train to whom the catching of one of these connections may mean just as much as to your husband. My business is to serve the community by maintaining the most trustworthy railway service that is possible."

There is a further word for the individual, a message which I think covers his individual problem; but our illustration does show us the only possible basis on which a train service can be run and—more importantly—the only possible basis on which a world can be run.

It is a commonplace to say that if two consequences both follow from a given proposition we cannot plaintively ask to have the one without the other, even though the one may strike us as pleasing and beneficial and the other seem evil and hurtful.[4]

This world is not a finished piece of work. God is still at work on it and in it. It is not yet "the best of all possible worlds" but it is the world of best possibilities. If we allow that the basis on which God has arranged human life is the best, we cannot com-

---

[4] I have taken some paragraphs here from an earlier book, *Why Do Men Suffer?* (Nashville: Abingdon Press, 1936, an Apex reprint).

plain at those inescapable, painful consequences which flow from that basis—even when they appear so distressing as to seem to deny the love and power of God—any more than we can applaud because God has provided man with that necessity of life which we call water, and then curse him because someone drowns; or praise him for the inestimable benefits of fire and curse him because someone is burnt by it.

One is left with the uncomfortable feeling that if all the resources of the human family were devoted to the cure and prevention of disease and mental suffering, the men who dream of landing on the moon could, within one generation, banish the amount of suffering which constitutes a problem.

Chapter 5

Is my suffering
just a bit of bad luck?

In answering that question everything depends on what we mean by luck. We live in an ordered universe. Everything that happens has its cause—indeed, a whole string of causes. The universe is cosmos everywhere and chaos nowhere. Further, when we say that something is a chance happening or an accident or a piece of good or bad luck, we must not suppose that, however it may surprise *us,* God is also surprised. The Christian believes that God knows everything that happens and that he knew the future before it happened. Let it be quite clear, then, that God knew you were going to have this illness but, as we said in chapter 3, his knowing did not make it happen.

I am writing these words during a spell of bronchitis. God knew it would happen. But that knowing was not causative. The east wind and a cold church and a constitutional weakness going back to early childhood and bacilli in the respiratory passages were contributory causes, and God knew all about them and what they would bring upon me.

Now turn back to the matter of chance or luck. For myself I leave a place in my philosophy of life for chance happenings as long as I am allowed to define what I mean by chance or luck— and I mean by it an event which God did not intend and which man could not foresee. We have already seen that many things happen which God did not intend to happen. He allows many things which he did not intend. All sin is allowed, but not in-

39

tended. Unless it were allowed man would have no free will. God allowed the sin a man did yesterday, but he knew it would happen before it did. But neither God's knowledge nor his allowing caused it to happen.

Every day thousands of things happen which could be called chance or accident or luck. I heard only recently of a golf ball badly driven by a beginner which struck a motorcyclist in the eye on an adjacent road. The cyclist swerved and a bus driver, in seeking to avoid the swerving cyclist, drove the bus off the road into a gully, where it turned over and injured half a dozen people. Unless we imagine that God ought to work a miracle to prevent all accidents—in which case man would never learn—then in a world made like this, accidents—defined as events which God did not intend and which man could not foresee—are inevitable. How foolish it would be for one of those bus passengers—even if stricken by blindness through splintered glass from the bus windows—to suppose that his disability was the will of God, or that God had ceased to be loving, or that man's folly was greater than God's power. How would man learn anything if his foolishness, carelessness, stupidity, ignorance, and sin were always overcome and safeguarded against evil consequences by some expression of interfering power on the part of omnipotence? To prevent, by a use of omnipotence, foolishness from producing its consequences, would fill the earth with unteachable fools. I do not deny that there are many things God *could* do by the use of his power. I suppose he could, in the illustration above, prevent the golf ball ever going off the fairway. (As a bad golfer I wish he would!) He could make the cyclist evade the ball, and so on. But more and more clearly I feel that while no one can answer the question as to what God can or cannot do, there are many things which God *must* not do, even though we wish he would, and we imagine that if only we had his power we would do them.

It is interesting to note that the more man learns about the laws by which God runs the universe the more he can exclude what we call luck. We toss up a coin and say that whether it falls heads or tails is purely a matter of luck. But if I knew all the factors involved in tossing up a coin—its weight, the number of revolutions it made, the air resistance, the force used, and so on—then presumably the way it fell could be calculated mathematically. The more man knows about the laws which govern the universe and the more wisely he acts as a result of his knowledge, the more will he be able to eliminate those "accidents" and "bad luck" which bring him disaster.

But I must guard against a faulty deduction some reader may make. He may feel, "Well, if one allows that an element of luck enters into life then anything may happen!" No! Anything cannot happen. I am quite sure of the most important fact that God has guarded this universe. Its laws are not infinite in number and therefore only a certain number of possible things can happen. Of course I don't know what this number is. Nobody does. The permutations and combinations of all the possibilities that could happen on a planet governed by laws which God ordained are beyond the scope of man's mind. Perhaps if some brilliant supermathematician knew all the laws and all the possibilities, he could work out the sum, but by faith in the wisdom and love of God—not by any scientific guess—I am quite sure that there are only a certain number of things that can happen.

To see this, let us go back to the parable of the nursery. The parents who allow their child to stumble and fall in it as he learns to walk do not, we said, put eiderdowns on the floor and have the walls padded. Even then the child can get a nasty tumble. He

41

can hurt himself fairly badly. *But the parents have excluded razor blades and bottles of sulphuric acid and arsenic.* In other words, they have guarded the nursery. It is not true to say that *anything* might happen. *Nothing can possibly happen with which the child, in co-operation with loving parents, cannot cope as he learns to walk.* Nothing can happen from which he cannot win a definite gain. I believe that the whole environment of man is guarded by our loving Father in the same way. Some terrible things can happen, but it is not true to say that *anything* can happen. Nothing can possibly happen from which gain cannot be won. Nothing can possibly happen with which it is utterly beyond our powers to cope.

If a thing happens to you, therefore, God knows all about it. He knows it can happen, that it is going to happen, that it has happened. But he knows also that nothing can possibly happen in this nursery of a universe that of itself has power to defeat his own purposes, and that if man grasps his opportunities and uses his resources and seeks also his Father's aid—just as a child might stretch up a hand when he stumbles—real good can be won from everything that seems like unfortunate accident. From that fact a profound truth emerges to me: the apparent evil in any happening that can occur to man is the measure of God's challenge to man to transform it into advantage. If the measure of the supposed evil becomes the measure of our right reaction, it will be the measure of our gain from anything which God allows. No happening would be allowed if it could defeat God, just as razor blades and acid would not be allowed in a nursery by the most Spartan parent.

Look at it like this. Man is very proud of what he calls his scientific discoveries—and indeed they are tremendous. But from a religious point of view it is true to say that he can discover nothing unless God reveals it. What the scientist discovers, God allows him to discover. The progress of the scientist's mind which allows him, benefiting from the discoveries of his predecessors, to startle the world with some new discovery is only an unveiling of one of the secrets of God by God himself, and *man never made a discovery until he was in sight of power to cope with that discovery*. If we could bring back our great-great-great-grandfathers and put them in the modern world, their sanity would be overturned. They would find that coping with the modern world was more than they could manage, for their minds would be utterly unattuned to its demands. Man has slowly climbed to his discoveries, and they have become discoveries only when he could use them for the happiness of his fellows and the glory of God. Yes, I know you are thinking of atomic energy. So am I. But don't let the horror of it disguise the fact that it *can* be used in man's service, even in his highest service. And here again the measure of the wonder of the discovery is God's challenge that it be used in his service. God is trusting us to use all new discoveries to further his plans.

So there are no accidents or chance happenings or bits of luck that are outside the scope of God's knowledge and man's power to deal with them adequately. Nothing can ever happen to us but that in co-operation with God we can turn it into a spiritual gain. I mean that literally. Do not just meet the liability with an asset that is its equivalent, but turn the liability itself into an asset. So don't say, "Well, it's just a matter of luck, and all life is chance, and instead of purpose there are accidents." Remember the parable of the nursery. Nothing is allowed to happen that could ultimately defeat the purposes of God.

As I have thought about the problem of the place of chance in the Christian life, I have found a kind of daydream taking shape in my mind. It has seemed to me as though a number of people were scattered through the length of a muddy lane, along which a laborer with a cart full of broken pieces of tile slowly passed, and to each person he gave a spadeful of fragments, which somehow the recipient knew he had to fit together into a pattern and the pattern into a pavement. In my dream many cried out to the laborer and said that of all those broken pieces of ill-assorted shapes and sizes they could make hardly any use at all, let alone make something beautiful. Then I saw in my dream that the more thoughtful people turned the fragments over, or exchanged some of theirs for others doled out to the people near them, and getting together made not only a beautiful pattern, but a firm pavement where there had been mud. It was a strange dream. The people who moved in its shadows complained loudly of injustice, for some got beautiful, colored stones, and these lucky people were able at once to make them into a pattern and set the pattern into the pavement. But others got rough-edged stones, dull of color, and they complained bitterly of their bad luck. But in my dream joy came to my heart when some of the most humble people who said nothing, heard, as from an angel voice, the advice, "Turn them over!" and on doing so found they were holding precious stones.

I could not help feeling that somehow life is like that. This man has good luck, and that man has bad luck, but I wonder whether, in the sight of God, there is any real difference between good luck and bad luck. So often the latter is a frozen asset which ultimately brings immense spiritual wealth. Dives thought he had good luck and Lazarus bad, but in the next world things looked very different (Luke 16:19-31), and—if we *must* use time words—we shall be longer there than here. I would like you to think about that. Life cannot ultimately be unjust. I have seen the lucky ones finish their lives having made a very poor thing of their luck, and I have seen the unlucky ones turn the rough stones of ill luck over and find they were jewels, and turn the things we call calamities into a pattern of loveliness and a pathway for other feet. I think it is God's purpose that the lucky ones and the unlucky ones should make a pattern and a pavement, and cry out at last with Jeremy Taylor:

> Lord, come away;
> Why dost Thou stay?
> Thy road is ready and Thy paths made straight
> With longing expectation wait
> The consecration of Thy beauteous feet.

For "All things work together for good to them that love God" (Rom. 8:28 K.J.V.) or, as C. H. Dodd translates the famous text, "In everything . . . he [God] co-operates for good with those who love God" (N.E.B.).

Your illness may be bad luck, in the sense defined. It is something God did not intend and you could not foresee. But it cannot of itself defeat God's final purposes, nor has it in itself any power to defeat you. It contains a challenge which, rightly responded to, can bring treasure.

Chapter 6

Where do God's goodness and omnipotence come in?

IT IS VERY NATURAL THAT A SUFFERER SHOULD WONDER WHY, if God has immeasurable power and infinite goodness, he does not either prevent disease and calamity or else do something quickly remedial when they overtake us. Many men and women in their hearts have felt as the philosopher John Stuart Mill felt. If God is good, the suffering in the world must mean that it happens because he cannot help it. In that case he is not all-powerful. If he is all-powerful and does not prevent or speedily end it, it must be because he is not good. So, runs the argument, either he is all-powerful and not good, or good but not all-powerful. He cannot be both.

Let us look at this problem.

First of all I am myself driven to the belief that God is good. The reason which most convinces me is that man at his best is good. The reader of this book is good. He or she would not smite a child with cancer or wreck his life with polio or insanity. Indeed, I can say with safety that the reader of this book is unlikely to do anything deliberately cruel or unkind. If we do fall into unkindness, cruelty, or what we call "sin," we reproach ourselves. We know, if we know anything at all, that goodness is better than badness; kindness is better than cruelty; love is better than lust; self-denial and sacrifice are better than self-aggression and selfishness. If there is a God at all, his nature must contain and express all those good things. If his

46

nature does not contain them, then we, his creatures, are better than he is, for we despise the opposites to, or absence of, the good. We may not as yet be able to *see,* as the work of a good God, many things he does and allows any more than a tiny boy whose father is a surgeon can see it to be a good thing to make a patient unconscious and then stretch him out on a table and cut him open with a knife. But the child who knows his father's nature from other evidence has to leave that problem in abeyance, awaiting further light, and he has to hold on to the fact that his father is good and is doing good. So, when Christ tells us that God is good, when Christ lives a good life himself and tells us that God is like that, we have to hold many things like disease in abeyance, awaiting further light, and we have to hold on to the fact that it is impossible to believe that God is evil. If he is, where does goodness come from? We have replaced the mystery of evil by a greater mystery of good.

There is, of course, another alternative, and that is that God is well-meaning and also very powerful, but stupid. I do not think we need stay on that point. All man's discoveries are divine revelations and no one is going to believe that this amazing universe, the discoveries about which nearly take our breath away, if it came from a divine hand at all, was made by an intensely powerful imbecile!

Is it then that God is not as powerful as we thought; that he cannot help the suffering that overtakes us? Yet surely one fleeting thought of the power of wind and wave, of flashing lightning and tearing hurricane, of volcano and earthquake,[1] apart altogether from the terrifying energy locked up in the atom, con-

[1] I have discussed the suffering that follows natural disasters in *Why Do Men Suffer? op. cit.,* pp. 89-105.

47

vince us that the creator of this universe could fitly be called the Lord of power.

But here we must consider the whole question of the nature of power. I think the concept of power is misunderstood because we imagine it to mean ability to do anything. Let us make up another illustration from the hockey field. Let us suppose that you and I are on the sidelines watching a game—which I must confess I love to do—and a huge giant of a man who is completely ignorant of the game comes along and asks what all the struggle is about. Supposing someone tells him that it is an effort to get the ball into the net, either at one end or the other. Supposing that, thinking to please, the giant stalks onto the field, knocks men right and left, picks up the ball, brushes off the goalkeeper, and puts it into the net. What a riot there would be! And what an interfering so-and-so the giant would be called! And what would happen to the game of hockey if that sort of behavior occurred?

You may think it a foolish illustration, but think back in imagination to 1665 when the great plague was raging. How many prayed that it should end! How many people must have prayed God to walk off the sidelines, as it were, and end men's struggle! Many prayers must have ascended that this or that individual might be healed. But if those prayers had been answered *plague would have been with us still*. Men would never have bothered to find out the causes and thus *prevent* plague. They would have put a prayer in the slot, so to speak, and drawn out a cure. We shall ask in a subsequent chapter why the germs of diseases were ever created at all; but part of the game of life is man's struggle for mastery, and to end the struggle by a show of what is popularly thought of as "omnipotence" makes the game —and all man learns from it—meaningless.

The sufferer may say, "That's all very well, but if I had had plague it would not have comforted me to know that God must not intervene because one day men would learn how to prevent it, and that his intervention would stop their struggle. I should have wanted him to heal *me*. And while I haven't got plague, I've got another disease, and that is what I want. I want him to do something for me and to do it *now*. Are you telling me he is only interested in the race and not in individuals?"

It is a fair question, and God's care for the individual so tremendously underlined by Jesus, I want to deal with in chapter 7. But for the moment let us continue to study what power really is.

I want to offer the definition that *power is ability to achieve purpose*. Many things look like power, feel like power, and are called power, but if they defeat purpose they are really weakness. The giant at the hockey match looked like the incarnation of power, but he defeated the whole purpose of the game. When we indulge in capital punishment it looks like power, the power of life and death, but surely the purpose of the state is to make its citizens, however bad, into good citizens. To kill one of them because he killed another defeats the whole purpose of punishment. The state does not exercise power. It accepts defeat.

To the schoolboy turned out of the class, the action of the schoolmaster must feel like power, and to the other boys it looks like power, but in the light of the purpose of teaching may not the schoolmaster wonder if his action should not be called weakness and defeat?

Again and again, the ways in which we imagine and wish that God would act and "show forth his mighty power" would, because they would defeat his holy and righteous purposes, really be weakness and show the same kind of futility as the giant at the hockey match. Paul saw the point clearly. "Why," said the bystanders at the Crucifixion, "doesn't Christ call on God? Surely a God of power could save his own Son! Let God come and save him." The Cross looked like defeat, felt like defeat, and was called defeat. Paul called it "the power of God" (I Cor. 1:18). What would a divine rescue of the Crucified have done compared with the power of the Cross to change men's lives through twenty centuries of its preaching in every nation under heaven?

Let us make up another illustration. The nursery floor is covered with toy wooden building blocks. Several little brothers are playing with them and they resolve to build a beautiful tower which their father, very good, very strong, and very wise, has described to them. But they quarrel as to who shall do this and who shall do that and as to what the pattern shall be. When one has got the tower partly built, another knocks it down again. Accidents happen too. Boys do not watch where they put their feet. They do not know when a tower will stand and the conditions which will make it likely to fall.

The father enters the nursery. He knows exactly how it should be done and what it should look like and how happy everyone would be were it finished. What are the possibilities open to him? I can think of four:

1. He can turn all the little boys out of the nursery and build the tower by himself. (God did not ask man to help him build the Himalayas.)

2. He can—let us imagine—intervene to prevent accidents and the results of ignorance and folly, staying the careless foot and the angry, hostile hand.

3. He can beat into subjection the unruly boys who quarrel, making them spineless, terrified slaves, or he can throw them out of the nursery.

4. He can see the tower built slowly, often unsoundly. He can see it fall, or be knocked down, or its building ruined by ignorance and folly, or by angry impatience, or jealousy and hate, and yet with infinite patience, without violence, try to teach the little brothers how to build again, how alone the tower can be made both beautiful and safe, how to get on with one another, one doing this and one doing that, until at last the tower arises erect, firmly founded, beautiful to see, and fulfilling the father's dreams both as to the final beauty and stability of the tower and the effect of building it thus on the builders.

The first three methods sound like power, but they would not fulfill nearly such a glorious purpose as the fourth method, even though at the end the boys say that they built the tower by themselves and had no help from anyone! The fourth method alone makes them brothers and enables them to fulfill their possibilities. It is the way of God with men. And we really must realize that *God's choice of his own restraint* is an expression of power, not weakness. Again and again, as civilizations rise and pass away, he sees his plans in ruins and his dreams trodden under foot. And in that disaster individual men suffer much pain. But this is the noblest way. For a *God,* this is the only way, since any other way would be less good.

This being so, we can see clearly that there are some things God *must* not do.

1. He must not have favorites. We shall look at prayer in chapter 8 and see it as *one* of the ways by which the little brothers can learn to combat some forms of disease. But we must not expect God to leap out of heaven, so to speak, and rescue the individual from evil consequence in response to prayer. If he did, the human family would never learn how to prevent and cure disease. Further, God would make religion an insurance against

51

catastrophe and men would rush to pay the premium by means of a spurious piety. Who would not start being religious and saying his prayers if by that means he could be made immune from cancer? And what a calculating travesty of religion it would be! As we read the Gospels we feel that Christ went out of his way to tell his men, not that following him would make them immune from trouble, but that following him would get them into it. They must be prepared, not only to face all that others faced but to have persecution added also (Matt. 10:22).

2. God must not achieve an end as though the means did not matter. That would be like putting the ball in the net; like doing Tommy's homework for him; like filling in for us, surreptitiously, the blank squares in our crossword puzzle by the one who made it.

3. God must not do things for you that would be unfair to me or vice versa. As we saw in the illustration of the express train, God must not intervene in a way which, for others, would cause disruption and an inability ever to learn those trustworthy laws on which the universe is run.

This does not deny miracle. A miracle means that laws we have not yet learned or understood are at work, some of them laws operating on a higher plane than we have yet reached and effecting as remarkable results as, say, penicillin would achieve among uneducated Eskimos, astonishing them as miracles astonish us. God often employs miracle. He never employs magic—by which I mean those imaginary happenings utterly outside law, whether material, psychological, psychical, or spiritual.

4. God must not give me what I ask, if he knows that to do so would defeat his purpose. Life is full of illustrations. How pathetically a typhoid patient pleads for food! How cruel it seems to deny a human being food! Yet food could prove fatal. In one

situation, my own son, a child of four, cried for something to drink. Yet even a drink of water would have defeated the purpose of the doctor whose skill saved his life. How terrible it would be if God, as it were, closed with us and granted some of our petitions. It would be as foolish as if a father, when his child of five announced that he wanted to be an engine driver, closed with the prayer and shut all other doors to usefulness. My own beloved little daughter for years told us that all she wanted to do in life was to "look after little doggies." She even specified the number as seventeen. But I think as an honors graduate in science and the wife of a research scientist and the mother of three lovely children, she has been of more use in the world. Said one saint, "Thou didst save me by thy hard refusals." My own faith is that such is the power of God to weave our suffering into his final plan that we shall have no regrets at last. All that we suffer is being woven into a plan of incredible beauty far, far beyond our power to understand yet. But nothing can defeat him. If it could, he would exclude it. James Russell Lowell once said that God wouldn't let us get hold of the matchbox unless the universe were fireproof. And we are in good hands, the hands of one utterly good beyond all our dreaming and *finally* omnipotent. For him all purposes will one day be fulfilled and all his dreams come true.

Chapter 7

What sense is there in all this suffering?

SOMETIMES I FEEL THAT I WANT TO APPEAL FOR MORE AGNOSTI-cism in our Christian thinking. I mean by that a willingness, while holding tightly to Christian essentials—which, in my view, are very few—to be willing to accept the fact that puny, insect man, adrift on this wayside planet amid a million galaxies, cannot even hope to understand all the purposes and plans which are in the mind of the creator of a universe such as modern science shows this to be.

I referred earlier to a little boy whose father was a surgeon being unable to understand what his father was about when a surgical operation took place. But of course the situation ought to be far more severely contrasted than that. Once when I was preaching in my beloved City Temple in London, where I was minister for nearly a quarter of a century, I saw an ant (I am sure it was an ant!) crawling along the pulpit cushion. When it came to a gap in the cushions on the pulpit edge, it hesitated, turned this way and turned that, seemingly hesitant as to which way to go. Possibly its wife was waiting for it to come home to lunch and would be irritable if it was late! The crack in the cushions seemed a major problem! I meditated long on the problem it raised and told my people about it. That little ant had never heard of the City Temple! It had no idea it was in one of the most famous pulpits in the world! It had never heard of London, or England, or Great Britain, or Europe, or America, or Russia, or China. The existence of the world was quite unknown to it, let alone the vast problems which perplex man on it and concerning it. As for other planets and the millions of stars in space, it was totally incapable of knowing anything about them.

We rightly believe that in terms of *love* we are individually precious to God, and to that problem we shall soon turn. But intellectually, would it not be wise to realize that we have little more idea of what plans God is working out than an ant in the City Temple has of what goes on when there is a meeting of the United Nations or an attempted journey to the moon?

A message like this needs carefully safeguarding. *As a beloved object* every man is infinitely precious to God, as a tiny child is to a father. But as one who can comprehend, how can any of us hope to encompass the thoughts of God?

Another point must be made clear. In Jesus we can become certain of the nature and quality of God, just as a cupful of sea water will tell the chemist all there is to know about the nature, the chemical composition of the Atlantic. But what can a cupful of sea water reveal to a shut-in child of the grandeur and majesty of a storm in mid-ocean; of the *activities* of the sea; of the vast life in its depths? Jesus reveals the nature and character of God. A good man, to the extent to which he is good, reveals the nature of God. A perfect man perfectly reveals the nature of God. But the Atlantic cannot be contained in a cup, and *all* the attributes and activities and purposes of God cannot be compressed within the human life of the Man of Nazareth. For though he was divine he never ceased to be human. He never escaped *some* of the limits of our humanity.

Perhaps the whole matter is summed up in the very simple lines of Whittier,

> I know not where His islands lift
> Their fronded palms in air;
> I only know I cannot drift
> Beyond His love and care.

I know not what space holds or even what space is like. I do not know what may be happening on a million other planets, for all I know, inhabited as this is with perhaps totally different forms of life, possibly far more spiritually and scientifically advanced than our own, possibly inhabiting the interior rather than the surface of their planets. I only know that because even I would have a concern about beings created with the capability of loving me and whom I love, God must have a concern about me, and that his greatness, so far from making me feel a mere ant or insect, makes me feel that his greatness and power are at my disposal, just as all the surgeon's abilities would be at the disposal of one who was a son even if the son could not understand one tenth of his father's activities.

This thought is worth a moment's pause. It is very interesting that the Bible never *so* exalts God's greatness as to belittle man. It exalts God's greatness to prove how vast are the resources at man's disposal. "When I look at thy heavens . . . what is man?" But note how the psalm goes on.

> Thou hast made him little less than God,
> and dost crown him with glory and honor.
>
> . . . .
>
> thou hast put all things under his feet.
> —Ps. 8:3-6.

Another psalm says of God, "He telleth the number of the stars" (a statement that is as true now as when the psalmist looked up to the night sky and counted some six thousand glowing points of light!). But he puts another sentence in close apposition, as if they held together. "He healeth the broken in heart, and bindeth up their wounds." (Ps. 147:3-4.)

When men cry out against, or deny the existence of, God because of human suffering—as they often do—I find comfort in the thought that I should be foolish to draw final conclusions when the purposefulness of God was only partially revealed. How silly I should be to walk through a theater and, from a few minutes' experience of the first act, make a deduction about the plot of the whole play or the character of the author. Yet this is what we do about God. We see human suffering and pain. We note the earthquake and the typhoon. We experience—as I have—two world wars and the continual threat of another, and petulantly we say, "There cannot be a God. If there is some kind of mental force behind the universe it is callous or careless, impotent or unloving, stupid or malevolent, or a mixture of all."

I have felt like that too. And then I have remembered odd facts from my reading. Sir John Jeans, for instance, says that if you stuck a stamp on the top of Cleopatra's Needle on the Embankment in London, the thickness of the stamp would, compared with the height of the monument, give you a true comparison between the time man had been on the earth compared with the time there had been an earth! I remembered some other writer saying that if the history of the world were divided into seven thousand equal parts, then one of them would represent the history of man! There is a well-known saying of the geologist Gheyselinck, in his book, *The Restless Earth,* that if the whole history of the world from the Archaean Age until today were compressed into a film scheduled to run for twenty-four hours, man would not *appear* until *the last five seconds of the film!* Why, the play has hardly started yet, has it? The Bible teaches that when the curtain comes down on the drama of God's world purposes, no one will be dissatisfied, and that every human life is very precious to God, always within his care; and that within his life, unbeaten by pain and suffering and any kind of disaster One who is both utterly good and finally omnipotent is working out a plan.

In his teaching there was nothing Jesus emphasized so much as the fact that the individual, whatever he has done, whatever he believes, and whatever catastrophe may fall upon him, either through his own sin or because he belongs to a worldwide family whose liabilities may through mischance fall upon him, is infinitely precious to God. Not a sparrow falls, says Jesus, without God's knowledge; without God doing something adequate about it. "Even the hairs of your head are all numbered," says Jesus in that lovely kind of Eastern exaggeration which made men smile but which got his message home.

One mistake we make is to think of God as a big man trying to keep up with all the things that happen to millions of people; with "so many children that he doesn't know what to do." But one Bible writer says, "In him we live and move and have our being." Suppose that is a bit nearer the truth! Do you realize that there are more cells in your brain than there are people on this planet? You don't watch over them. What happens to them happens to *you*. What happens to us, in a very real sense, happens to God. Not physically, of course, but in an identity of being which love involves. I must not stay to work that out, but if that little girl in your home fell and hurt herself, her mother would hold her, closely, as if the mother were trying to take the little body back into her own and bear the pain. God's sympathy is more than that. *In him,* we live and move and have our being. He knows and feels what happens to us because, in a sense, it happens to him. In a mysterious way, I believe all our suffering is caught up into the divine life. God is not standing apart watching our suffering; the distress happens also to him, and only God could bear it. When the late D. R. Davies visited Spain in 1937 and noted the wretchedness of the poor, he wrote: "I passed through an experience in which I felt the magnitude of human frustration, pain and defeat. For a moment I gathered up in myself the suffering of hungry, baffled men and women. It went a long way to push me to my final despair." That experience was an important factor in bringing him back to God. He adds, "In my bedroom before getting into bed I knelt down for the first time for years and cried, 'Oh, God!' That was all, but though I knew not God, that was, I believe, the deepest prayer I had ever uttered." [1]

If we could *know* from without the suffering, sorrow, and sin of a tiny hamlet, we should break down. If we knew it from within, we should go mad. God knows from within, is implicated in, and identified with, all the suffering, sorrow, and sin of all the world through all the ages. Immanence means that "in all our afflictions he is afflicted"; that what men suffer is a faint reflection of what he suffers, and inasmuch as men do wrong to one another they do it unto him.

Here is a loving father whose boy is living a wastrel life in a great city. We watch the father's hair whiten, his face become drawn and lined, his shoulders become bowed, his gait feeble. His son's sins are bringing him down by reason of their burden. Anyone who further injures the soul of that boy aims a yet greater blow at his father. But the father, however sympathetic and involved, is *outside* the boy. "How much more shall your

[1] D. R. Davies, *In Search of Myself* (London: Geoffrey Bles, 1961), pp. 174, 177.

59

heavenly Father" bear that burden! He is purer and therefore more sensitive to sin. And he is *within* the boy's being. Still "wounded for our transgressions." No longer will I ask petulantly of any human tragedy, "Why does God allow this to happen?" I will at least complete the question, "Why does God allow this to happen *to himself?*" "Oh, who am I, that for my sake, my Friend should bear my load and carry my sorrows and be stabbed with my sins?"

How well I remember visiting a leper settlement in India, speaking to the lepers, spending the day with them, and then—having sympathized and done any small thing or said any small word intended to help—I went to my bungalow, changed my clothes, and sat down to dinner. But when Jesus saw a leper he became a leper. He did not, of course, develop the symptoms. But which is the worst part of disease, the physical symptom or the psychological syndrome—what it feels like to be a leper? The latter is the worst: the loneliness, the mental anguish, the sense of being an outcast. Jesus did not sympathize merely. Certainly he did not patronize. Nor did he bend down in pity, as one who says, "Yes, I know what he feels." He *felt* it all. He identified himself with all the horror of it until he could get his shoulder under the burden and lift and dispel it forever. The poet Walt Whitman said that when he saw someone suffering he did not just feel deeply sympathetic. His words were, "I myself become the wounded person." How much more involved a loving, immanent God must be!

So, if suffering has ever made you bitter, do try to believe that you have not cast yourself out of God's caring and loving and sharing. Even if your suffering is your own fault, he shares the fault; he was "made sin on our behalf." The Good Shepherd is searching for his lost sheep *until he find it*. Listen to these words of assurance: They are mine and "they shall never perish and no one shall snatch them out of my hand." (John 10:28.) The coin will not be left in the dust ultimately to disintegrate. It bears the image of the King. It is part of his treasure. And where his treasure is, there will his heart be also.

Chapter 8

Why is there
such a thing as disease?

THIS INDEED HAS LONG SEEMED TO ME THE CRUX OF THE WHOLE problem we are studying: not so much, "Why did my saintly mother get cancer?"—the question that comes up every time questions on religion are asked—but rather, "Why is there such a terrible thing as cancer *to be got by anyone*?" If disease is often the result of ignorance, folly, or sin somewhere far back—and how far back no one can say—why should such a terrible price have to be paid for it? Opposition to the laws of the universe paid for by *discomfort* we could understand. We don't blench when a child puts his finger on the hot bars of the grate and gets a burn and a blister no bigger than a dime. We know he must learn the danger, as well as the comfort, of heat. But cancer, polio, paresis, smallpox, leprosy, insanity! . . . I speak feelingly because my mother and both my sisters died of cancer. One of my sisters suffered for nearly three years. All three maintained an unbroken faith to the end, but they were all convinced and radiant Christians before that. They didn't need pain to pull them up. Again and again, without Christian faith, one might conclude, not that folly or sin were met with a just consequence, but that a powerful fiend had set a trap for a child in the dark and landed him in an agony of mind and body quite undeserved and wholly unforeseen.

I think the only answer I can give to the question at the head of this chapter is that God, who *must* be good and is obviously a being of immense power, has not yet finished making his universe. The story of creation in Genesis is a marvelous guess in an appealing literary framework. But God did not "rest the seventh day" as one might sit back and say, "Well, that is finished and it is very good!" [1] Jesus is a greater authority than the editor of the first book in the Bible and he said, "My Father has never yet ceased his work" (John 5:17 N.E.B.).

One thing we can say in advance of studying the subject of this chapter is this: *God* must have an answer to the problem of man's pain. And that pain is such a problem that the commensurate answer must be an amazingly glorious one. If, feeling the poignancy of human pain (including the agonies of little children and the sufferings of animals, both terrified by fear and darkness as well as by pain) man at last will be able to say spontaneously, "Now I understand," then God's answer must be a very wonderful one and provide an experience of unimaginable joy. We *are* promised that an answer will be given. Jesus said, "You do not understand now . . . , but one day you will." (John 13:7 N.E.B.) What an answer it will be if, in the light of it, there are no questions about pain left to ask! Paul shared this belief through faith. He, the man who could cure others but was chronically ill himself (II Cor. 12:7), said, "My knowledge now is partial; then it will be whole" (I Cor. 13:12 N.E.B.). If, then, God's final purpose is more than commensurate with man's pain, man's faith in God must be stretched to that same compass.

When all this has been said; when, in fact, I have admitted that the short answer to the question at the head of this chapter

---

[1] "God saw everything that he had made, and behold, it was very good. . . . And on the seventh day God finished his work which he had done, and he rested on the seventh day from all his work." (Gen. 1:31; 2:2.)

is, "I don't know," we are free to speculate, and this I find it interesting and not unhelpful to do as follows:

1. Let us bear in mind the undoubted fact that disease did not begin with man. Those who "explain" all disease as being due to man's sin must be hard pressed when they are confronted by the indubitable facts disclosed by scientific research. Those who tell us that if we lived "closer to nature" we should all be perfectly well, forget that primitive tribes suffer from terrible diseases and that even plants and animals are all liable to disease—and, as far as man can discover, always have been. "It is known," says G. G. Dawson,

that disease is a phenomenon much older than man. The fossilized bones of animals now extinct show unmistakable evidence of disease. The earliest example of vertebrate disease due to infection known to scientists is that of a reptile which broke one of its dorsal spines. This became infected so that an incurable inflammatory condition arose known today as osteomyelitis.[2]

The date given to this case of disease on earth is 130 million years ago! Dawson adds,

Amongst other fossilized remains are those of a dinosaur which had bone tumour, whilst some exhibit pathological conditions due to bacterial infection. It is a remarkable fact that bacteria of the micrococcus and diplococcus orders have been found in coal measures, in the fossilized faeces of fish and in the vertebrate and other remains belonging to the Carboniferous Era, some 160 million years ago. . . . It is evident then, that disease existed on the earth before man's advent, and continued its course during the days of our prehistoric ancestors.[3]

[2] *Healing, Pagan and Christian* (London: S.P.C.K., 1935), p. 1.
[3] *Ibid.*, pp. 2-3.

Of course, this solves nothing in regard to the *origin* of disease. It only pushes the problem far enough back to absolve man from responsibility *for* its origin.[4] Some have speculated that there may have been a species of "fall" amongst men who are now extinct but who were once higher in attainment, both spiritually and physically, than anything to which man as we know him has ever attained since, and that the wickedness of these supermen originally brought chaos and disease into the world. For myself, I know of no real support for this theory, which seems determined to saddle man with a responsibility for disease which the facts do not warrant. Others believe that the world was full of spiritual intelligences even more closely in the image of God than man is and that they morally "fell" and became evil intelligences— hence the devil and his angels—which brought havoc into God's world and upset his plans; evil intelligences who had earlier derived from God enough power to create those forms of life like—say—the hooded cobra, the giant squid, and the polio virus, which now pester man. But for this speculation I find little support and no attractiveness.

2. A view to which I think we are driven is that the world was not created with only man's freedom from danger and suffering in view. One dreams of a Utopia in which "the wolf shall dwell with the lamb, and the leopard shall lie down with the kid" and the child can touch a deadly snake without fear (Isa. 11:6-9). And it may be that we shall reach that state one day. In the meantime, the world of created animals, including man, looks like a vast arena where each organism must fight for its existence,

---

[4] I am afraid John Wesley was wrong when in his preface to *Primitive Physic* he argues, "Why is there pain in the world?" and answers, "Because there is sin. Had there been no sin, there would have been no pain. Pain is the necessary effect of sin." (London: Epworth Press, 1960.)

and Jesus seems to have recognized that no divine protection stopped the wolf from snatching the lamb if it could do so (John 10:12). When a lion carries off a missionary, Christian people find it at once a problem that God should let it happen, but the psalmist sings:

> The high mountains are for the wild goats;
> the rocks are a refuge for the badgers.
>
> .   .   .   .
>
> Thou makest darkness, and it is night,
> when all the beasts of the forest creep forth.
> The young lions roar for their prey,
> seeking their food from God.
>
> —Ps. 104:18, 20-21

The Christian prays that the lions, young or old, will keep away from missionaries, but there is more than humor in this limerick:

> There was a young lady of Ryde
> Who was carried away by the tide,
>   But a man-eating shark
>   Was heard to remark,
> "I knew that the Lord would provide."

And seriously, man must realize that every organism in the world including himself is fighting for its life, seeking its food that it may continue to live.

Not many centuries ago, in this my "island home," wolves came down in winter from the forests on the hilltops, and, unable to find their normal food, attacked villagers who had to fight them and destroy them or they would themselves have been destroyed, together with their sheep, cattle, and poultry. Even as I was writing these words, *The Times* reported as follows from Spain:

Nearly all the dogs of the village of Lubian, in Zamora province, have been killed by a pack of wolves.

Apparently reduced to extreme hunger, the wolves without fear of anything or anybody, according to a report from Zamora, came down from their lairs in the snow-covered mountains during the night and roamed around the streets of Lubian. They broke into corrals and killed virtually all the watchdogs in the village.

The mountains to the north of Zamora, which form a labyrinth of peaks and ridges, valleys and ravines, are known for their many wolves. Every winter hunting parties are organized by the authorities to protect the sheep, cattle, and poultry from their raids, prizes being awarded to the hunters who bag the highest number.[5]

Still the fight goes on. Many diseases are caused by germs or more minute organisms. We have all heard of a virus infection. Our commonest enemies now are smaller than wolves. We may not shoot them as our forefathers shot the wolves, but the battle is the same and the problem is the same. It is the battle man fights for survival.

Man has been told that he is to rule supreme in the creation. "Let them have dominion over the fish of the sea, and over the birds of the air, and over the cattle, and over all the earth, and over every creeping thing that creeps upon the earth" (Gen. 1:26); but he has had to fight for that dominion and the battle still goes on. The psalmist cries that man is to have authority over all sheep and oxen, the beasts of the field, the fowl of the air, the fish of the sea, and all the works of God's hands (Ps. 8:6-8),

[5] *The Times* (London), December 23, 1961. Reprinted by permission of *The Times*.

and those who are vegetarians on principle have to remember that Jesus went fishing with his men and is reported more than once to have prepared a meal of fish for his disciples.[6] But to have *authority* over an enemy does not mean that the desired *power* over him has been reached, as any policeman thinking of the criminals who elude him would be quick to acknowledge. He has authority but not power. (One wishes that one's conscience had as much power as it has authority!) How true and salutary is that wise word in the Epistle to the Hebrews, "We do not yet see everything in subjection to him" (Heb. 2:8). That word "yet" hints at a glorious possibility, but in the meantime man's battle for supremacy must go forward and he will learn more in the battle than if all were done for him, just as the hockey player in our illustration learns by playing the game, not by having someone put the ball in the net by irresistible power.

3. There is, however, a view about germs which I think may be part of the answer to the question, "Why were the germs of disease ever created?"

Most people know that the human body contains bacteria—which are healthy and friendly to man. They are called saprophytes. Some of them live in, and feed on, the various secretions of the body. Most people also know that the very chemical constitution of the secretions of the body can be altered by the emotions of the deep mind. It was found, for example, that when a nursing mother who was breast-feeding her baby was forced to watch a fight between her husband whom she loved and a man who had attempted to seduce her and whom she hated, the hate in the mother's mind was of such intensity that

[6] Matt. 14:17; 15:34; Mark 6:38; 8:7; Luke 5:6; 9:13; John 6:9; 21:6; and especially 21:9-13.

her breast milk was turned to poison and the baby fell dead from her breast.[7]

Dr. H. P. Newsholme, formerly Medical Officer of Health for Birmingham, with whom I talked and corresponded on this point, agrees in his famous book, *Health, Disease and Integration,* that "there is no essential difference in mechanism between the secretion of milk by the breast glands and the secretion of saliva by the salivary glands and *of mucus by the mucous glands.*" (Italics mine.)

During a lecture at Cambridge I heard a most interesting story of which I made notes:

Dr. Harold Wolff and Dr. Stewart Wolf of Cornell University in America experimented on a willing patient called Tom who was employed in their hospital. As a result of an accident years earlier, Tom had to feed himself through a specially constructed opening directly into his stomach *which could be observed.*

Tom was told he was being dismissed for inefficiency. Not only did his face grow red and angry but the lining of his stomach became congested and engorged with blood even to the point of bleeding at the merest touch. When he was told that the alleged dismissal had been concocted, his stomach returned to normal. Further experiments showed that if Tom was depressed and dejected his stomach became gray and covered with mucus.

Dr. Stafford-Clark tells of a cat who was induced to eat a meal containing barium so that in X rays the outline of stomach and digestive organs could plainly be seen on a screen. When a dog was brought into the room and the cat securely held "the whole contour and behaviour of its stomach altered completely, the

[7] See Eric Pritchard in *Infant Education*, quoted by Dr. H. P. Newsholme in *Health, Disease and Integration* (London: Allen and Unwin), p. 55.

valves at each end closed tight while the rest of the stomach sagged and digestive movements ceased." [8]

Emotion, therefore, especially if intense, and/or long sustained, can produce chemical and other changes in the saliva or *the mucus* which covers certain tissues. With this in mind I want to quote from the researches of Dr. J. G. Adami. He writes:

Every pathogenic microbe has closely related forms or species differing from it in little beyond the fact that the one is virulent, the other non-virulent. Next, it is to be noted that these allied species are found suggestively growing in the cavities or on the mucous surfaces of the body, in the same habitat as the virulent forms, or again in water and foodstuffs. . . . This state of affairs in itself leads to the conclusion that pathogenic microbes at some period, or periods, have originated from the microbes saprophytic upon [=friendly to] the body surfaces, or existing commonly in the water and foodstuffs; that they have originated by adaptation of these forms to growth, not merely on, but within the tissues.

He writes again, "According to the environment so do bacteria assume special qualities." [9]

What does all this amount to in simple English? To this, I think: that germs, friendly to human health and feeding happily on mucus and other secretions within us, find that, through our emotional reactions, the nature and composition of these secretions alters and becomes unsuitable to them. They therefore naturally move to some other feeding ground where they find food but where their activities interfere with our health and well-being. From being benign baccilli, therefore, they become malign. But

---

[8] David Stafford-Clark, *Psychiatry Today* (Baltimore: Penguin Books, 1959, a Pelican Book), p. 238. Dr. Clark also verifies the story of Tom.

[9] *Medical Contributions to the Study of Evolution* (London: Duckworth, 1918), pp. 23, 42.

if man has himself changed the composition of his own secretions by harboring emotions like excessive worry or guilt or resentment or hate, and has thus driven friendly germs to become hostile germs, he can hardly cry out petulantly to God, "I don't know why you ever created these enemies of my peace." I find it very, very hard to believe that the germ or baccillus of small-pox was once a friendly little fellow ministering to my total health, and the idea that *all* the germs of disease were once friendly and benign has not been put forward by anyone; but, before we pass on, listen to Dr. Adami on the germ of diphtheria.

Diptheria gains its simplest explanation as being due to the acquirement within recent times of virulent properties by some *previously harmless* diphtheroid bacillus growing in the throat and upper respiratory passages. And so it has been with . . . infections in general. . . . I admit that there may be contradictory causes, that particular environments may favour the origin or reappearance of particular diseases, as again that local tissue environment may determine particular selective development of virulence.[10]

Dr. Newsholme himself went so far as to say that

nervous activity arising from *primary acute emotion* or from cerebral irritation, may conceivably produce living particulate enzymes or "viruses" capable of causing catabolism[11] and capable of conveying "disease" to the individual and to others. In other words, the "filtrable virus" need not necessarily be derived from a source, always the same, external to the body, but may be the product of the unhealthy body itself.[12]

It will be interesting if, after death, we are allowed to ask

[10] J. G. Adami, *op cit.*, p. 42.
[11] Catabolism means the breaking down and destruction of the cells of the body.
[12] Dr. H. P. Newsholme, *Health, Disease and Integration, op. cit.*, p. 68.

71

questions and challenge God with making disease germs, to learn that man is himself responsible for the virulence and hostility of some of them. One begins to wonder and speculate whether many forms of life, which in the evolutionary scale are below man and which develop hostility to him, may be prisons in which spirit-entities express some primitive striving or some anger against conditions for which man is responsible! The saints sometimes seem able to make friends even with leopards.[18]

Alas, in every field of human inquiry there is so little that we know. When, during the First World War, I served in Mesopotamia as an officer in the Indian army and later as a chaplain, disease was a greater enemy than the Turks and cost us more men's lives. We used to curse the sandflies which brought us down in hundreds with a particular brand of fever. I remember how lustily the men going on leave would sing a chorus which went:

> I wouldn't choose
> To live with the Jews
> Or the Arab tribes we see.
> Farewell, little hell,
> Sandfly, goodbye.
> There's a Blighty girl waiting for me.

But the "Arab tribes" (who, be it noted, seemed not to suffer from the bites of these tiny demons) said, "Sandflies are our friends. They fertilize our date palms. No sandflies, no dates."

I would willingly, at one time, have consigned all wasps to perdition. But a well-qualified writer in *The Times* wrote,

[18] See my *His Life and Ours* (Nashville: Abingdon Press, 1933, 1961), pp. 98-100.

Nine tenths of the activities of wasps are beneficent to man. From late spring to early autumn they seek out and destroy vast multitudes of caterpillars and grubs, which, if left unchecked, would destroy our crops, our vegetables, our orchards, and our trees.[14]

Do we know enough about germs and viruses to say that all their activities are, from our point of view, evil? Would human life be more difficult without them?

This does not stop me from "swatting" a wasp in my study or from trying to murder disease germs in my body, but it lights up a point of view which should be included as we try to work out a Christian philosophy of suffering.

It is incredible that God is responsible for the creation of anything essentially evil. That God, as it were, sat down one afternoon and thought out, planned, and created a virus which later, multiplied by thousands, would torment, wreck the happiness of, and perhaps painfully kill an innocent and lovely baby is impossible of belief by anyone of undistorted mind.

That God is still at work in his world, that he is hindered, possibly by nonhuman, nonincarnate evil intelligences, and certainly by human ignorance, folly, and sin, that much which he planned as good has been turned into temporary evil in the terrific struggle going on in every part of his creation, and that man has not yet found his proper place in the universe, all this does seem a possible clue where so much is dark.

One thing is clear. We must ally ourselves with God in every way open to us, knowing that our complete health is his ideal will and that even if for a dozen reasons we do not win back physical wholeness he will let nothing be lost; and that we *can* turn what

[14] August 22, 1934.

is not his will into his ultimate glory and our ultimate gain. "The team" will win the game. The victory is promised on what Livingstone called "the word of a Gentleman," and our private sorrows and suffering, however sore now, desolating to our present faith, and puzzling to the intellect, will finally form such a glowing part of God's victory, that joy will fill our hearts. So far from everlastingly complaining, we shall be saying, "Fancy God being able to make *that* out of my pain! Blessed be his glorious name forever."

Chapter 9

How can I fight this illness?

MY OLD FRIEND AND TEACHER, FROM WHOM I LEARNED SO MUCH, the late Rev. Dr. W. R. Maltby, used to say: "It is not wicked to be ill, but it is wicked to be more ill than you need be." What a true word that is! Illness means that we can serve the community with less efficiency and possibly hinder those who look after us from fullness of life and service. I hope that does not sound unkind. I know that the invalid who prays and loves and offers his suffering to God does far more good in the world than thousands of fit and healthy people do, but he doesn't *have* to be ill before he can pray and love and offer himself to God. Jesus said, "I have come that men may have life, and may have it in all its fullness." (John 10:10 N.E.B.) Would John Wesley, who prayed and loved and endlessly toiled for the greater part of a century, have done more if, physically handicapped, he had prayed in his bedroom? It is hard to answer perhaps, but I adhere to my first principle that God's ideal will is complete fitness of body, mind, and spirit. Let me offer God as fit an instrument as I can for his service! Paul says, "I beseech you therefore, brethren, by the mercies of God, to present your bodies a living sacrifice, holy [healthy], well-pleasing to God which is your spiritual worship." (Rom. 12:1, English Revised Version margin.) In other words, maximum spiritual service can ideally be rendered if one has a healthy body and a sound mind dedicated to God.

I can safely suppose that any reader of this chapter who is ill has called in his doctor. The doctor's training includes all that has been usefully learned about healing the body and mind since Hippocrates, who lived about 450 B.C. At the same time no good doctor pretends that he has thought of everything. Nor will he object to "another's opinion" being sought. Consultants have been derided for "knowing more and more about less and less," but I can speak from experience of inestimable help being usually given by them.

Osteopaths are derided too, but again I can speak from experience of weeks of pain, including the pain, discomfort, and time-consuming nuisance of hot poultices applied every few hours—ended in half an hour by adequate osteopathy, and just recently, when a young woman was referred to me because her pain was supposed to be "psychological," a medically qualified osteopath found a partially dislocated hip, and in my presence relieved her of pain in a few minutes though she had had months of fussing with steel belts, plaster jackets, and rest, including weeks of lying on her back.

If I were ill I would turn to anyone who could put me right if I trusted him enough to feel that he would not make matters worse; and in my opinion there is a place for the psychiatrist, the dietitian, the nature-cure therapist, the manipulator, and for treament by radiesthesia or, as I prefer to call it, odic force.[1] As for the physiotherapist, the masseuse, and the efficient and conscientious nurse, I can think of no more worthwhile job for a young woman to take up. Such a person, properly trained and qualified, renders a tremendous service to the community.

But when all such help has been considered is there nothing

---

[1] I have described odic force and given instances of its successful use in my book, *Wounded Spirits* to be published by Abingdon Press in 1963.

else to be done? What about religion, with its emphasis on faith and prayer? Do we not read of "faith healing" and of healing through prayer?

I must not repeat here what I have written in other books on this subject,[2] but some simple things may be said.

In my opinion, by far the best way for the sufferer to think out the relationship of religion to his suffering would be for him to ask an instructed minister or clergyman whom he trusted to visit him. This would give him an opportunity for confession— if this were felt necessary—and for discussion.

It could not be anything but a contribution to the regaining of health for a sufferer to make sure that his religious life was in good order. We all know in these days to what an extent the bottling up of hate or fear or resentment or worry or malice or guilt can set off illness and delay recovery from illnesses that have a physical origin. Doctors too are increasingly aware of this. They now do not only ask the patient with a gastric ulcer what he has been eating; they ask him what he is worrying about. Ministers could do a great service to patients—since we have all sinned— in declaring the loving forgiveness of God and making sure that the patient not only assents but *receives* into the depths of his mind that healing truth.

Prayer for healing is to be encouraged as long as the patient understands clearly what he is doing, or, if prayer is made for him in church, what intercession aims at doing for him. It aims to bring the patient into as complete a unity with God as is

[2] *Why Do Men Suffer?*; *Prescription for Anxiety*; *Psychology, Religion, and Healing*; *Psychology and Life* (Abingdon Press). *Psychology in Service of the Soul* (Epworth Press). *Wounded Spirits* (to be published by Abingdon Press in 1963).

possible. Clearly it follows the reception of forgiveness. Equally clearly prayer is not a cure-all. It frequently fails to cure because it is not the relevant way of healing that particular illness. It will not be wasted, but frankly it does not usually bring physical cure. You would not say, "O God make me better," if you had a toothache. You would go to the dentist. Do we really expect God to deliver us from an illness which may have a similarly physical origin just because we do not know the relevant person to whom to go? But health is harmonious correspondence with environment; the body with the physical world, the mind with the world of true ideas, and the soul with God. Prayer at any rate can bring health to the soul, and the interrelation of body, mind, and spirit is so close that health in one relationship indubitably increases total health, and if the dis-ease, even though physically suffered, is an expression of a spiritual or emotional malaise, prayer, with the reconciliation with God which it brings, could well be the main therapeutic factor.

In regard to faith a lot of misunderstanding is current. We are told by some to "have faith," as if one could do so like turning on a tap. We fit and healthy people only make others feel guilty and miserable by telling them to "have faith." *Christ knew how to call out faith*. We so rarely do that for people. I dislike the term "faith healing," for some "healers" make us feel that if only we had faith we could be cured of anything. This, I think, is nonsense. It must be most comforting to some "faith healers" to move about the country holding missions. If people are healed or their symptoms removed (often only temporarily, though this is not publicized), then the healer adds them to his list of successes. If the patients are unhealed (and thus driven into a deeper depression than ever), then it is because they had insufficient "faith." Heads the healer wins, tails the patient loses! In such missions the determining factor, if the patient appears healed, is often not true faith at all but a species of accidental suggestibility which is part of the patient's temperamental makeup and no more a credit or discredit to him than the fact that he has a long nose or ginger hair.

True faith in this connection is a different thing altogether and has nothing whatever to do with believing theological propositions. What did the people whom Jesus healed know of theology? Professor Macmurray says that "Christ's use of the term 'faith' does not allow us to take it as the equivalent of 'belief' in the ordinary sense of holding certain views." Believing *in* a person is quite a different thing from believing the truth of propositions about him, and it is the former that is so essential. Christ's words, his very voice, his eyes, his quiet authority, and the lovely life he lived would make men know intuitively that they could trust him, that they were accepted just as they were. The word "faith" should always be reserved for *a person*. To talk of having "faith" in castor oil or some other material thing is, in my view, a misuse of language.

Faith, then, is quietly trusting the God who is like Jesus *whether one is healed or not,* knowing that we are safe, that God loves us, is at work in us and through us, and will use the suffering, if, for various reasons, it cannot yet be ended. We *can* have that kind of faith by constantly looking at him as the Gospels teach us to regard him, and by talking with him, listening, looking, and loving. In that utterly reliable and loving presence the querulous, rebellious complaint dies. We still want to be well but we can bear the delay even if complete healing only comes after death, when we throw off, like a tattered old overcoat, the physical covering of a spirit that without hindrance enters joyously into the heritage of that health which has always been God's will.[3]

---

[3] Those who want an excellent essay on true faith and its relevance to our subject would find it in a shilling pamphlet by Dr. Denis V. Martin, called, *The Meaning of Faith in Faith-Healing* (London: Epworth Press, 1954). There is also a chapter on "The Nature and Place of Faith in Faith Healing" in my *Psychology, Religion, and Healing, op. cit.*, p. 423, and a chapter entitled "The Weapon of Faith" in *Why Do Men Suffer? op cit.*, pp. 164 ff.

Appendix to Chapter 9

Healing Missions

I feel that I must warn the sufferer against missions and meetings and services held by various kinds of "healers" because they have done so much harm to people I know that I feel very strongly about them, though I will summarize here views which I have expressed more fully elsewhere.[4]

There can be no objection to a quiet service, with or without the laying on of hands, in the presence of the patient's relatives or a few carefully selected friends. But the patient should be instructed beforehand by the ministrant so that if disappointed by the continuance of his illness, he does not lose faith or make mistaken deductions about faith and about God.

Healing services open to the general public are not allowed in Methodist churches by a resolution of the Methodist Conference of 1952. The reasons I gave when proposing this resolution may be summarized as follows:

A. *Emotional Perils*

1. It is impossible for a large number of sick people to be gathered in a congregation and invited to come forward for healing without intense emotion being aroused in both the patients and the onlookers. This has frequently resulted in outbreaks of hysteria, with terrifying results for all.

2. A few people may claim to be healed there and then, though in two much-advertised and crowded "healing missions" in Liver-

[4] *Psychology, Religion, and Healing, op. cit.,* and *Wounded Spirits, op. cit.*

pool and Birkenhead some years ago no one even claimed healing.[5] Those who claim healing thrust the unhealed into a grim disappointment and share it themselves when, as so often happens, the apparently healed relapse into illness again, a fact not advertised by anyone and as far as possible concealed from everyone.

3. There is fostered a confusion between faith and suggestibility. The unhealed feel that they had insufficient faith and the healed congratulate themselves on having it, when the differentiating factor is often suggestibility, which is a temperamental quality we either have or have not; whereas true faith is a splendid quality which has to be worked for and *which does not necessarily insure healing*. We can have true faith without healing and we can have healing without faith.

4. Other faulty conclusions are secretly accepted by the unhealed, such as that religion is "no good," or that God has favorites, or that they themselves are unworthy. None of these conclusions is sound.

B. *Physical Perils*

1. The postponement of surgical help while waiting for the "healer" to visit the patient's area can render the surgeon's task harder or even impossible.

2. The transitory nature of the relief and the return of the symptoms increases the depression of the patient and lowers his morale in his fight for health.

3. The lack of discrimination on the part of the healer, such as in a case known to me of a little fellow with a club foot being promised football boots after his visit to a "healer," so that he

---

[5] *Birkenhead News,* June 10, 1939.

could play like other boys. His mental state on returning unhealed makes one angry about the whole farce. It should be remembered that Christ has more in common with the modern surgeon than with some faith healers, for he knew what was the matter and altered his treatment accordingly, whereas some healers lay hands on everyone without knowledge or insight and sometimes, by implication, blame the unhealed for not "having faith."

4. Most importantly, in certain cases of psychosomatic illness, the *symptom* of disease is banished and seen no more after the healing service. Thereupon a cure is announced and everybody is deeply impressed. But, *if the psychological condition which set up the symptom in the first place is not dealt with and healed, the unconscious mind will produce another symptom far more difficult to cure, or else set up mental or emotional symptoms which had been finding a certain expression in the physical ones.*

This truth lies behind Christ's words, which sound so stern, spoken to the man whom he cured by the pool of Bethesda, "Now that you are well again, leave your sinful ways, or you may suffer something worse" (John 5:14 N.E.B.). If the man's illness had been psychosomatic, a translation of inner guilt into bodily illness, then the unconscious mind would not repeat the same symptoms; it would find another so that its bluff could not easily be called and its activities be obvious. Jesus is not *threatening* the man, "Sin no more, that nothing worse befall you." He is stating a truth which anyone who has followed up the activities of "healing missions" could illustrate. For instance: "a duodenal ulcer is in many cases a substitute for conscious anxiety." [6] If the ulcer alone is "cured," the deep mind will either produce a more serious symptom, or else the anxiety will be expressed as conscious terror

[6] Arthur Guirdham, *A Theory of Disease* (London: Allen and Unwin, 1957), p. 88.

which is much harder to bear. It is easier to bear our sufferings in the body than in the mind. Many patients whose physical symptoms expressed mental dis-ease, have, after having merely the symptom cured, fallen into mental illness or "nervous breakdown."

Canon Grensted in his Bampton Lectures wrote:

The great danger of missions of healing is that by their very prestige and by their impressive setting they act with immense power along these (hysteria-producing) lines. They attract and profoundly affect hysterics of all kinds. But they give little guarantee that the cures achieved are radical. Even if the patients develop a new and edifying piety, this may easily be nothing more than a new phase of their hysteria, as far removed from true religion as fantasy is from fact.[7]

5. A fifth and very serious objection to the healing mission is that it encourages the patient to use God as a means of getting well, with the only too well-evidenced likelihood that if he recovers he will forget God. This puts God in the same category as a treatment. "Deep X ray failed, penicillin was ineffective, let's try religion." A man actually said to me, "I tried everything else so I thought I'd try a spot of prayer!" But it seems to me a serious heresy to regard God as a means to our end. We are means to his. The aim of prayer is hardly the same as the aim of a pill.

[7] I cannot refrain here from quoting further from Canon Grensted's Bampton Lectures: "To cure the symptom only invites the appearance of other symptoms which may be at least as serious. The story is told of a doctor who by repeated suggestion cured a patient of the conviction that he was a dog. The cure was reported triumphantly with the appended note, 'Unfortunately he now believes that he is a water-rat.' Of an enormous number of religious healings the same criticism must be made." L. W. Grensted, Oriel Professor of the Philosophy of the Christian Religion in the University of Oxford, *Psychology and God* (London: Longmans, Green & Co. Ltd., 1930), p. 117.

Those who desire healing through religion should sincerely seek to be forgiven and to get a new realization of the love and power of God. If healing comes, it will be a by-product and of course is to be welcomed. But we must face the fact that if we are honest we are far more interested in the health of our bodies than in that of our souls. We would far rather be cured of our cancer than of our meannesses, lusts, and hypocrisy. But we must not suppose that God's order of importance is the same as ours.

Some will feel that I am hard on "healing missions" and will quote the New Testament in support of them, pointing out that Christ healed people in the street. I would reply that repeatedly Christ sought privacy for his healings and after a healing told the patient, "Tell no man!" Consider Matt. 8:4 K.J.V., "See thou tell no man"; Matt. 9:30 K.J.V., "See that no man know it"; Mark 5:43 K.J.V., "He charged them . . . that no man should know it"; Mark 7:24 K.J.V., "[He] would have no man know it"; Mark 7:36 K.J.V., "He charged them that they should tell no man"; and Mark 8:30; 9:9; and so on. Jesus sent a leper to the priest so that he could get his "discharge certificate" but added, "Tell no man" (Luke 5:14 K.J.V.).

As for Christ healing in the street, I feel that this is no precedent for the modern church. Christ was Christ. He had insight and *knew* what was wrong with a patient without being told. He changed his technique accordingly. He knew whom he could heal and whom he couldn't. No one surely believes that Christ could have given sight to a man whose eyes had been gouged out, or healed the lameness of a man with a missing leg, and so on. Many illnesses with which ignorant healers try to deal are in the same category.

How different from Christ's methods is the setup of the healing mission of today. At its worst there is much advertisement beforehand. Patients, *whatever their disease,* are encouraged to come many miles. Soft music or the repetition of sentimental hymn tunes intentionally works up the emotion. The healer enters dramatically (with appropriate comments in the press later about his or her dress and "wonderful hands," etc.) and the performance begins. The "healer" does not understand one thing about anatomy, psychology, disease, or medicine; and without any sifting of cases, or variations in technique, or previous consultation with the doctor, or talk with the patient, he lays hands on the *head* of every kneeling suppliant. If the healer possesses "odic force" or if the patient is highly suggestible and has hysterical symptoms, there may be the appearance of a cure. This is blazoned next day in the press, which I have never known to report the frequent relapses in which mental depression is added to the return of the symptoms.

For myself I am glad that the Methodist Church, to which I belong, has banned from its premises such travesties, such exhibitions of primitive mumbo-jumbo. I believe in faith, but we do not live in the first century when faith was a projection from credulity. We live in a scientific age when faith is a projection from science; a loving commitment which travels as far as possible along the road of scientific knowledge and then takes its leap into the unprovable *in the direction of the trend of the evidence,* depending on the trustworthiness of God's nature and character as Christ revealed him.

Chapter 10

If I don't get better,
is God's plan defeated?

THE ANSWER TO THIS QUESTION MUST BE A TRIUMPHANT "NO!"
A God who could be ultimately defeated by factors which he had
allowed to function in his universe would be no God at all. The
very idea of omnipotence is not that everything that happens does
so because God wills it in the sense of intending it. The truth
about omnipotence is that nothing that does happen, even though
it springs from man's misused free will, or from the human
family's mass ignorance, or from folly or sin can *finally* defeat
God. That is where omnipotence comes in.

If a sufferer reaches the point when he can no longer believe
that he is going to recover in this life, even then I think he should
try to co-operate with those who are doing their best to make
him well. He need not regard his suffering even from the human
standpoint as dead loss. His physicians may learn something by
which they can help other sufferers, and who knows when a cure
of his particular malady may be found?

At the same time, I feel I must write down my long-considered
opinion that where a patient is in constant agony for which no
relief can be found, and from which, humanly speaking, nothing
can be learned, the quiet committing of the soul to God and the
ending of physical life would not win from me censure of the
doctor or criticism of the patient. Into this vexed and difficult
question of euthanasia—or easy death, as it is called—I must not
take the space to enter fully; but when one remembers how for-

tuitously, through the passion of parents, a life is sometimes begun, how ready a doctor is to destroy an infant life if the mother's is endangered; how men in millions have been led to death in war, or have been executed by the processes of the law or by tyrants like Hitler; how bravely, thinking of others, men like Captain Oates have gone to their deaths, and how determined men are to punish those who make an animal linger in long-continued pain, I see no reason in logic or religion why a patient for whom life has become unendurable and who can see no end to physical suffering, no value in it, no cowardly retreat from sharing responsibilities he ought not to evade, and only relief for those who look on, should not be allowed to slip away before the dignity of human nature is lowered any further. Were this made legal, all other outcomes having been discussed from a Christian and medical angle, I would myself give such a patient Holy Communion and stay with him while the doctor, whose responsibility I should thus share, did what was necessary to help one life to end and another begin. As yet it is not legal—though it is widely practiced—and we must keep the law.

This being so, the Christian attitude to continued suffering must be acceptance and co-operation. These are the words which seem to me the best to describe man's ideal attitude to the suffering which he cannot remedy.

Acceptance of a share, still more the willing acceptance of more than our full share, in the tragedy of life—a tragedy in which God, as well as man, is an actor—is positive; it has about it something vitalizing. . . . Those who meet pain clear-eyed, and with a positive and active acceptance, who "face the music" as the slang phrase has it; those who are not only ready to do their bit, but to share their bit in the world's sorrow, make a great discovery. They find not only that they are enabled to bear their sorrow in a way which hurts less—for that which hurts most in the bearing is that which is most resented; what is most freely accepted hurts least—but that they achieve an enrichment and a growth in personality which makes them centers of influence and light in ways of which they never suspected the possibility. Few things can so inspire and re-create the human heart as the spectacle of crushing misfortune cheerfully and heroically borne; and the unconscious influence which those exert is far greater than they or others comprehend. Suffering lightly borne is constructive work . . . for pain conquered is power.[1]

Such acceptance takes a man right into the secret places of God's purposes, and into a fellowship which includes some of the finest souls who have ever breathed. And while we assert that suffering is not the will of God, it can never be too emphatically stated that there is an opportunity in suffering which it is God's will we should take and turn to our own, and the world's, highest advantage. A thousand things which are not the will of God will happen to us in a world arranged as this is, but nothing can happen to us which cannot be captured for God by taking the right attitude. There is an alchemy which turns all things into spiritual gold, and that alchemy is the right attitude to them. Ultimately, what happens to us does not matter. But our reaction to what happens to us matters greatly. *142671*

The experiences of pain will come to us all. But nothing can ever come to us that may not be captured for God and for the gain of our personal character by an adoption of the right attitude. To one man a set of experiences are great mysteries, baffling problems, heavy burdens. To another those selfsame experiences will be, in Samuel Rutherford's phrase, the kind of burden

[1] Lily Dougall, *God's Way with Man* (London: Student Christian Movement Press, 1924).

that "sails are to a ship, that wings are to a bird." What are to
Martin Chuzzlewit desolating blows of fate are to Mark Tapley
opportunities "for coming out strong." To one man, life's experiences are those of dark valleys, steep mountains, rough places.
To another every valley becomes exalted, every mountain and hill
is brought low, the rough places are made plain, because he has
found an attitude which, applied to them, subdues them.

There are still many questions that we cannot answer about
pain. Why could not God have brought about the same ends by a
different means, cutting out the possibility of pain? There is no
answer except to say that to all Wisdom the way he took was
the best way. We may ask why God ever made a body and mind
capable of feeling such pain; and if some answer that only such
a being as man could climb, as man does, till his stride takes in
the very stars, then others will say the price paid is too high. We
have no faculty for a complete answer, but the lines of thought
we have pursued in their cumulative strength seem to us to go
as far as one need go. For the rest we may take as a parable an
incident from Egypt.

When the Nile spread its obliterating deposit of black mud over
fields hardly won from the desert, and watered at great cost of patient
toil, the victor over it was not the engineer stemming its current with
his barricade, but the inspired peasant who, greatly daring, flung his
precious rice into the forbidding ooze, and waited for God to send the
rich harvest.[2]

That is acceptance and co-operation. Where we cannot fight and
overcome suffering, we are to take such an attitude to it that
by co-operation with God we may bring a great harvest which

[2] John Oman, *Grace and Personality* (London: Cambridge University Press,
1919), p. 10.

shall enrich the spiritual wealth of the world and make glad the heart of God.

If even the heart is not satisfied, it will find its anchorage on that fundamental with which we began—the goodness of God. And it will find its final argument, not in the brain, but in those reasons which the heart alone can give.

> Yet, in the maddening maze of things,
>   And tossed by storm and flood,
> To one fixed trust my spirit clings;
>   I know that God is good!

"I KNOW." The world's thinking sufferers, from Job to Browning, have all said that triumphant word: "I know that my redeemer liveth"; "I know in whom I have believed."

> Sorrow is hard to bear and doubt is slow to clear;
>   Each sufferer has his say, his scheme of the weal and woe.
> But God has a few of us whom He whispers in the ear,
>   The rest may reason and welcome; 'tis we musicians *know*.

We cannot understand pain altogether, nor justify it, nor explain it, but we know him. That assurance runs like a silver cord through all the maze of men's experience through all the ages as they are confronted by this mystery. Better men than ourselves have found that just to hold to that cord and trust in the dark is in itself the defeat of pain. Though there should be every reason in the world to prove that God is a devil; that evil is more powerful than good; that there is no order, no purpose, no living design, no meaning in life at all, yet in the face of all argument to say, "I know," that is to keep alive the undying fire of faith and to

91

make of the very things that would quench it, fuel that shall make it a blazing furnace.

Thus we may not solve the mystery entirely, but we may rise above it, rob it of its power to quell us; more than that, we may turn its fruit of doubt into faith, its depression into victory, its evil into a power for good that none can stay, knowing if "God were one whit less than He is, He dare not put us into a world that carries so many arguments against Him." [8]

I should like to end the book by looking again at Jesus, the beloved Son who only sought to do his Father's will. How justifiably he might have asked the questions which stand at the head of some of the foregoing chapters! Did God know? Why should this happen to me? Where do God's goodness and omnipotence come in? What sense is there in it all? If I am killed, will God's plan be defeated?

I cannot myself avoid the conclusion that the Cross was no more the will of God than any other brutal murder. It was the work of wicked men, as Peter said on the day of Pentecost. Wicked men do not do the will of God. And I think the awful agony in the Garden of Gethsemane was our Lord's dread lest God's plan should be defeated. He had hoped to convince the multitudes himself. When that looked like failing he hoped the twelve would carry the good news through the land. And what good news it was! God was the loving Father of all, and all were brothers. All men of all nations were dear to him and all could bring from the North and the South and the East and the West their treasures of mind and heart and make one world kingdom with no nation but humanity and with no king but God.

Then he had been betrayed, deserted, arrested, and the Cross

[8] Letters to his friends for private circulation by Forbes Robinson.

looked like, and felt like, and was called the end. As that Cross loomed up, no wonder that he who had said so confidently, "With God all things are possible," cried out, *"If it be possible,* let this cup pass." (Matt. 19:26; 26:39.)

For some sufferer who reads this book something similar may have happened. A young mother faces death and wonders, as Christ did, however the purposes of God can possibly be worked out. She may be leaving young children. A young man is taken, as Christ was, at the height of his powers. A young father, the breadwinner, dies, leaving a little family behind. . . .

Yet still those things that God did not plan or intend can be woven into a pattern which serves his purposes and which none can destroy. The Cross has meant that far more spiritual power has been released into the world than if Jesus had lived to a ripe old age and died in quiet retirement. And God can weave our lesser sorrows and sufferings into a plan which will leave us with no sense of loss at last. God can flash to us code messages by means of lamps which he did not light. Jesus might have said to Caiaphas and those who plotted his death what Joseph said to his brethren, "You meant evil against me; but God meant it for good" (Gen. 50:20). And those whose sorrows have been brought upon them by evil men will one day say the same.

Even death itself, I think, matters hardly at all if only we can glimpse the perspective of God's age-long plan. Whether I continue to live and work on this plane or on the next, on this side of death or on the other, probably makes no more difference to God's purposes than whether I live in Manchester or Leeds.

For life goes on. I am as sure of that as of any tenet in the Christian creed. I feel I want to say to anyone suffering from what is called incurable diesease: "Only the body dies. To answer the question at the head of this chapter, you *will* get better. You

93

will wake up on a spiritual plane of love and activity and service and eternal youth, unhampered by pain and disease and the limitations of old age, creaky muscles, hardened arteries, and laboring breath; and you will find that you have only parted with a worn-out overcoat called the body. The real 'you' is immortal, and you will greet your dear ones again and go on spiritually where you left off here."

No one at death has exhausted his possibilities. Some at death have hardly begun to live. If death meant annihilation, then nature would be as irrational as would be the death of every bird before it left its shell. Within that imprisoning shell are wings and a throat and the structure of eyes. One day, when the shell is broken, they will function. The difference will be that of the huddled body, cramped up in a shell, and a skylark on poised wing in the sunlit air pouring out its song in the glory of a new life. We too shall enter a new phase of activity and realized possibility.

So, dear sufferer, I salute you, knowing that no words of mine can ease your pain, hoping only that in a world in which none of us can see very far, a thought here and there may ease a bewildered mind or a troubled spirit, "to give light to them that sit in darkness and in the shadow of death; and to guide our feet into the way of peace."

A Prayer

O GOD, WHO DWELLEST IN UNAPPROACHABLE MYSTERY AND whose ways are far beyond our understanding, help us to rest our minds in the certainty that we are dear to thee in spite of all our weaknesses and failures. Forgive us if, sometimes, suffering fills all our horizon and we find no comfort in any word of man or any thought of thee. Draw very near to us in the tenderness and compassion which overflowed from thee into the heart of Christ, and, for his sake, keep alive the flickering flame of our faith and hope and love. Show us the pathway of thy will for us in each day and in each circumstance. If it may be, lighten our burden, gladden our eyes, comfort our hearts, heal the sick body, and quiet the troubled mind. But whatever may lie ahead, give us the assurance that thy friendliness enwraps us, that a wondrous purpose that cannot be defeated is being worked out in our lives, and that nothing can ever snatch us from thy loving care. So at last, without regret and without dishonor, bring us to our journey's end in peace. AMEN.

BY WILL DURANT

The Story of Philosophy

Transition

The Pleasures of Philosophy

Adventures in Genius

BY WILL AND ARIEL DURANT

THE STORY OF CIVILIZATION:

I. *Our Oriental Heritage*

II. *The Life of Greece*

III. *Caesar and Christ*

IV. *The Age of Faith*

V. *The Renaissance*

VI. *The Reformation*

VII. *The Age of Reason Begins*

VIII. *The Age of Louis XIV*

IX. *The Age of Voltaire*

X. *Rousseau and Revolution*

The Lessons of History

THE
LESSONS
OF
HISTORY

by

Will and Ariel Durant

SIMON AND SCHUSTER

NEW YORK

PUBLISHED BY SIMON AND SCHUSTER
ROCKEFELLER CENTER, 630 FIFTH AVENUE
NEW YORK, NEW YORK 10020

ELEVENTH PRINTING

LIBRARY OF CONGRESS CATALOG CARD NUMBER: 68-19949
DESIGNED BY RICHARD C. KARWOSKI
MANUFACTURED IN THE UNITED STATES OF AMERICA

Contents

Preface

This postlude needs little preface. After finishing *The Story of Civilization* to 1789, we reread the ten volumes with a view to issuing a revised edition that would correct many errors of omission, fact, or print. In that process we made note of events and comments that might illuminate present affairs, future probabilities, the nature of man, and the conduct of states. (The references, in the text, to various volumes of the *Story* are offered not as authorities but as instances or elucidations so come upon.) We tried to defer our conclusions until we had completed our survey of the narrative, but doubtless our preformed opinions influenced our selection of illustrative material. The following essay is the result. It repeats many ideas that we, or others before us, have already expressed; our aim is not originality but inclusiveness; we offer a survey of human experience, not a personal revelation.

Here, as so often in the past, we must gratefully acknowledge the help and counsel given us by our daughter Ethel.

WILL AND ARIEL DURANT

THE
LESSONS
OF
HISTORY

I. Hesitations

As his studies come to a close the historian faces the challenge: Of what use have your studies been? Have you found in your work only the amusement of recounting the rise and fall of nations and ideas, and retelling "sad stories of the death of kings"? Have you learned more about human nature than the man in the street can learn without so much as opening a book? Have you derived from history any illumination of our present condition, any guidance for our judgments and policies, any guard against the rebuffs of surprise or the vicissitudes of change? Have you found such regularities in the sequence of past events that you can predict the future actions of mankind or the fate of states? Is it possible that, after all, "history has no sense," [1] that it teaches us nothing, and that the immense past was only the weary rehearsal of the mistakes that the future is destined to make on a larger stage and scale?

At times we feel so, and a multitude of doubts assail our enterprise. To begin with, do we really know what the past was, what actually happened, or is history "a fable" not quite "agreed upon"? Our knowledge of any past event is always incomplete, probably inaccurate, beclouded by ambivalent evidence and biased historians, and perhaps distorted by our own patriotic or religious partisanship. "Most history is guessing, and the rest is prejudice." [2] Even the historian who thinks to rise above partiality for his country, race, creed, or class betrays his secret predilection in his choice of materials, and in the nuances of his adjectives. "The historian always oversimplifies, and hastily selects a manageable minority of facts and faces out of a crowd of souls and events whose multitudinous complexity he can never quite embrace or comprehend." [3] — Again, our conclusions from the past to the future are made more hazardous than ever by the acceleration of change. In 1909 Charles Péguy thought that "the world changed less since Jesus Christ than in the last thirty years";[4] and perhaps some young doctor of philosophy in physics would now add that his science has changed more since 1909 than in all recorded time before. Every year—sometimes, in war, every month—some new invention, method, or situation compels a fresh adjustment of behavior and ideas. — Furthermore, an element of chance, perhaps of freedom, seems to enter into the conduct of metals and men. We are no longer confident that atoms, much less organisms, will respond in the future as we think they have responded in the past. The electrons, like Cowper's God, move in mysterious ways their wonders to perform, and some quirk of character or circumstance may upset national equations, as when Alexander drank himself to death and let his new empire fall apart (323 B.C.), or as when Frederick the Great was saved from disaster by the accession of a Czar infatuated with Prussian ways (1762).

Obviously historiography cannot be a science. It can only be an industry, an art, and a philosophy—an industry by ferreting out the facts, an art by establishing a meaningful order in the chaos of materials, a philosophy by seeking perspective and enlightenment. "The present is the past rolled up for action, and the past is the present unrolled for understanding" [5]—or so we believe and hope. In philosophy we try to see the part in the light of the whole; in the "philos-ophy of history" we try to see this moment in the light of the past. We know that in both cases this is a counsel of perfection; total per-spective is an optical illusion. We do not know the whole of man's history; there were probably many civilizations before the Sumerian or the Egyptian; we have just begun to dig! We must operate with partial knowledge, and be provisionally content with probabilities; in history, as in science and politics, relativity rules, and all formulas should be suspect. "History smiles at all attempts to force its flow into theoretical patterns or logical grooves; it plays havoc with our gen-eralizations, breaks all our rules; history is baroque." [6] Perhaps, within these limits, we can learn enough from history to bear reality patiently, and to respect one another's delusions.

Since man is a moment in astronomic time, a transient guest of the earth, a spore of his species, a scion of his race, a composite of body, character, and mind, a member of a family and a community, a be-liever or doubter of a faith, a unit in an economy, perhaps a citizen in a state or a soldier in an army, we may ask under the corresponding heads—astronomy, geology, geography, biology, ethnology, psy-chology, morality, religion, economics, politics, and war—what his-tory has to say about the nature, conduct, and prospects of man. It is a precarious enterprise, and only a fool would try to compress a hun-dred centuries into a hundred pages of hazardous conclusions. We proceed.

II. History and the Earth

Let us define history, in its troublesome duplexity, as the events or record of the past. Human history is a brief spot in space, and its first lesson is modesty. At any moment a comet may come too close to the earth and set our little globe turning topsy-turvy in a hectic course, or choke its men and fleas with fumes or heat; or a fragment of the smiling sun may slip off tangentially—as some think our planet did a few astronomic moments ago—and fall upon us in a wild embrace ending all grief and pain. We accept these possibilities in our stride, and retort to the cosmos in the words of Pascal: "When the universe has crushed him man will still be nobler than that which kills him, because he knows that he is dying, and of its victory the universe knows nothing." [7]

History is subject to geology. Every day the sea encroaches somewhere upon the land, or the land upon the sea; cities disappear under the water, and sunken cathedrals ring their melancholy bells. Mountains rise and fall in the rhythm of emergence and erosion; rivers swell and flood, or dry up, or change their course; valleys become deserts, and isthmuses become straits. To the geologic eye all the

surface of the earth is a fluid form, and man moves upon it as inse-
curely as Peter walking on the waves to Christ.

Climate no longer controls us as severely as Montesquieu and
Buckle supposed, but it limits us. Man's ingenuity often overcomes
geological handicaps: he can irrigate deserts and air-condition the
Sahara; he can level or surmount mountains and terrace the hills with
vines; he can build a floating city to cross the ocean, or gigantic birds
to navigate the sky. But a tornado can ruin in an hour the city that
took a century to build; an iceberg can overturn or bisect the floating
palace and send a thousand merrymakers gurgling to the Great Certainty. Let rain become too rare, and civilization disappears under
sand, as in Central Asia; let it fall too furiously, and civilization will
be choked with jungle, as in Central America. Let the thermal average rise by twenty degrees in our thriving zones, and we should
probably relapse into lethargic savagery. In a semitropical climate a
nation of half a billion souls may breed like ants, but enervating heat
may subject it to repeated conquest by warriors from more stimulating habitats. Generations of men establish a growing mastery over
the earth, but they are destined to become fossils in its soil.

Geography is the matrix of history, its nourishing mother and dis-
ciplining home. Its rivers, lakes, oases, and oceans draw settlers to
their shores, for water is the life of organisms and towns, and offers
inexpensive roads for transport and trade. Egypt was "the gift of the
Nile," and Mesopotamia built successive civilizations "between the
rivers" and along their effluent canals. India was the daughter of the
Indus, the Brahmaputra and the Ganges; China owed its life and sorrows to the great rivers that (like ourselves) often wandered from
their proper beds and fertilized the neighborhood with their over-
flow. Italy adorned the valleys of the Tiber, the Arno, and the Po.
Austria grew along the Danube, Germany along the Elbe and the

Rhine, France along the Rhone, the Loire, and the Seine. Petra and Palmyra were nourished by oases in the desert.

When the Greeks grew too numerous for their boundaries, they founded colonies along the Mediterranean ("like frogs around a pond," said Plato[8]) and along the Euxine, or Black, Sea. For two thousand years—from the battle of Salamis (480 B.C.) to the defeat of the Spanish Armada (1588)—the northern and southern shores of the Mediterranean were the rival seats of the white man's ascendancy. But in and after 1492 the voyages of Columbus and Vasco da Gama invited men to brave the oceans; the sovereignty of the Mediterranean was challenged; Genoa, Pisa, Florence, Venice declined; the Renaissance began to fade; the Atlantic nations rose, and finally spread their suzerainty over half the world. "Westward the course of empire takes its way," wrote George Berkeley about 1730. Will it continue across the Pacific, exporting European and American industrial and commercial techniques to China, as formerly to Japan? Will Oriental fertility, working with the latest Occidental technology, bring the decline of the West?

The development of the airplane will again alter the map of civilization. Trade routes will follow less and less the rivers and seas; men and goods will be flown more and more directly to their goal. Countries like England and France will lose the commercial advantage of abundant coast lines conveniently indented; countries like Russia, China, and Brazil, which were hampered by the excess of their land mass over their coasts, will cancel part of that handicap by taking to the air. Coastal cities will derive less of their wealth from the clumsy business of transferring goods from ship to train or from train to ship. When sea power finally gives place to air power in transport and war, we shall have seen one of the basic revolutions in history.

The influence of geographic factors diminishes as technology grows. The character and contour of a terrain may offer opportunities for agriculture, mining, or trade, but only the imagination and initiative of leaders, and the hardy industry of followers, can transform the possibilities into fact; and only a similar combination (as in Israel today) can make a culture take form over a thousand natural obstacles. Man, not the earth, makes civilization.

III. Biology and History

History is a fragment of biology: the life of man is a portion of the vicissitudes of organisms on land and sea. Sometimes, wandering alone in the woods on a summer day, we hear or see the movement of a hundred species of flying, leaping, creeping, crawling, burrowing things. The startled animals scurry away at our coming; the birds scatter; the fish disperse in the brook. Suddenly we perceive to what a perilous minority we belong on this impartial planet, and for a moment we feel, as these varied denizens clearly do, that we are passing interlopers in their natural habitat. Then all the chronicles and achievements of man fall humbly into the history and perspective of polymorphous life; all our economic competition, our strife for mates, our hunger and love and grief and war, are akin to the seeking, mating, striving, and suffering that hide under these fallen trees or leaves, or in the waters, or on the boughs.

Therefore the laws of biology are the fundamental lessons of history. We are subject to the processes and trials of evolution, to the struggle for existence and the survival of the fittest to survive. If some of us seem to escape the strife or the trials it is because our group protects us; but that group itself must meet the tests of survival.

So the first biological lesson of history is that life is competition. Competition is not only the life of trade, it is the trade of life—peaceful when food abounds, violent when the mouths outrun the food. Animals eat one another without qualm; civilized men consume one another by due process of law. Co-operation is real, and increases with social development, but mostly because it is a tool and form of competition; we co-operate in our group—our family, community, club, church, party, "race," or nation—in order to strengthen our group in its competition with other groups. Competing groups have the qualities of competing individuals: acquisitiveness, pugnacity, partisanship, pride. Our states, being ourselves multiplied, are what we are; they write our natures in bolder type, and do our good and evil on an elephantine scale. We are acquisitive, greedy, and pugnacious because our blood remembers millenniums through which our forebears had to chase and fight and kill in order to survive, and had to eat to their gastric capacity for fear they should not soon capture another feast. War is a nation's way of eating. It promotes co-operation because it is the ultimate form of competition. Until our states become members of a large and effectively protective group they will continue to act like individuals and families in the hunting stage.

The second biological lesson of history is that life is selection. In the competition for food or mates or power some organisms succeed and some fail. In the struggle for existence some individuals are better equipped than others to meet the tests of survival. Since Nature (here meaning total reality and its processes) has not read very carefully the American Declaration of Independence or the French Revolutionary Declaration of the Rights of Man, we are all born unfree and unequal: subject to our physical and psychological heredity, and to the customs and traditions of our group; diversely endowed in health and strength, in mental capacity and qualities of character. Nature loves difference as the necessary material of selection and evolution; identical twins differ in a hundred ways, and no two peas are alike.

Inequality is not only natural and inborn, it grows with the complexity of civilization. Hereditary inequalities breed social and artificial inequalities; every invention or discovery is made or seized by the exceptional individual, and makes the strong stronger, the weak relatively weaker, than before. Economic development specializes functions, differentiates abilities, and makes men unequally valuable to their group. If we knew our fellow men thoroughly we could select thirty per cent of them whose combined ability would equal that of all the rest. Life and history do precisely that, with a sublime injustice reminiscent of Calvin's God.

Nature smiles at the union of freedom and equality in our utopias. For freedom and equality are sworn and everlasting enemies, and when one prevails the other dies. Leave men free, and their natural inequalities will multiply almost geometrically, as in England and America in the nineteenth century under *laissez-faire*. To check the growth of inequality, liberty must be sacrificed, as in Russia after 1917. Even when repressed, inequality grows; only the man who is below the average in economic ability desires equality; those who are conscious of superior ability desire freedom; and in the end superior ability has its way. Utopias of equality are biologically doomed, and the best that the amiable philosopher can hope for is an approximate equality of legal justice and educational opportunity. A society in which all potential abilities are allowed to develop and function will have a survival advantage in the competition of groups. This competition becomes more severe as the destruction of distance intensifies the confrontation of states.

The third biological lesson of history is that life must breed. Nature has no use for organisms, variations, or groups that cannot reproduce abundantly. She has a passion for quantity as prerequisite to the selection of quality; she likes large litters, and relishes the struggle that picks the surviving few; doubtless she looks on approvingly at the upstream race of a thousand sperms to fertilize one ovum. She is more interested in the species than in the individual, and makes little difference between civilization and barbarism. She does not care that a high birth rate has usually accompanied a culturally low civilization, and a low birth rate a civilization culturally high; and she (here meaning Nature as the process of birth, variation, competition, selection, and survival) sees to it that a nation with a low birth rate shall be periodically chastened by some more virile and fertile group. Gaul survived against the Germans through the help of Roman legions in Caesar's days, and through the help of British and American legions in our time. When Rome fell the Franks rushed in from Germany and made Gaul France; if England and America should fall, France, whose population remained almost stationary through the nineteenth century, might again be overrun.

If the human brood is too numerous for the food supply, Nature has three agents for restoring the balance: famine, pestilence, and war. In a famous *Essay on Population* (1798) Thomas Malthus explained that without these periodic checks the birth rate would so far exceed the death rate that the multiplication of mouths would nullify any increase in the production of food. Though he was a clergyman and a man of good will, Malthus pointed out that the issuance of relief funds or supplies to the poor encouraged them to marry early and breed improvidently, making the problem worse. In a second

edition (1803) he advised abstention from coitus except for reproduction, but he refused to approve other methods of birth control.
Having little hope of acceptance for this counsel of sanctity, he predicted that the balance between mouths and food would be maintained in the future, as in the past, by famine, pestilence, and war.

The advances of agricultural and contraceptive technology in the
nineteenth century apparently refuted Malthus: in England, the
United States, Germany, and France the food supply kept pace with
births, and the rising standard of living deferred the age of marriage
and lowered the size of the family. The multiplication of consumers
was also a multiplication of producers: new "hands" developed new
lands to raise more food. The recent spectacle of Canada and the
United States exporting millions of bushels of wheat while avoiding
famine and pestilence at home seemed to provide a living answer to
Malthus. If existing agricultural knowledge were everywhere applied, the planet could feed twice its present population.

Malthus would answer, of course, that this solution merely
postpones the calamity. There is a limit to the fertility of the soil;
every advance in agricultural technology is sooner or later canceled
by the excess of births over deaths; and meanwhile medicine, sanita-
tion, and charity nullify selection by keeping the unfit alive to multiply their like. To which hope replies: the advances of industry, ur-
banization, education, and standards of living, in countries that now
endanger the world by their fertility, will probably have the same
effect there, in reducing the birth rate, as they have had in Europe
and North America. Until that equilibrium of production and reproduction comes it will be a counsel of humanity to disseminate the
knowledge and means of contraception. Ideally parentage should be
a privilege of health, not a by-product of sexual agitation.

Is there any evidence that birth control is dysgenic—that it lowers
the intellectual level of the nation practicing it? Presumably it has

been used more by the intelligent than by the simple, and the labors of educators are apparently canceled in each generation by the fertility of the uninformed. But much of what we call intelligence is the result of individual education, opportunity, and experience; and there is no evidence that such intellectual acquirements are transmitted in the genes. Even the children of Ph.D.s must be educated and go through their adolescent measles of errors, dogmas, and isms; nor can we say how much potential ability and genius lurk in the chromosomes of the harassed and handicapped poor. Biologically, physical vitality may be, at birth, of greater value than intellectual pedigree; Nietzsche thought that the best blood in Germany was in peasant veins; philosophers are not the fittest material from which to breed the race.

Family limitation played some part in the history of Greece and Rome. It is amusing to find Julius Caesar offering (59 B.C.) rewards to Romans who had many children, and forbidding childless women to ride in litters or wear jewelry. Augustus renewed this campaign some forty years later, with like futility. Birth control continued to spread in the upper classes while immigrant stocks from the Germanic North and the Greek or Semitic East replenished and altered the population of Italy.[9] Very probably this ethnic change reduced the ability or willingness of the inhabitants to resist governmental incompetence and external attack.

In the United States the lower birth rate of the Anglo-Saxons has lessened their economic and political power; and the higher birth rate of Roman Catholic families suggests that by the year 2000 the Roman Catholic Church will be the dominant force in national as well as in municipal or state governments. A similar process is helping to restore Catholicism in France, Switzerland, and Germany; the lands of Voltaire, Calvin, and Luther may soon return to the papal fold. So the birth rate, like war, may determine the fate of theologies; just as the defeat of the Moslems at Tours (732) kept France and Spain from replacing the Bible with the Koran, so the superior organization, discipline, morality, fidelity, and fertility of Catholics may cancel the Protestant Reformation and the French Enlightenment. There is no humorist like history.

IV. Race and History

There are some two billion colored people on the earth, and some nine hundred million whites. However, many palefaces were delighted when Comte Joseph-Arthur de Gobineau, in an *Essai sur l'inégalité des races humaines* (1853–55), announced that the species man is composed of distinct races inherently different (like individuals) in physical structure, mental capacity, and qualities of character; and that one race, the "Aryan," was by nature superior to all the rest.

> Everything great, noble, or fruitful in the works of man on this planet, in science, art, and civilization, derives from a single starting point, is the development of a single germ; . . . it belongs to one family alone, the different branches of which have reigned in all the civilized countries of the universe. . . . History shows that all civilization derives from the white race, that none can exist without its help, and that a society is great and brilliant only so far as it preserves the blood of the noble group that created it.[10]

Environmental advantages (argued Gobineau) cannot explain the rise of civilization, for the same kind of environment (e.g., soil-fertilizing rivers) that watered the civilizations of Egypt and the Near East produced no civilization among the Indians of North America, though they lived on fertile soil along magnificent streams. Nor do institutions make a civilization, for this has risen under a diversity, even a contrariety, of institutions, as in monarchical Egypt and "democratic" Athens. The rise, success, decline, and fall of a civilization depend upon the inherent quality of the race. The degeneration of a civilization is what the word itself indicates—a falling away from the genus, stock, or race. "Peoples degenerate only in consequence of the various mixtures of blood which they undergo." [11] Usually this comes through intermarriage of the vigorous race with those whom it has conquered. Hence the superiority of the whites in the United States and Canada (who did not intermarry with the Indians) to the whites in Latin America (who did). Only those who are themselves the product of such enfeebling mixtures talk of the equality of races, or think that "all men are brothers." [12] All strong characters and peoples are race conscious, and are instinctively averse to marriage outside their own racial group.

In 1899 Houston Stewart Chamberlain, an Englishman who had made Germany his home, published *Die Grundlagen des neunzehnten Jahrhunderts* (*The Foundations of the Nineteenth Century*), which narrowed the creative race from Aryans to Teutons: "True history begins from the moment when the German with mighty hand seizes the inheritance of antiquity." Dante's face struck Chamberlain as characteristically German; he thought he heard unmistakably German accents in St. Paul's Epistle to the Galatians; and though he was not quite sure that Christ was a German, he was confident that "whoever maintains that Christ was a Jew is either ignorant or dishonest." [13] German writers were too polite to contradict their guest: Treitschke and Bernhardi admitted that the Germans were the greatest of modern peoples; Wagner put the theory to music; Alfred Rosenberg made German blood and soil the inspiring "myth of the twentieth century"; and Adolf Hitler, on this basis, roused the Germans to slaughter a people and to undertake the conquest of Europe.

An American, Madison Grant, in *The Passing of the Great Race* (1916), confined the achievements of civilization to that branch of the Aryans which he called "Nordics"—Scandinavians, Scythians, Baltic Germans, Englishmen, and Anglo-Saxon Americans. Cooled to hardness by northern winters, one or another tribe of these fair-haired, blue-eyed "blond beasts" swept down through Russia and the Balkans into the lazy and lethargic South in a series of conquests marking the dawn of recorded history. According to Grant the "Sacae" (Scythians?) invaded India, developed Sanskrit as an "Indo-European" language, and established the caste system to prevent their deterioration through intermarriage with dark native stocks. The Cimmerians poured over the Caucasus into Persia, the Phrygians into Asia Minor, the Achaeans and Dorians into Greece and Crete, the Umbrians and Oscans into Italy. Everywhere the Nordics were adventurers, warriors, disciplinarians; they made subjects or slaves of the temperamental, unstable, and indolent "Mediterranean" peoples of the South, and they intermarried with the intermediate quiet and acquiescent "Alpine" stocks to produce the Athenians of the Periclean apogee and the Romans of the Republic. The Dorians intermarried least, and became the Spartans, a martial Nordic caste ruling "Mediterranean" helots. Intermarriage weakened and softened the Nordic stock in Attica, and led to the defeat of Athens by Sparta in the Peloponnesian War, and the subjugation of Greece by the purer Nordics of Macedonia and Republican Rome.

In another inundation of Nordics—from Scandinavia and northern Germany—Goths and Vandals conquered Imperial Rome; Angles and Saxons conquered England and gave it a new name; Franks conquered Gaul and gave it their name. Still later, the Nordic Normans conquered France, England, and Sicily. The Nordic Lombards followed their long beards into Italy, intermarried, and vitalized Milan and Florence into a Renaissance. Nordic Varangians conquered Russia, and ruled it till 1917. Nordic Englishmen colonized America and Australia, conquered India, and set their sentinels in every major Asiatic port.

In our time (Grant mourned) this Nordic race is abandoning its mastery. It lost its footing in France in 1789; as Camille Desmoulins told his café audience, the Revolution was a revolt of the indigenous Gauls ("Alpines") against the Teutonic Franks who had subjugated them under Clovis and Charlemagne. The Crusades, the Thirty Years' War, the Napoleonic Wars, the First World War depleted the Nordic stock and left it too thin to resist the higher birth rate of Alpine and Mediterranean peoples in Europe and America. By the year 2000, Grant predicted, the Nordics will have fallen from power, and with their fall Western civilization will disappear in a new barbarism welling up everywhere from within and from without. He wisely conceded that the Mediterranean "race," while inferior in bodily stamina to both the Nordics and the Alpines, has proved superior in intellectual and artistic attainments; to it must go the credit for the classic flowering of Greece and Rome; however, it may have owed much to intermarriage with Nordic blood.

Some weaknesses in the race theory are obvious. A Chinese scholar would remind us that his people created the most enduring civilization in history—statesmen, inventors, artists, poets, scientists, philosophers, saints from 2000 B.C. to our own time. A Mexican scholar could point to the lordly structures of Mayan, Aztec, and Incan cultures in pre-Columbian America. A Hindu scholar, while acknowledging "Aryan" infiltration into north India some sixteen hundred years before Christ, would recall that the black Dravidic peoples of south India produced great builders and poets of their own; the temples of Madras, Madura, and Trichinopoly are among the most impressive structures on earth. Even more startling is the towering shrine of the Khmers at Angkor Wat. History is color-blind, and can develop a civilization (in any favorable environment) under almost any skin.

Difficulties remain even if the race theory is confined to the white man. The Semites would recall the civilizations of Babylonia, Assyria, Syria, Palestine, Phoenicia, Carthage, and Islam. The Jews gave the Bible and Christianity to Europe, and much of the Koran to Mohammed. The Mohammedans could list the rulers, artists, poets, scientists, and philosophers who conquered and adorned a substantial portion of the white man's world from Baghdad to Cordova while Western Europe groped through the Dark Ages (c. 565–c. 1095).

The ancient cultures of Egypt, Greece, and Rome were evidently the product of geographical opportunity and economic and political development rather than of racial constitution, and much of their civilization had an Oriental source.[14] Greece took its arts and letters from Asia Minor, Crete, Phoenicia, and Egypt. In the second millennium B.C. Greek culture was "Mycenaean," partly derived from Crete, which had probably learned from Asia Minor. When the "Nordic" Dorians came down through the Balkans, toward 1100 B.C., they destroyed much of this proto-Greek culture; and only after an interval of several centuries did the historic Greek civilization emerge in the Sparta of "Lycurgus," the Miletus of Thales, the Ephesus of Heracleitus, the Lesbos of Sappho, the Athens of Solon. From the sixth century B.C. onward the Greeks spread their culture along the Mediterranean at Durazzo, Taranto, Crotona, Reggio Calabria, Syracuse, Naples, Nice, Monaco, Marseilles, Málaga. From the Greek cities of south Italy, and from the probably Asiatic culture of Etruria, came the civilization of ancient Rome; from Rome came the civilization of Western Europe; from Western

Europe came the civilization of North and South America. In the third and following centuries of our era various Celtic, Teutonic, or Asiatic tribes laid Italy waste and destroyed the classic cultures. The South creates the civilizations, the North conquers them, ruins them, borrows from them, spreads them: this is one summary of history.

Attempts to relate civilization to race by measuring the relation of brain to face or weight have shed little light on the problem. If the Negroes of Africa have produced no great civilization it is probably because climatic and geographical conditions frustrated them; would any of the white "races" have done better in those environments? It is remarkable how many American Negroes have risen to high places in the professions, arts, and letters in the last one hundred years despite a thousand social obstacles.

The role of race in history is rather preliminary than creative. Varied stocks, entering some locality from diverse directions at divers times, mingle their blood, traditions, and ways with one another or with the existing population, like two diverse pools of genes coming together in sexual reproduction. Such an ethnic mixture may in the course of centuries produce a new type, even a new people; so Celts, Romans, Angles, Saxons, Jutes, Danes, and Normans fused to produce Englishmen. When the new type takes form its cultural expressions are unique, and constitute a new civilization—a new physiognomy, character, language, literature, religion, morality, and art. It is not the race that makes the civilization, it is the civilization that makes the people: circumstances geographical, economic, and political create a culture, and the culture creates a human type. The Englishman does not so much make English civilization as it makes him; if he carries it wherever he goes, and dresses for dinner in Timbuktu, it is not that he is creating his civilization there anew, but that he acknowledges even there its mastery over his soul. In the long run such differences of tradition or type yield to the influence of the environment. Northern peoples take on the characteristics of southern peoples after living for generations in the tropics, and the grandchildren of peoples coming up from the leisurely South fall into the quicker tempo of movement and mind which they find in the North.

Viewed from this point, American civilization is still in the stage of racial mixture. Between 1700 and 1848 white Americans north of Florida were mainly Anglo-Saxon, and their literature was a flowering of old England on New England's soil. After 1848 the doors of America were opened to all white stocks; a fresh racial fusion began, which will hardly be complete for centuries to come. When, out of this mixture, a new homogeneous type is formed, America may have its own language (as different from English as Spanish is from Italian), its indigenous literature, its characteristic arts; already these are visibly or raucously on their way.

"Racial" antipathies have some roots in ethnic origin, but they are also generated, perhaps predominantly, by differences of acquired culture—of language, dress, habits, morals, or religion. There is no cure for such antipathies except a broadened education. A knowledge of history may teach us that civilization is a co-operative product, that nearly all peoples have contributed to it; it is our common heritage and debt; and the civilized soul will reveal itself in treating every man or woman, however lowly, as a representative of one of these creative and contributory groups.

V. Character and History

Society is founded not on the ideals but on the nature of man, and the constitution of man rewrites the constitutions of states. But what is the constitution of man?

We may define human nature as the fundamental tendencies and feelings of mankind. The most basic tendencies we shall call instincts, though we recognize that much doubt has been cast upon their inborn quality. We might describe human nature through the "Table of Character Elements" given on the following page. In this analysis human beings are normally equipped by "nature" (here meaning heredity) with six positive and six negative instincts, whose function it is to preserve the individual, the family, the group, or the species. In positive personalities the positive tendencies predominate, but most individuals are armed with both sets of instincts—to meet or to avoid (according to mood or circumstance) the basic challenges or opportunities of life. Each instinct generates habits and is accompanied by feelings. Their totality is the nature of man.

But how far has human nature changed in the course of history? Theoretically there must have been some change; natural selection has presumably operated upon psychological as well as upon physio-

TABLE OF CHARACTER ELEMENTS

INSTINCTS		HABITS		FEELINGS	
Positive	Negative	Positive	Negative	Positive	Negative
Action	Sleep	Play	Rest	Buoyancy	Fatigue
		Work	Sloth	Energy	Inertia
		Curiosity	Indifference	Eagerness	Boredom
		Manipulation	Hesitation	Wonder	Doubt
		Thought	Dreaming	Absorption	Vacuity
		Innovation	Imitation	Resolution	Acceptance
		Art	Disorder	Aesthetic feeling	Confusion
Fight	Flight	Approach	Retreat	Courage	Anxiety
		Competition	Co-operation	Rivalry	Friendliness
		Pugnacity	Timidity	Anger	Fear
		Mastery	Submission	Pride	Humility
Acquisition	Avoidance	Eating	Rejection	Hunger	Disgust
		Hoarding	Spending	Greed	Prodigality
		Property	Poverty	Possessiveness	Insecurity
Association	Privacy	Communication	Solitude	Sociability	Secretiveness
		Seeking approval	Fearing disapproval	Vanity	Shyness
		Generosity	Selfishness	Kindliness	Hostility
Mating	Refusal	Sexual activity	Sexual perversion	Sexual imagination	Sexual neurosis
		Courtship	Blushing	Sexual love	Modesty
Parental care	Filial dependence	Homemaking	Filial rebellion	Parental love	Filial resentment

logical variations. Nevertheless, known history shows little altera-
tion in the conduct of mankind. The Greeks of Plato's time behaved
very much like the French of modern centuries; and the Romans
behaved like the English. Means and instrumentalities change; motives and ends remain the same: to act or rest, to acquire or give, to
fight or retreat, to seek association or privacy, to mate or reject, to
offer or resent parental care. Nor does human nature alter as between
classes: by and large the poor have the same impulses as the rich,
with only less opportunity or skill to implement them. Nothing is
clearer in history than the adoption by successful rebels of the methods they were accustomed to condemn in the forces they deposed.

Evolution in man during recorded time has been social rather than
biological: it has proceeded not by heritable variations in the species,
but mostly by economic, political, intellectual, and moral innovation
transmitted to individuals and generations by imitation, custom, or
education. Custom and tradition within a group correspond to type
and heredity in the species, and to instincts in the individual; they
are ready adjustments to typical and frequently repeated situations.
New situations, however, do arise, requiring novel, unstereotyped
responses; hence development, in the higher organisms, requires a capacity for experiment and innovation—the social correlates of variation and mutation. Social evolution is an interplay of custom with
origination.

Here the initiative individual—the "great man," the "hero," the
"genius"—regains his place as a formative force in history. He is not
quite the god that Carlyle described; he grows out of his time and
land, and is the product and symbol of events as well as their agent
and voice; without some situation requiring a new response his new
ideas would be untimely and impracticable. When he is a hero of
action, the demands of his position and the exaltation of crisis develop and inflate him to such magnitude and powers as would in nor-

mal times have remained potential and untapped. But he is not merely an effect. Events take place through him as well as around him; his ideas and decisions enter vitally into the course of history. At times his eloquence, like Churchill's, may be worth a thousand regiments; his foresight in strategy and tactics, like Napoleon's, may win battles and campaigns and establish states. If he is a prophet like Mohammed, wise in the means of inspiring men, his words may raise a poor and disadvantaged people to unpremeditated ambitions and surprising power. A Pasteur, a Morse, an Edison, a Ford, a Wright, a Marx, a Lenin, a Mao Tse-tung are effects of numberless causes, and causes of endless effects.

In our table of character elements imitation is opposed to innovation, but in vital ways it co-operates with it. As submissive natures unite with masterful individuals to make the order and operation of a society, so the imitative majority follows the innovating minority, and this follows the originative individual, in adapting new responses to the demands of environment or survival. History in the large is the conflict of minorities; the majority applauds the victor and supplies the human material of social experiment.

Intellect is therefore a vital force in history, but it can also be a dissolvent and destructive power. Out of every hundred new ideas ninety-nine or more will probably be inferior to the traditional responses which they propose to replace. No one man, however brilliant or well-informed, can come in one lifetime to such fullness of understanding as to safely judge and dismiss the customs or institutions of his society, for these are the wisdom of generations after centuries of experiment in the laboratory of history. A youth boiling with hormones will wonder why he should not give full freedom to his sexual desires; and if he is unchecked by custom, morals, or laws, he may ruin his life before he matures sufficiently to understand that sex is a river of fire that must be banked and cooled by a hundred restraints if it is not to consume in chaos both the individual and the group.

So the conservative who resists change is as valuable as the radical who proposes it—perhaps as much more valuable as roots are more vital than grafts. It is good that new ideas should be heard, for the sake of the few that can be used; but it is also good that new ideas should be compelled to go through the mill of objection, opposition, and contumely; this is the trial heat which innovations must survive before being allowed to enter the human race. It is good that the old should resist the young, and that the young should prod the old; out of this tension, as out of the strife of the sexes and the classes, comes a creative tensile strength, a stimulated development, a secret and basic unity and movement of the whole.

VI. Morals and History

Morals are the rules by which a society exhorts (as laws are the rules by which it seeks to compel) its members and associations to behavior consistent with its order, security, and growth. So for sixteen centuries the Jewish enclaves in Christendom maintained their continuity and internal peace by a strict and detailed moral code, almost without help from the state and its laws.

A little knowledge of history stresses the variability of moral codes, and concludes that they are negligible because they differ in time and place, and sometimes contradict each other. A larger knowledge stresses the universality of moral codes, and concludes to their necessity.

Moral codes differ because they adjust themselves to historical and environmental conditions. If we divide economic history into three stages—hunting, agriculture, industry—we may expect that the moral code of one stage will be changed in the next. In the hunting stage a man had to be ready to chase and fight and kill. When he had caught his prey he ate to the cubic capacity of his stomach, being uncertain when he might eat again; insecurity is the mother of greed, as cruelty is the memory—if only in the blood—of a time when the

37

test of survival (as now between states) was the ability to kill. Presumably the death rate in men—so often risking their lives in the hunt—was higher than in women; some men had to take several women, and every man was expected to help women to frequent pregnancy. Pugnacity, brutality, greed, and sexual readiness were advantages in the struggle for existence. Probably every vice was once a virtue—i.e., a quality making for the survival of the individual, the family, or the group. Man's sins may be the relics of his rise rather than the stigmata of his fall.

History does not tell us just when men passed from hunting to agriculture—perhaps in the Neolithic Age, and through the discovery that grain could be sown to add to the spontaneous growth of wild wheat. We may reasonably assume that the new regime demanded new virtues, and changed some old virtues into vices. Industriousness became more vital than bravery, regularity and thrift more profitable than violence, peace more victorious than war. Children were economic assets; birth control was made immoral. On the farm the family was the unit of production under the discipline of the father and the seasons, and paternal authority had a firm economic base. Each normal son matured soon in mind and self-support; at fifteen he understood the physical tasks of life as well as he would understand them at forty; all that he needed was land, a plow, and a willing arm. So he married early, almost as soon as nature wished; he did not fret long under the restraints placed upon premarital relations by the new order of permanent settlements and homes. As for young women, chastity was indispensable, for its loss might bring unprotected motherhood. Monogamy was demanded by the approximate numerical equality of the sexes. For fifteen hundred years this agricultural moral code of continence, early marriage, divorceless monogamy, and multiple maternity maintained itself in Christian

Europe and its white colonies. It was a stern code, which produced some of the strongest characters in history.

Gradually, then rapidly and ever more widely, the Industrial Revolution changed the economic form and moral superstructure of European and American life. Men, women, and children left home and family, authority and unity, to work as individuals, individually paid, in factories built to house not men but machines. Every decade the machines multiplied and became more complex; economic maturity (the capacity to support a family) came later; children no longer were economic assets; marriage was delayed; premarital continence became more difficult to maintain. The city offered every discouragement to marriage, but it provided every stimulus and facility for sex. Women were "emancipated"—i.e., industrialized; and contraceptives enabled them to separate intercourse from pregnancy. The authority of father and mother lost its economic base through the growing individualism of industry. The rebellious youth was no longer constrained by the surveillance of the village; he could hide his sins in the protective anonymity of the city crowd. The progress of science raised the authority of the test tube over that of the crosier; the mechanization of economic production suggested mechanistic materialistic philosophies; education spread religious doubts; morality lost more and more of its supernatural supports. The old agricultural moral code began to die.

In our time, as in the times of Socrates (d. 399 B.C.) and Augustus (d. A.D. 14), war has added to the forces making for moral laxity. After the violence and social disruption of the Peloponnesian War Alcibiades felt free to flout the moral code of his ancestors, and Thrasymachus could announce that might was the only right. After the wars of Marius and Sulla, Caesar and Pompey, Antony and Octavius, "Rome was full of men who had lost their economic footing and their moral stability: soldiers who had tasted adventure and had learned to kill; citizens who had seen their savings consumed in the taxes and inflation caused by war; . . . women dizzy with freedom, multiplying divorces, abortions, and adulteries. . . . A shallow sophistication prided itself upon its pessimism and cynicism." [15] It is almost a picture of European and American cities after two world wars.

History offers some consolation by reminding us that sin has flourished in every age. Even our generation has not yet rivaled the popularity of homosexualism in ancient Greece or Rome or Renaissance Italy. "The humanists wrote about it with a kind of scholarly affection, and Ariosto judged that they were all addicted to it"; Aretino asked the Duke of Mantua to send him an attractive boy.[16] Prostitution has been perennial and universal, from the state-regulated brothels of Assyria[17] to the "night clubs" of West-European and American cities today. In the University of Wittenberg in 1544, according to Luther, "the race of girls is getting bold, and run after the fellows into their rooms and chambers and wherever they can, and offer them their free love." [18] Montaigne tells us that in his time (1533–92) obscene literature found a ready market;[19] the immorality of our stage differs in kind rather than degree from that of Restoration England; and John Cleland's *Memoirs of a Woman of Pleasure* —a veritable catena of coitus—was as popular in 1749 as in 1965.[20] We have noted the discovery of dice in the excavations near the site of Nineveh;[21] men and women have gambled in every age. In every age men have been dishonest and governments have been corrupt; probably less now than generally before. The pamphlet literature of sixteenth-century Europe "groaned with denunciations of wholesale adulteration of food and other products." [22] Man has never reconciled himself to the Ten Commandments. We have seen Voltaire's view of history as mainly "a collection of the crimes, follies, and misfortunes" of mankind,[23] and Gibbon's echo of that summary.[24]

We must remind ourselves again that history as usually written (*peccavimus*) is quite different from history as usually lived: the historian records the exceptional because it is interesting—because it is exceptional. If all those individuals who had no Boswell had found their numerically proportionate place in the pages of historians we should have a duller but juster view of the past and of man. Behind the red façade of war and politics, misfortune and poverty, adultery and divorce, murder and suicide, were millions of orderly homes, devoted marriages, men and women kindly and affectionate, troubled and happy with children. Even in recorded history we find so many instances of goodness, even of nobility, that we can forgive, though not forget, the sins. The gifts of charity have almost equaled the cruelties of battlefields and jails. How many times, even in our sketchy narratives, we have seen men helping one another—Farinelli providing for the children of Domenico Scarlatti, divers people succoring young Haydn, Conte Litta paying for Johann Christian Bach's studies at Bologna, Joseph Black advancing money repeatedly to James Watt, Puchberg patiently lending and lending to Mozart. Who will dare to write a history of human goodness?

So we cannot be sure that the moral laxity of our times is a herald of decay rather than a painful or delightful transition between a moral code that has lost its agricultural basis and another that our industrial civilization has yet to forge into social order and normality. Meanwhile history assures us that civilizations decay quite leisurely. For 250 years after moral weakening began in Greece with the Sophists, Hellenic civilization continued to produce masterpieces of literature and art. Roman morals began to "decay" soon after the conquered Greeks passed into Italy (146 B.C.), but Rome continued to have great statesmen, philosophers, poets, and artists until the death of Marcus Aurelius (A.D. 180). Politically Rome was at nadir when Caesar came (60 B.C.); yet it did not quite succumb to the barbarians till A.D. 465. May we take as long to fall as did Imperial Rome!

Perhaps discipline will be restored in our civilization through the military training required by the challenges of war. The freedom of the part varies with the security of the whole; individualism will diminish in America and England as geographical protection ceases. Sexual license may cure itself through its own excess; our unmoored children may live to see order and modesty become fashionable; clothing will be more stimulating than nudity. Meanwhile much of our moral freedom is good: it is pleasant to be relieved of theological terrors, to enjoy without qualm the pleasures that harm neither others nor ourselves, and to feel the tang of the open air upon our liberated flesh.

VII. Religion and History

Even the skeptical historian develops a humble respect for religion, since he sees it functioning, and seemingly indispensable, in every land and age. To the unhappy, the suffering, the bereaved, the old, it has brought supernatural comforts valued by millions of souls as more precious than any natural aid. It has helped parents and teachers to discipline the young. It has conferred meaning and dignity upon the lowliest existence, and through its sacraments has made for stability by transforming human covenants into solemn relationships with God. It has kept the poor (said Napoleon) from murdering the rich. For since the natural inequality of men dooms many of us to poverty or defeat, some supernatural hope may be the sole alternative to despair. Destroy that hope, and class war is intensified. Heaven and utopia are buckets in a well: when one goes down the other goes up; when religion declines Communism grows.

Religion does not seem at first to have had any connection with morals. Apparently (for we are merely guessing, or echoing Petronius, who echoed Lucretius) "it was fear that first made the gods" [25] —fear of hidden forces in the earth, rivers, oceans, trees, winds, and sky. Religion became the propitiatory worship of these forces through offerings, sacrifice, incantation, and prayer. Only when priests used these fears and rituals to support morality and law did religion become a force vital and rival to the state. It told the people that the local code of morals and laws had been dictated by the gods. It pictured the god Thoth giving laws to Menes for Egypt, the god Shamash giving Hammurabi a code for Babylonia, Yahveh giving the Ten Commandments and 613 precepts to Moses for the Jews, and the divine nymph Egeria giving Numa Pompilius laws for Rome. Pagan cults and Christian creeds proclaimed that earthly rulers were appointed and protected by the gods. Gratefully nearly ever state shared its lands and revenues with the priests.

Some recusants have doubted that religion ever promoted morality, since immorality has flourished even in ages of religious domination. Certainly sensuality, drunkenness, coarseness, greed, dishonesty, robbery, and violence existed in the Middle Ages; but probably the moral disorder born of half a millennium of barbarian invasion, war, economic devastation, and political disorganization would have been much worse without the moderating effect of the Christian ethic, priestly exhortations, saintly exemplars, and a calming, unifying ritual. The Roman Catholic Church labored to reduce slavery, family feuds, and national strife, to extend the intervals of truce and peace, and to replace trial by combat or ordeal with the judgments of established courts. It softened the penalties exacted by Roman or barbarian law, and vastly expanded the scope and organization of charity.

Though the Church served the state, it claimed to stand above all states, as morality should stand above power. It taught men that patriotism unchecked by a higher loyalty can be a tool of greed and crime. Over all the competing governments of Christendom it promulgated one moral law. Claiming divine origin and spiritual hegemony, the Church offered itself as an international court to which all rulers were to be morally responsible. The Emperor Henry IV recognized this claim by submitting to Pope Gregory VII at Canossa (1077); and a century later Innocent III raised the authority and prestige of the papacy to a height where it seemed that Gregory's ideal of a moral superstate had come to fulfillment.

The majestic dream broke under the attacks of nationalism, skepticism, and human frailty. The Church was manned with men, who often proved biased, venal, or extortionate. France grew in wealth and power, and made the papacy her political tool. Kings became strong enough to compel a pope to dissolve that Jesuit order which had so devotedly supported the popes. The Church stooped to fraud, as with pious legends, bogus relics, and dubious miracles; for centuries it profited from a mythical "Donation of Constantine" that had allegedly bequeathed Western Europe to Pope Sylvester I (r. 314–35), and from "False Decretals" (c. 842) that forged a series of documents to give a sacred antiquity to papal omnipotence.[26] More and more the hierarchy spent its energies in promoting orthodoxy rather than morality, and the Inquisition almost fatally disgraced the Church. Even while preaching peace the Church fomented religious wars in sixteenth-century France and the Thirty Years' War in seventeenth-century Germany. It played only a modest part in the outstanding advance of modern morality—the abolition of slavery. It allowed the philosophers to take the lead in the humanitarian movements that have alleviated the evils of our time.

History has justified the Church in the belief that the masses of mankind desire a religion rich in miracle, mystery, and myth. Some minor modifications have been allowed in ritual, in ecclesiastical costume, and in episcopal authority; but the Church dares not alter the doctrines that reason smiles at, for such changes would offend and disillusion the millions whose hopes have been tied to inspiring and consolatory imaginations. No reconciliation is possible between religion and philosophy except through the philosophers' recognition that they have found no substitute for the moral function of the Church, and the ecclesiastical recognition of religious and intellectual freedom.

Does history support a belief in God? If by God we mean not the creative vitality of nature but a supreme being intelligent and benevolent, the answer must be a reluctant negative. Like other departments of biology, history remains at bottom a natural selection of the fittest individuals and groups in a struggle wherein goodness receives no favors, misfortunes abound, and the final test is the ability to survive. Add to the crimes, wars, and cruelties of man the earthquakes, storms, tornadoes, pestilences, tidal waves, and other "acts of God" that periodically desolate human and animal life, and the total evidence suggests either a blind or an impartial fatality, with incidental and apparently haphazard scenes to which we subjectively ascribe order, splendor, beauty, or sublimity. If history supports any theology this would be a dualism like the Zoroastrian or Manichaean: a good spirit and an evil spirit battling for control of the universe and men's souls. These faiths and Christianity (which is essentially Manichaean) assured their followers that the good spirit would win in the end; but of this consummation history offers no guarantee. Nature and history do not agree with our conceptions of good and bad; they define good as that which survives, and bad as that which goes under; and the universe has no prejudice in favor of Christ as against Genghis Khan.

The growing awareness of man's minuscule place in the cosmos has furthered the impairment of religious belief. In Christendom we may date the beginning of the decline from Copernicus (1543). The process was slow, but by 1611 John Donne was mourning that the earth had become a mere "suburb" in the world, and that "new philosophy calls all in doubt"; and Francis Bacon, while tipping his hat occasionally to the bishops, was proclaiming science as the religion of modern emancipated man. In that generation began the "death of God" as an external deity.

So great an effect required many causes besides the spread of science and historical knowledge. First, the Protestant Reformation, which originally defended private judgment. Then the multitude of Protestant sects and conflicting theologies, each appealing to both Scriptures and reason. Then the higher criticism of the Bible, displaying that marvelous library as the imperfect work of fallible men. Then the deistic movement in England, reducing religion to a vague belief in a God hardly distinguishable from nature. Then the growing acquaintance with other religions, whose myths, many of them pre-Christian, were distressingly similar to the supposedly factual bases of one's inherited creed. Then the Protestant exposure of Catholic miracles, the deistic exposure of Biblical miracles, the general exposure of frauds, inquisitions, and massacres in the history of religion. Then the replacement of agriculture—which had stirred men to faith by the annual rebirth of life and the mystery of growth—with industry, humming daily a litany of machines, and suggesting a world machine. Add meanwhile the bold advance of skeptical scholarship, as in Bayle, and of pantheistic philosophy, as in Spinoza; the massive attack of the French Enlightenment upon Christianity; the revolt of Paris against the Church during the French Revolution. Add, in our own time, the indiscriminate slaughter of civilian populations in modern war. Finally, the awesome triumphs of scientific technology, promising man omnipotence and destruction, and challenging the divine command of the skies.

In one way Christianity lent a hand against itself by developing in many Christians a moral sense that could no longer stomach the vengeful God of the traditional theology. The idea of hell disappeared from educated thought, even from pulpit homilies. Presbyterians became ashamed of the Westminster Confession, which had pledged them to belief in a God who had created billions of men and women despite his foreknowledge that, regardless of their virtues and crimes, they were predestined to everlasting hell. Educated Christians visiting the Sistine Chapel were shocked by Michelangelo's picture of Christ hurling offenders pell-mell into an inferno whose fires were never to be extinguished; was this the "gentle Jesus, meek and mild," who had inspired our youth? Just as the moral development of the Hellenes had weakened their belief in the quarrelsome and adulterous deities of Olympus ("A certain proportion of mankind," wrote Plato, "do not believe at all in the existence of the gods." [27]), so the development of the Christian ethic slowly eroded Christian theology. Christ destroyed Jehovah.

The replacement of Christian with secular institutions is the culminating and critical result of the Industrial Revolution. That states should attempt to dispense with theological supports is one of the many crucial experiments that bewilder our brains and unsettle our ways today. Laws which were once presented as the decrees of a god-given king are now frankly the confused commands of fallible men. Education, which was the sacred province of god-inspired priests, becomes the task of men and women shorn of theological robes and awe, and relying on reason and persuasion to civilize young rebels who fear only the policeman and may never learn to reason at all. Colleges once allied to churches have been captured by businessmen and scientists. The propaganda of patriotism, capitalism, or Communism succeeds to the inculcation of a supernatural creed and moral code. Holydays give way to holidays. Theaters are full even on Sundays, and even on Sundays churches are half empty. In Anglo-Saxon families religion has become a social observance and protective coloration; in American Catholic families it flourishes; in upper- and middle-class France and Italy religion is "a secondary sexual characteristic of the female." A thousand signs proclaim that Christianity is undergoing the same decline that fell upon the old Greek religion after the coming of the Sophists and the Greek Enlightenment.

Catholicism survives because it appeals to imagination, hope, and the senses; because its mythology consoles and brightens the lives of the poor; and because the commanded fertility of the faithful slowly regains the lands lost to the Reformation. Catholicism has sacrificed the adherence of the intellectual community, and suffers increasing defections through contact with secular education and literature; but it wins converts from souls wearied with the uncertainty of reason, and from others hopeful that the Church will stem internal disorder and the Communist wave.

If another great war should devastate Western civilization, the resultant destruction of cities, the dissemination of poverty, and the disgrace of science may leave the Church, as in A.D. 476, the sole hope and guide of those who survive the cataclysm.

One lesson of history is that religion has many lives, and a habit of resurrection. How often in the past have God and religion died and been reborn! Ikhnaton used all the powers of a pharaoh to destroy the religion of Amon; within a year of Ikhnaton's death the religion of Amon was restored.[28] Atheism ran wild in the India of Buddha's youth, and Buddha himself founded a religion without a god; after his death Buddhism developed a complex theology including gods, saints, and hell.[29] Philosophy, science, and education depopulated the Hellenic pantheon, but the vacuum attracted a dozen Oriental faiths rich in resurrection myths. In 1793 Hébert and Chaumette, wrongly interpreting Voltaire, established in Paris the atheistic worship of the Goddess of Reason; a year later Robespierre, fearing chaos and inspired by Rousseau, set up the worship of the Supreme Being; in 1801 Napoleon, versed in history, signed a concordat with Pius VII, restoring the Catholic Church in France. The irreligion of eight-eenth-century England disappeared under the Victorian compromise with Christianity: the state agreed to support the Anglican Church, and the educated classes would muffle their skepticism, on the tacit understanding that the Church would accept subordination to the state, and the parson would humbly serve the squire. In America the rationalism of the Founding Fathers gave place to a religious revival in the nineteenth century.

Puritanism and paganism—the repression and the expression of the senses and desires—alternate in mutual reaction in history. Generally religion and puritanism prevail in periods when the laws are feeble and morals must bear the burden of maintaining social order; skepticism and paganism (other factors being equal) progress as the rising power of law and government permits the decline of the church, the family, and morality without basically endangering the stability of the state. In our time the strength of the state has united with the several forces listed above to relax faith and morals, and to allow paganism to resume its natural sway. Probably our excesses will bring another reaction; moral disorder may generate a religious revival; atheists may again (as in France after the debacle of 1870) send their children to Catholic schools to give them the discipline of religious belief. Hear the appeal of the agnostic Renan in 1866:

> Let us enjoy the liberty of the sons of God, but let us take care lest we become accomplices in the diminution of virtue which would menace society if Christianity were to grow weak. What should we do without it? . . . If Rationalism wishes to govern the world without regard to the religious needs of the soul, the experience of the French Revolution is there to teach us the consequences of such a blunder.[30]

Does history warrant Renan's conclusion that religion is necessary to morality—that a natural ethic is too weak to withstand the savagery that lurks under civilization and emerges in our dreams, crimes, and wars? Joseph de Maistre answered: "I do not know what the heart of a rascal may be; I know what is in the heart of an honest man; it is horrible." [31] There is no significant example in history, before our time, of a society successfully maintaining moral life without the aid of religion. France, the United States, and some other nations have divorced their governments from all churches, but they have had the help of religion in keeping social order. Only a few Communist states have not merely dissociated themselves from religion but have repudiated its aid; and perhaps the apparent and provisional success of this experiment in Russia owes much to the temporary acceptance of Communism as the religion (or, as skeptics would say, the opium) of the people, replacing the church as the vendor of comfort and hope. If the socialist regime should fail in its efforts to destroy relative poverty among the masses, this new religion may lose its fervor and efficacy, and the state may wink at the restoration of supernatural beliefs as an aid in quieting discontent. "As long as there is poverty there will be gods." [32]

VIII. Economics and History

History, according to Karl Marx, is economics in action—the contest, among individuals, groups, classes, and states, for food, fuel, materials, and economic power. Political forms, religious institutions, cultural creations, are all rooted in economic realities. So the Industrial Revolution brought with it democracy, feminism, birth control, socialism, the decline of religion, the loosening of morals, the liberation of literature from dependence upon aristocratic patronage, the replacement of romanticism by realism in fiction—and the economic interpretation of history. The outstanding personalities in these movements were effects, not causes; Agamemnon, Achilles, and Hector would never have been heard of had not the Greeks sought commercial control of the Dardanelles; economic ambition, not the face of Helen "fairer than the evening air clad in the beauty of a thousand stars," launched a thousand ships on Ilium; those subtle Greeks knew how to cover naked economic truth with the fig leaf of a phrase.

Unquestionably the economic interpretation illuminates much history. The money of the Delian Confederacy built the Parthenon; the treasury of Cleopatra's Egypt revitalized the exhausted Italy of Augustus, gave Virgil an annuity and Horace a farm. The Crusades, like the wars of Rome with Persia, were attempts of the West to capture trade routes to the East; the discovery of America was a result of the failure of the Crusades. The banking house of the Medici financed the Florentine Renaissance; the trade and industry of Nuremberg made Dürer possible. The French Revolution came not because Voltaire wrote brilliant satires and Rousseau sentimental romances, but because the middle classes had risen to economic leadership, needed legislative freedom for their enterprise and trade, and itched for social acceptance and political power.

Marx did not claim that individuals were always actuated by economic interest; he was far from imagining that material considerations led to Abélard's romance, or the gospel of Buddha, or the poems of Keats. But perhaps he underestimated the role played by noneconomic incentives in the behavior of masses: by religious fervor, as in Moslem or Spanish armies; by nationalistic ardor, as in Hitler's troops or Japan's kamikazes; by the self-fertilizing fury of mobs, as in the Gordon riots of June 2–8, 1780, in London, or the massacres of September 2–7, 1792, in Paris. In such cases the motives of the (usually hidden) leaders may be economic, but the result is largely determined by the passions of the mass. In many instances political or military power was apparently the cause rather than the result of economic operations, as in the seizure of Russia by the Bolsheviks in 1917, or in the army coups that punctuate South American history. Who would claim that the Moorish conquest of Spain, or the Mongol conquest of Western Asia, or the Mogul conquest of India, was the product of economic power? In these cases the poor proved stronger than the rich; military victory gave political ascendancy, which brought economic control. The generals could write a military interpretation of history.

Allowing for these cautions, we may derive endless instruction from the economic analysis of the past. We observe that the invading barbarians found Rome weak because the agricultural population which had formerly supplied the legions with hardy and patriotic warriors fighting for land had been replaced by slaves laboring listlessly on vast farms owned by one man or a few. Today the inability of small farms to use the best machinery profitably is again forcing agriculture into large-scale production under capitalistic or communistic ownership. It was once said that "civilization is a parasite on the man with the hoe," [33] but the man with the hoe no longer exists; he is now a "hand" at the wheel of a tractor or a combine. Agriculture becomes an industry, and soon the farmer must choose between being the employee of a capitalist and being the employee of a state.

At the other end of the scale history reports that "the men who can manage men manage the men who can manage only things, and the men who can manage money manage all." [34] So the bankers, watching the trends in agriculture, industry, and trade, inviting and directing the flow of capital, putting our money doubly and trebly to work, controlling loans and interest and enterprise, running great risks to make great gains, rise to the top of the economic pyramid. From the Medici of Florence and the Fuggers of Augsburg to the Rothschilds of Paris and London and the Morgans of New York, bankers have sat in the councils of governments, financing wars and popes, and occasionally sparking a revolution. Perhaps it is one secret of their power that, having studied the fluctuations of prices, they know that history is inflationary, and that money is the last thing a wise man will hoard.

The experience of the past leaves little doubt that every economic system must sooner or later rely upon some form of the profit motive to stir individuals and groups to productivity. Substitutes like slavery, police supervision, or ideological enthusiasm prove too unproductive, too expensive, or too transient. Normally and generally men are judged by their ability to produce—except in war, when they are ranked according to their ability to destroy.

Since practical ability differs from person to person, the majority of such abilities, in nearly all societies, is gathered in a minority of men. The concentration of wealth is a natural result of this concentration of ability, and regularly recurs in history. The rate of concentration varies (other factors being equal) with the economic freedom permitted by morals and the laws. Despotism may for a time retard the concentration; democracy, allowing the most liberty, accelerates it. The relative equality of Americans before 1776 has been overwhelmed by a thousand forms of physical, mental, and economic differentiation, so that the gap between the wealthiest and the poorest is now greater than at any time since Imperial plutocratic Rome. In progressive societies the concentration may reach a point where the strength of number in the many poor rivals the strength of ability in the few rich; then the unstable equilibrium generates a critical situation, which history has diversely met by legislation redistributing wealth or by revolution distributing poverty.

In the Athens of 594 B.C., according to Plutarch, "the disparity of fortune between the rich and the poor had reached its height, so that the city seemed to be in a dangerous condition, and no other means for freeing it from disturbances . . . seemed possible but despotic power." [35] The poor, finding their status worsened with each year—the government in the hands of their masters, and the corrupt courts deciding every issue against them—began to talk of violent revolt. The rich, angry at the challenge to their property, prepared to defend themselves by force. Good sense prevailed; moderate elements secured the election of Solon, a businessman of aristocratic lineage, to the supreme archonship. He devaluated the currency, thereby easing the burden of all debtors (though he himself was a creditor); he reduced all personal debts, and ended imprisonment for debt; he can-

celed arrears for taxes and mortgage interest; he established a gradu-
ated income tax that made the rich pay at a rate twelve times that
required of the poor; he reorganized the courts on a more popular
basis; and he arranged that the sons of those who had died in war for
Athens should be brought up and educated at the government's ex-
pense. The rich protested that his measures were outright confisca-
tion; the radicals complained that he had not redivided the land; but
within a generation almost all agreed that his reforms had saved
Athens from revolution.[36]

The Roman Senate, so famous for its wisdom, adopted an uncom-
promising course when the concentration of wealth approached an
explosive point in Italy; the result was a hundred years of class and
civil war. Tiberius Gracchus, an aristocrat elected as tribune of the
people, proposed to redistribute land by limiting ownership to 333
acres per person, and alloting surplus land to the restive proletariat of
the capital. The Senate rejected his proposals as confiscatory. He ap-
pealed to the people, telling them, "You fight and die to give wealth
and luxury to others; you are called the masters of the world, but
there is not a foot of ground that you can call your own."[37] Contrary
to Roman law, he campaigned for re-election as tribune; in an
election-day riot he was slain (133 B.C.). His brother Caius, taking
up his cause, failed to prevent a renewal of violence, and ordered his
servant to kill him; the slave obeyed, and then killed himself (121
B.C.); three thousand of Caius' followers were put to death by Sena-
torial decree. Marius became the leader of the plebs, but withdrew
when the movement verged on revolution. Catiline, proposing to
abolish all debts, organized a revolutionary army of "wretched pau-
pers"; he was inundated by Cicero's angry eloquence, and died in
battle against the state (62 B.C.). Julius Caesar attempted a compromise, but was cut down by the patricians (44 B.C.) after five years of
civil war. Mark Antony confused his support of Caesar's policies

with personal ambitions and romance; Octavius defeated him at Actium, and established the "Principate" that for 210 years (30 B.C. – A.D. 180) maintained the Pax Romana between the classes as well as among the states within the Imperial frontiers.[38]

After the breakdown of political order in the Western Roman Empire (A.D. 476), centuries of destitution were followed by the slow renewal and reconcentration of wealth, partly in the hierarchy of the Catholic Church. In one aspect the Reformation was a redistribution of this wealth by the reduction of German and English payments to the Roman Church, and by the secular appropriation of ecclesiastical property and revenues. The French Revolution attempted a violent redistribution of wealth by Jacqueries in the countryside and massacres in the cities, but the chief result was a transfer of property and privilege from the aristocracy to the bourgeoisie. The government of the United States, in 1933–52 and 1960–65, followed Solon's peaceful methods, and accomplished a moderate and pacifying redistribution; perhaps someone had studied history. The upper classes in America cursed, complied, and resumed the concentration of wealth.

We conclude that the concentration of wealth is natural and inevitable, and is periodically alleviated by violent or peaceable partial redistribution. In this view all economic history is the slow heartbeat of the social organism, a vast systole and diastole of concentrating wealth and compulsive recirculation.

IX. Socialism and History

The struggle of socialism against capitalism is part of the historic rhythm in the concentration and dispersion of wealth. The capitalist, of course, has fulfilled a creative function in history: he has gathered the savings of the people into productive capital by the promise of dividends or interest; he has financed the mechanization of industry and agriculture, and the rationalization of distribution; and the result has been such a flow of goods from producer to consumer as history has never seen before. He has put the liberal gospel of liberty to his use by arguing that businessmen left relatively free from transportation tolls and legislative regulation can give the public a greater abundance of food, homes, comfort, and leisure than has ever come from industries managed by politicians, manned by governmental employees, and supposedly immune to the laws of supply and demand. In free enterprise the spur of competition and the zeal and zest of ownership arouse the productiveness and inventiveness of men; nearly every economic ability sooner or later finds its niche and reward in the shuffle of talents and the natural selection of skills; and a basic democracy rules the process insofar as most of the articles to be produced, and the services to be rendered, are determined by public demand rather than by governmental decree. Meanwhile competition compels the capitalist to exhaustive labor, and his products to ever-rising excellence.

There is much truth in such claims today, but they do not explain why history so resounds with protests and revolts against the abuses of industrial mastery, price manipulation, business chicanery, and irresponsible wealth. These abuses must be hoary with age, for there have been socialistic experiments in a dozen countries and centuries. We read that in Sumeria, about 2100 B.C.,

> the economy was organized by the state. Most of the arable land was the property of the crown; labourers received rations from the crops delivered to the royal storehouses. For the administration of this vast state economy a very differentiated hierarchy was developed, and records were kept of all deliveries and distributions of rations. Tens of thousands of clay tablets inscribed with such records were found in the capital Ur itself, in Lagash, Umma . . . Foreign trade also was carried out in the name of the central administration.[39]

In Babylonia (c. 1750 B.C.) the law code of Hammurabi fixed wages for herdsmen and artisans, and the charges to be made by physicians for operations.[40]

In Egypt under the Ptolemies (323 B.C. – 30 B.C.) the state owned the soil and managed agriculture: the peasant was told what land to till, what crops to grow; his harvest was measured and registered by government scribes, was threshed on royal threshing floors, and was conveyed by a living chain of fellaheen into the granaries of the king. The government owned the mines and appropriated the ore. It nationalized the production and sale of oil, salt, papyrus, and textiles. All commerce was controlled and regulated by the state; most retail trade was in the hands of state agents selling state-produced goods. Banking was a government monopoly, but its operation might be delegated to private firms. Taxes were laid upon every person, industry, process, product, sale, and legal document. To keep track of taxable transactions and income, the government maintained a swarm of scribes and a complex system of personal and property registration. The revenue of this system made the Ptolemaic the richest state of the time.[41] Great engineering enterprises were completed, agriculture was improved, and a large proportion of the profits went to develop and adorn the country and to finance its cultural life. About 290 B.C. the famous Museum and Library of Alexandria were founded. Science and literature flourished; at uncertain dates in this Ptolemaic era some scholars made the "Septuagint" translation of the Pentateuch into Greek. Soon, however, the pharaohs took to expensive wars, and after 246 B.C. they gave themselves to drink and venery, allowing the administration of the state and the economy to fall into the hands of rascals who ground every possible penny out of the poor. Generation after generation the government's exactions grew. Strikes increased in number and violence. In the capital, Alexandria, the populace was bribed to peace by bounties and spectacles, but it was watched by a large military force, was allowed no voice in the government, and became in the end a violent mob. Agriculture and industry decayed through lack of incentive; moral disintegration spread; and order was not restored until Octavius brought Egypt under Roman rule (30 B.C.).

Rome had its socialist interlude under Diocletian. Faced with increasing poverty and restlessness among the masses, and with imminent danger of barbarian invasion, he issued in A.D. 301 an *Edictum de pretiis*, which denounced monopolists for keeping goods from the market to raise prices, and set maximum prices and wages for all important articles and services. Extensive public works were undertaken to put the unemployed to work, and food was distributed gratis, or at reduced prices, to the poor. The government—which already owned most mines, quarries, and salt deposits—brought nearly all major industries and guilds under detailed control. "In every large town," we are told, "the state became a powerful employer, . . . standing head and shoulders above the private industrialists, who were in any case crushed by taxation." [42] When businessmen predicted ruin, Diocletian explained that the barbarians were at the gate, and that individual liberty had to be shelved until collective liberty could be made secure. The socialism of Diocletian was a war economy, made possible by fear of foreign attack. Other factors equal, internal liberty varies inversely as external danger.

The task of controlling men in economic detail proved too much for Diocletian's expanding, expensive, and corrupt bureaucracy. To support this officialdom—the army, the court, public works, and the dole—taxation rose to such heights that men lost incentive to work or earn, and an erosive contest began between lawyers finding devices to evade taxes and lawyers formulating laws to prevent evasion. Thousands of Romans, to escape the taxgatherer, fled over the frontiers to seek refuge among the barbarians. Seeking to check this elusive mobility, and to facilitate regulation and taxation, the government issued decrees binding the peasant to his field and the worker to his shop until all his debts and taxes had been paid. In this and other ways medieval serfdom began.[43]

China has had several attempts at state socialism. Szuma Ch'ien (b. c.145 B.C.) informs us that to prevent private individuals from "reserving to their sole use the riches of the mountains and the sea in order to gain a fortune, and from putting the lower classes into subjection to themselves," [44] the Emperor Wu Ti (r. 140 B.C. – 87 B.C.) nationalized the resources of the soil, extended governmental direction over transport and trade, laid a tax upon incomes, and established public works, including canals that bound the rivers together and irrigated the fields. The state accumulated stockpiles of goods, sold these when prices were rising, bought more when prices were falling; thus, says Szuma Ch'ien, "the rich merchants and large shopkeepers would be prevented from making big profits, . . . and prices would be regulated in the Empire." [45] For a time, we are told, China prospered as never before. A combination of "acts of God" with human deviltry put an end to the experiment after the death of the Emperor. Floods alternated with droughts, created tragic shortages, and raised prices beyond control. Businessmen protested that taxes were making them support the lazy and the incompetent. Harassed by the high cost of living, the poor joined the rich in clamoring for a return to the old ways, and some proposed that the inventor of the new system be boiled alive. The reforms were one by one rescinded, and were almost forgotten when they were revived by a Chinese philosopher-king.

Wang Mang (r. A.D. 9–23) was an accomplished scholar, a patron of literature, a millionaire who scattered his riches among his friends and the poor. Having seized the throne, he surrounded himself with men trained in letters, science, and philosophy. He nationalized the land, divided it into equal tracts among the peasants, and put an end to slavery. Like Wu Ti, he tried to control prices by the accumulation or release of stockpiles. He made loans at low interest to private enterprise. The groups whose profits had been clipped by his legislation united to plot his fall; they were helped by drought and flood and foreign invasion. The rich Liu family put itself at the head of a general rebellion, slew Wang Mang, and repealed his legislation. Everything was as before.[46]

A thousand years later Wang An-shih, as premier (1068–85), undertook a pervasive governmental domination of the Chinese economy. "The state," he held, "should take the entire management of commerce, industry, and agriculture into its own hands, with a view to succoring the working classes and preventing them from being ground into the dust by the rich." [47] He rescued the peasants from the moneylenders by loans at low interest. He encouraged new settlers by advancing them seed and other aid, to be repaid out of the later yield of their land. He organized great engineering works to control floods and check unemployment. Boards were appointed in every district to regulate wages and prices. Commerce was nationalized. Pensions were provided for the aged, the unemployed, and the poor. Education and the examination system (by which admission to governmental office was determined) were reformed; "pupils threw away their textbooks of rhetoric," says a Chinese historian, "and began to study primers of history, geography, and political economy." [48]

What undermined the experiment? First, high taxes, laid upon all to finance a swelling band of governmental employees. Second, conscription of a male in every family to man the armies made necessary by barbarian invasions. Third, corruption in the bureaucracy; China, like other nations, was faced with a choice between private plunder and public graft. Conservatives, led by Wang An-shih's brother, argued that human corruptibility and incompetence make governmental control of industry impracticable, and that the best economy is a *laissez-faire* system that relies on the natural impulses of men. The rich, stung by the high taxation of their fortunes and the monopoly of commerce by the government, poured out their resources in a campaign to discredit the new system, to obstruct its enforcement, and to bring it to an end. This movement, well organized, exerted constant pressure upon the Emperor. When another period of drought and flood was capped by the appearance of a terrifying comet, the Son of Heaven dismissed Wang An-shih, revoked his decrees, and called the opposition to power. [49]

The longest-lasting regime of socialism yet known to history was set up by the Incas in what we now call Peru, at some time in the thirteenth century. Basing their power largely on popular belief that the earthly sovereign was the delegate of the Sun God, the Incas organized and directed all agriculture, labor, and trade. A governmental census kept account of materials, individuals, and income; professional "runners," using a remarkable system of roads, maintained the network of communication indispensable to such detailed rule over so large a territory. Every person was an employee of the state, and seems to have accepted this condition cheerfully as a promise of security and food. This system endured till the conquest of Peru by Pizarro in 1533.

On the opposite slope of South America, in a Portuguese colony along the Uruguay River, 150 Jesuits organized 200,000 Indians into another socialistic society (c. 1620–1750). The ruling priests managed nearly all agriculture, commerce, and industry. They allowed each youth to choose among the trades they taught, but they required every able-bodied person to work eight hours a day. They provided for recreation, arranged sports, dances, and choral performances of a thousand voices, and trained orchestras that played European music. They served also as teachers, physicians, and judges, and devised a penal code that excluded capital punishment. By all accounts the natives were docile and content, and when the community was attacked it defended itself with an ardor and ability that surprised the assailants. In 1750 Portugal ceded to Spain territory including seven of the Jesuit settlements. A rumor having spread that the lands of these colonies contained gold, the Spanish in America insisted on immediate occupation; the Portuguese government under Pombal (then at odds with the Jesuits) ordered the priests and the natives to leave the settlements; and after some resistance by the Indians the experiment came to an end.[50]

In the social revolt that accompanied the Protestant Reformation in Germany, communistic slogans based on the Bible were advanced by several rebel leaders. Thomas Münzer, a preacher, called upon the

people to overthrow the princes, the clergy, and the capitalists, and
to establish a "refined society" in which all things were to be in common.[51] He recruited an army of peasants, inspired them with accounts of communism among the Apostles, and led them to battle.
They were defeated, five thousand of them were slain, Münzer was
beheaded (1525). Hans Hut, accepting Münzer's teachings, organized at Austerlitz an Anabaptist community that practiced communism for almost a century (c. 1530–1622). John of Leiden led a
group of Anabaptists in capturing control of Münster, the capital of
Westphalia; there, for fourteen months, they maintained a communistic regime (1534–35).[52]

In the seventeenth century a group of "Levellers" in Cromwell's
army begged him in vain to establish a communistic utopia in England. The socialist agitation subsided during the Restoration, but it
rose again when the Industrial Revolution revealed the greed and
brutality of early capitalism—child labor, woman labor, long hours,
low wages, and disease-breeding factories and slums. Karl Marx and
Friedrich Engels gave the movement its Magna Carta in the *Communist Manifesto* of 1847, and its Bible in *Das Kapital* (1867–95).
They expected that socialism would be effected first in England,
because industry was there most developed and had reached a stage
of centralized management that seemed to invite appropriation by
the government. They did not live long enough to be surprised by
the outbreak of Communism in Russia.

Why did modern socialism come first in a Russia where capitalism
was in its infancy and there were no large corporations to ease the
transition to state control? Centuries of peasant poverty and reams of
intellectual revolt had prepared the way, but the peasants had been
freed from serfdom in 1861, and the intellectuals had been inclined
toward an anarchism antipodal to an all-absorbing state. Probably the

Russian Revolution of 1917 succeeded because the Czarist government had been defeated and disgraced by war and bad management; the Russian economy had collapsed in chaos, the peasants returned from the front carrying arms, and Lenin and Trotsky had been given safe conduct and bon voyage by the German government. The Revolution took a Communistic form because the new state was challenged by internal disorder and external attack; the people reacted as any nation will react under siege—it put aside all individual freedom until order and security could be restored. Here too Communism was a war economy. Perhaps it survives through continued fear of war; given a generation of peace it would presumably be eroded by the nature of man.

Socialism in Russia is now restoring individualistic motives to give its system greater productive stimulus, and to allow its people more physical and intellectual liberty. Meanwhile capitalism undergoes a correlative process of limiting individualistic acquisition by semi-socialistic legislation and the redistribution of wealth through the "welfare state." Marx was an unfaithful disciple of Hegel: he interpreted the Hegelian dialectic as implying that the struggle between capitalism and socialism would end in the complete victory of socialism; but if the Hegelian formula of thesis, antithesis, and synthesis is applied to the Industrial Revolution as thesis, and to capitalism versus socialism as antithesis, the third condition would be a synthesis of capitalism and socialism; and to this reconciliation the Western world visibly moves. Year by year the role of Western governments in the economy rises, the share of the private sector declines. Capitalism retains the stimulus of private property, free enterprise, and competition, and produces a rich supply of goods; high taxation, falling heavily upon the upper classes, enables the government to provide for a self-limited population unprecedented services in education, health, and recreation. The fear of capitalism has compelled socialism to widen freedom, and the fear of socialism has compelled capitalism to increase equality. East is West and West is East, and soon the twain will meet.

X. Government and History

Alexander Pope thought that only a fool would dispute over forms of government. History has a good word to say for all of them, and for government in general. Since men love freedom, and the freedom of individuals in society requires some regulation of conduct, the first condition of freedom is its limitation; make it absolute and it dies in chaos. So the prime task of government is to establish order; organized central force is the sole alternative to incalculable and disruptive force in private hands. Power naturally converges to a center, for it is ineffective when divided, diluted, and spread, as in Poland under the *liberum veto;* hence, the centralization of power in the monarchy by Richelieu or Bismarck, over the protest of feudal barons, has been praised by historians. A similar process has centered power in the federal government in the United States; it was of no use to talk of "states' rights" when the economy was ignoring state boundaries and could be regulated only by some central authority. Today international government is developing as industry, commerce, and finance override frontiers and take international forms.

Monarchy seems to be the most natural kind of government, since it applies to the group the authority of the father in a family or of the chieftain in a warrior band. If we were to judge forms of government from their prevalence and duration in history we should have to give the palm to monarchy; democracies, by contrast, have been hectic interludes.

After the breakdown of Roman democracy in the class wars of the Gracchi, Marius, and Caesar, Augustus organized, under what in effect was monarchical rule, the greatest achievement in the history of statesmanship—that Pax Romana which maintained peace from 30 B.C. to A.D. 180 throughout an empire ranging from the Atlantic to the Euphrates and from Scotland to the Black Sea. After him monarchy disgraced itself under Caligula, Nero, and Domitian; but after them came Nerva, Trajan, Hadrian, Antoninus Pius, and Marcus Aurelius—"the finest succession of good and great sovereigns," Renan called them, "that the world has ever had." [53] "If," said Gibbon, "a man were called upon to fix the period during which the condition of the human race was most happy and prosperous, he would without hesitation name that which elapsed from the accession of Nerva to the death of Marcus Aurelius. Their united reigns are possibly the only period of history in which the happiness of a great people was the sole object of government." [54] In that brilliant age, when Rome's subjects complimented themselves on being under her rule, monarchy was adoptive: the emperor transmitted his authority not to his offspring but to the ablest man he could find; he adopted this man as his son, trained him in the functions of government, and gradually surrendered to him the reins of power. The system worked well, partly because neither Trajan nor Hadrian had a son, and the sons of Antoninus Pius died in childhood. Marcus Aurelius had a son, Commodus, who succeeded him because the philosopher failed to name another heir; soon chaos was king.*

---

* We should add that some historians consider the age of the Antonines as an unsuccessful "rally" in the decay of Rome. See Arnold J. Toynbee, *A Study of History* (London, 1934 f.), IV, 60.

All in all, monarchy has had a middling record. Its wars of succession brought mankind as much evil as the continuity or "legitimacy" of the monarchy brought good. When it is hereditary it is likely to be more prolific of stupidity, nepotism, irresponsibility, and extravagance than of nobility or statesmanship. Louis XIV has often been taken as the paragon of modern monarchs, but the people of France rejoiced at his death. The complexity of contemporary states seems to break down any single mind that tries to master it.

Hence most governments have been oligarchies—ruled by a minority, chosen either by birth, as in aristocracies, or by a religious organization, as in theocracies, or by wealth, as in democracies. It is unnatural (as even Rousseau saw) for a majority to rule, for a majority can seldom be organized for united and specific action, and a minority can. If the majority of abilities is contained in a minority of men, minority government is as inevitable as the concentration of wealth; the majority can do no more than periodically throw out one minority and set up another. The aristocrat holds that political selection by birth is the sanest alternative to selection by money or theology or violence. Aristocracy withdraws a few men from the exhausting and coarsening strife of economic competition, and trains them from birth, through example, surroundings, and minor office, for the tasks of government; these tasks require a special preparation that no ordinary family or background can provide. Aristocracy is not only a nursery of statesmanship, it is also a repository and vehicle of culture, manners, standards, and tastes, and serves thereby as a stabilizing barrier to social fads, artistic crazes, or neurotically rapid changes in the moral code. See what has happened to morals, manners, style, and art since the French Revolution.

Aristocracies have inspired, supported, and controlled art, but they have rarely produced it. The aristocrat looks upon artists as manual laborers; he prefers the art of life to the life of art, and would never think of reducing himself to the consuming toil that is usually the price of genius. He does not often produce literature, for he thinks of writing for publication as exhibitionism and salesmanship. The result has been, in modern aristocracies, a careless and dilettante hedonism, a lifelong holiday in which the privileges of place were enjoyed to the full, and the responsibilities were often ignored. Hence the decay of some aristocracies. Only three generations intervened between *"L'état c'est moi"* and *"Après moi le déluge."*

So the services of aristocracy did not save it when it monopolized privilege and power too narrowly, when it oppressed the people with selfish and myopic exploitation, when it retarded the growth of the nation by a blind addiction to ancestral ways, when it consumed the men and resources of the state in the lordly sport of dynastic or territorial wars. Then the excluded banded together in wild revolt; the new rich combined with the poor against obstruction and stagnation; the guillotine cut off a thousand noble heads; and democracy took its turn in the misgovernment of mankind.

Does history justify revolutions? This is an old debate, well illustrated by Luther's bold break from the Catholic Church versus Erasmus' plea for patient and orderly reform, or by Charles James Fox's stand for the French Revolution versus Edmund Burke's defense of "prescription" and continuity. In some cases outworn and inflexible institutions seem to require violent overthrow, as in Russia in 1917. But in most instances the effects achieved by the revolution would apparently have come without it through the gradual compulsion of economic developments. America would have become the dominant factor in the English-speaking world without any revolution. The French Revolution replaced the landowning aristocracy with the money-controlling business class as the ruling power; but a similar result occurred in nineteenth-century England without bloodshed, and without disturbing the public peace. To break sharply with the past is to court the madness that may follow the shock of sudden blows or mutilations. As the sanity of the individual lies in the continuity of his memories, so the sanity of a group lies in the continuity of its traditions; in either case a break in the chain invites a neurotic reaction, as in the Paris massacres of September, 1792.*

Since wealth is an order and procedure of production and exchange rather than an accumulation of (mostly perishable) goods, and is a trust (the "credit system") in men and institutions rather than in the intrinsic value of paper money or checks, violent revolutions do not so much redistribute wealth as destroy it. There may be a redivision of the land, but the natural inequality of men soon re-creates an inequality of possessions and privileges, and raises to power a new minority with essentially the same instincts as in the old. The only real revolution is in the enlightenment of the mind and the improvement of character, the only real emancipation is individual, and the only real revolutionists are philosophers and saints.

In strict usage of the term, democracy has existed only in modern times, for the most part since the French Revolution. As male adult suffrage in the United States it began under Andrew Jackson; as adult suffrage it began in our youth. In ancient Attica, out of a total population of 315,000 souls, 115,000 were slaves, and only 43,000 were citizens with the right to vote.[55] Women, nearly all workingmen, nearly all shopkeepers and tradesmen, and all resident aliens were excluded from the franchise. The citizen minority was divided into two factions: the oligarchic—chiefly the landed aristocracy and the upper bourgeoisie; and the democratic—small landowners and

---

*See Taine's unforgettable description in *The French Revolution* (New York, 1931), II, 209–33.

small businessmen, and citizens who had lapsed into wage labor but still retained the franchise. During the ascendancy of Pericles (460–430 B.C.) the aristocracy prevailed, and Athens had her supreme age in literature, drama, and art. After his death, and the disgrace of the aristocracy through the defeat of Athens in the Peloponnesian War (431–404 B.C.), the *demos*, or lower class of citizens, rose to power, much to the disgust of Socrates and Plato. From Solon to the Roman conquest of Greece (146 B.C.) the conflict of oligarchs and democrats was waged with books, plays, orations, votes, ostracism, assassination, and civil war. At Corcyra (now Corfu), in 427 B.C., the ruling oligarchy assassinated sixty leaders of the popular party; the democrats overturned the oligarchs, tried fifty of them before a kind of Committee of Public Safety, executed all fifty, and starved hundreds of aristocratic prisoners to death. Thucydides' description reminds us of Paris in 1792–93.

> During seven days the Corcyreans were engaged in butchering those of their fellow citizens whom they regarded as their enemies. . . . Death raged in every shape, and, as usually happens at such times, there was no length to which violence did not go; sons were killed by their fathers, and suppliants were dragged from the altar or slain on it. . . . Revolution thus ran its course from city to city, and the places where it arrived last, from having heard what had been done before, carried to a still greater excess the . . . atrocity of their reprisals. . . . Corcyra gave the first example of these crimes, . . . of the revenge exacted by the governed (who had never experienced equitable treatment, or, indeed, aught but violence, from their rulers) and . . . of the savage and pitiless excesses into which men were hurried by their passions. . . . Meanwhile the moderate part of the citizens perished between the two [warring groups]. . . . The whole Hellenic world was convulsed.[56]

In his *Republic* Plato made his mouthpiece, Socrates, condemn the triumphant democracy of Athens as a chaos of class violence, cultural decadence, and moral degeneration. The democrats contemptuously rejected temperance as unmanliness. . . . Insolence they term breeding, and anarchy liberty, and waste magnificence, and impudence courage. . . . The father gets accustomed to descend to the level of his sons and to fear them, and the son to be on a level with his father, having no shame or fear of his parents. . . . The teacher fears and flatters his scholars, and the scholars despise their masters and tutors. . . . The old do not like to be thought morose and authoritative, and therefore they imitate the young. . . . Nor must I forget to tell of the liberty and equality of the two sexes in relation to each other. . . . The citizens chafe impatiently at the least touch of authority, and at length . . . they cease to care even for the laws, written or unwritten. . . . And this is the fair and glorious beginning out of which springs dictatorship [*tyrannis*]. . . . The excessive increase of anything causes a reaction in the opposite direction; . . . dictatorship naturally arises out of democracy, and the most aggravated form of tyranny and slavery out of the most extreme form of liberty.[57]

By the time of Plato's death (347 B.C.) his hostile analysis of Athenian democracy was approaching apparent confirmation by history. Athens recovered wealth, but this was now commercial rather than landed wealth; industrialists, merchants, and bankers were at the top of the reshuffled heap. The change produced a feverish struggle for money, a *pleonexia*, as the Greeks called it—an appetite for more and more. The *nouveaux riches* (*neoplutoi*) built gaudy mansions, bedecked their women with costly robes and jewelry, spoiled them with dozens of servants, rivaled one another in the feasts with which they regaled their guests. The gap between the rich and the poor widened; Athens was divided, as Plato put it, into "two cities: . . . one the city of the poor, the other of the rich, the one at war with the other." [58] The poor schemed to despoil the rich by legislation, taxation, and revolution; the rich organized themselves for protection against the poor. The members of some oligarchic organizations, says Aristotle, took a solemn oath: "I will be an adversary of the people" (i.e., the commonalty), "and in the Council I will do it all the evil that I can." [59] "The rich have become so unsocial," wrote Isocrates about 366 B.C., "that those who own property had rather throw their possessions into the sea than lend aid to the needy, while those who are in poorer circumstances would less gladly find a treasure than seize the possessions of the rich." [60] The poorer citizens captured control of the Assembly, and began to vote the money of the rich into the coffers of the state, for redistribution among the people through governmental enterprises and subsidies. The politicians strained their ingenuity to discover new sources of public revenue. In some cities the decentralizing of wealth was more direct: the debtors in Mytilene massacred their creditors en masse; the democrats of Argos fell upon the rich, killed hundreds of them, and confiscated their property. The moneyed families of otherwise hostile Greek states leagued themselves secretly for mutual aid against popular revolts. The middle classes, as well as the rich, began to distrust democracy as empowered envy, and the poor distrusted it as a sham equality of votes nullified by a gaping inequality of wealth. The rising bitterness of the class war left Greece internally as well as internationally divided when Philip of Macedon pounced down upon it in 338 B.C., and many rich Greeks welcomed his coming as preferable to revolution. Athenian democracy disappeared under Macedonian dictatorship.[61]

Plato's reduction of political evolution to a sequence of monarchy, aristocracy, democracy, and dictatorship found another illustration in the history of Rome. During the third and second centuries before Christ a Roman oligarchy organized a foreign policy and a disciplined army, and conquered and exploited the Mediterranean world. The wealth so won was absorbed by the patricians, and the commerce so developed raised to luxurious opulence the upper middle class.

Conquered Greeks, Orientals, and Africans were brought to Italy to serve as slaves on the *latifundia;* the native farmers, displaced from the soil, joined the restless, breeding proletariat in the cities, to enjoy the monthly dole of grain that Caius Gracchus had secured for the poor in 123 B.C. Generals and proconsuls returned from the provinces loaded with spoils for themselves and the ruling class; millionaires multiplied; mobile money replaced land as the source or instrument of political power; rival factions competed in the wholesale purchase of candidates and votes; in 53 B.C. one group of voters received ten million sesterces for its support.[62] When money failed, murder was available: citizens who had voted the wrong way were in some instances beaten close to death and their houses were set on fire. Antiquity had never known so rich, so powerful, and so corrupt a government.[63] The aristocrats engaged Pompey to maintain their ascendancy; the commoners cast in their lot with Caesar; ordeal of battle replaced the auctioning of victory; Caesar won, and established a popular dictatorship. Aristocrats killed him, but ended by accepting the dictatorship of his grandnephew and stepson Augustus (27 B.C.). Democracy ended, monarchy was restored; the Platonic wheel had come full turn.

We may infer, from these classic examples, that ancient democracy, corroded with slavery, venality, and war, did not deserve the name, and offers no fair test of popular government. In America democracy had a wider base. It began with the advantage of a British heritage: Anglo-Saxon law, which, from Magna Carta onward, had defended the citizens against the state; and Protestantism, which had opened the way to religious and mental liberty. The American Revolution was not only a revolt of colonials against a distant government; it was also an uprising of a native middle class against an imported aristocracy. The rebellion was eased and quickened by an abundance of free land and a minimum of legislation. Men who owned the soil they tilled, and (within the limits of nature) controlled the conditions under which they lived, had an economic footing for political freedom; their personality and character were rooted in the earth. It was such men who made Jefferson president—Jefferson who was as skeptical as Voltaire and as revolutionary as Rousseau. A government that governed least was admirably suited to liberate those individualistic energies that transformed America from a wilderness to a material utopia, and from the child and ward to the rival and guardian of Western Europe. And while rural isolation enhanced the freedom of the individual, national isolation provided liberty and security within protective seas. These and a hundred other conditions gave to America a democracy more basic and universal than history had ever seen.

Many of these formative conditions have disappeared. Personal isolation is gone through the growth of cities. Personal independence is gone through the dependence of the worker upon tools and capital that he does not own, and upon conditions that he cannot control. War becomes more consuming, and the individual is helpless to understand its causes or to escape its effects. Free land is gone, though home ownership spreads—with a minimum of land. The once self-employed shopkeeper is in the toils of the big distributor, and may echo Marx's complaint that everything is in chains. Economic freedom, even in the middle classes, becomes more and more exceptional, making political freedom a consolatory pretense. And all this has come about not (as we thought in our hot youth) through the perversity of the rich, but through the impersonal fatality of economic development, and through the nature of man. Every advance in the complexity of the economy puts an added premium upon superior ability, and intensifies the concentration of wealth, responsibility, and political power.

Democracy is the most difficult of all forms of government, since it requires the widest spread of intelligence, and we forgot to make ourselves intelligent when we made ourselves sovereign. Education has spread, but intelligence is perpetually retarded by the fertility of the simple. A cynic remarked that "you mustn't enthrone ignorance just because there is so much of it." However, ignorance is not long enthroned, for it lends itself to manipulation by the forces that mold public opinion. It may be true, as Lincoln supposed, that "you can't fool all the people all the time," but you can fool enough of them to rule a large country.

Is democracy responsible for the current debasement of art? The debasement, of course, is not unquestioned; it is a matter of subjective judgment; and those of us who shudder at its excesses—its meaningless blotches of color, its collages of debris, its Babels of cacophony—are doubtless imprisoned in our past and dull to the courage of experiment. The producers of such nonsense are appealing not to the general public—which scorns them as lunatics, degenerates, or charlatans—but to gullible middle-class purchasers who are hypnotized by auctioneers and are thrilled by the new, however deformed. Democracy is responsible for this collapse only in the sense that it has not been able to develop standards and tastes to replace those with which aristocracies once kept the imagination and individualism of artists within the bounds of intelligible communication, the illumination of life, and the harmony of parts in a logical sequence and a coherent whole. If art now seems to lose itself in *bizarreries,* this is not only because it is vulgarized by mass suggestion or domination, but also because it has exhausted the possibilities of old schools and forms, and flounders for a time in the search for new patterns and styles, new rules and disciplines.

All deductions having been made, democracy has done less harm, and more good, than any other form of government. It gave to human existence a zest and camaraderie that outweighed its pitfalls and defects. It gave to thought and science and enterprise the freedom essential to their operation and growth. It broke down the walls of privilege and class, and in each generation it raised up ability from every rank and place. Under its stimulus Athens and Rome became the most creative cities in history, and America in two centuries has provided abundance for an unprecedentedly large proportion of its population. Democracy has now dedicated itself resolutely to the spread and lengthening of education, and to the maintenance of public health. If equality of educational opportunity can be established, democracy will be real and justified. For this is the vital truth beneath its catchwords: that though men cannot be equal, their access to education and opportunity can be made more nearly equal. The rights of man are not rights to office and power, but the rights of entry into every avenue that may nourish and test a man's fitness for office and power. A right is not a gift of God or nature but a privilege which it is good for the group that the individual should have.

In England and the United States, in Denmark, Norway, and Sweden, in Switzerland and Canada, democracy is today sounder than ever before. It has defended itself with courage and energy against the assaults of foreign dictatorship, and has not yielded to dictatorship at home. But if war continues to absorb and dominate it, or if the itch to rule the world requires a large military establishment and appropriation, the freedoms of democracy may one by one succumb to the discipline of arms and strife. If race or class war divides us into hostile camps, changing political argument into blind hate, one side or the other may overturn the hustings with the rule of the sword. If our economy of freedom fails to distribute wealth as ably as it has created it, the road to dictatorship will be open to any man

who can persuasively promise security to all; and a martial government, under whatever charming phrases, will engulf the democratic
world.

XI. History and War

War is one of the constants of history, and has not diminished with civilization or democracy. In the last 3,421 years of recorded history only 268 have seen no war. We have acknowledged war as at present the ultimate form of competition and natural selection in the human species. "*Polemos pater panton,*" said Heracleitus; war, or competition, is the father of all things, the potent source of ideas, inventions, institutions, and states. Peace is an unstable equilibrium, which can be preserved only by acknowledged supremacy or equal power.

The causes of war are the same as the causes of competition among individuals: acquisitiveness, pugnacity, and pride; the desire for food, land, materials, fuels, mastery. The state has our instincts without our restraints. The individual submits to restraints laid upon him by morals and laws, and agrees to replace combat with conference, because the state guarantees him basic protection in his life, property, and legal rights. The state itself acknowledges no substantial restraints, either because it is strong enough to defy any interference with its will or because there is no superstate to offer it basic protection, and no international law or moral code wielding effective force.

In the individual, pride gives added vigor in the competitions of life; in the state, nationalism gives added force in diplomacy and war. When the states of Europe freed themselves from papal overlordship and protection, each state encouraged nationalism as a supplement to its army and navy. If it foresaw conflict with any particular country it fomented, in its people, hatred of that country, and formulated catchwords to bring that hatred to a lethal point; meanwhile it stressed its love of peace.

This conscription of the soul to international phobia occurred only in the most elemental conflicts, and was seldom resorted to in Europe between the Religious Wars of the sixteenth century and the Wars of the French Revolution. During that interval the peoples of conflicting states were allowed to respect one another's achievements and civilization; Englishmen traveled safely in France while France was at war with England; and the French and Frederick the Great continued to admire each other while they fought each other in the Seven Years' War. In the seventeenth and eighteenth centuries war was a contest of aristocracies rather than of peoples. In the twentieth century the improvement of communication, transport, weapons, and means of indoctrination made war a struggle of peoples, involving civilians as well as combatants, and winning victory through the wholesale destruction of property and life. One war can now destroy the labor of centuries in building cities, creating art, and developing habits of civilization. In apologetic consolation war now promotes science and technology, whose deadly inventions, if they are not forgotten in universal destitution and barbarism, may later enlarge the material achievements of peace.

In every century the generals and the rulers (with rare exceptions like Ashoka and Augustus) have smiled at the philosophers' timid dislike of war. In the military interpretation of history war is the final arbiter, and is accepted as natural and necessary by all but cowards and simpletons. What but the victory of Charles Martel at

Tours (732) kept France and Spain from becoming Mohammedan? What would have happened to our classic heritage if it had not been protected by arms against Mongol and Tatar invasions? We laugh at generals who die in bed (forgetting that they are more valuable alive than dead), but we build statues to them when they turn back a Hitler or a Genghis Khan. It is pitiful (says the general) that so many young men die in battle, but more of them die in automobile accidents than in war, and many of them riot and rot for lack of discipline; they need an outlet for their combativeness, their adventurousness, their weariness with prosaic routine; if they must die sooner or later why not let them die for their country in the anesthesia of battle and the aura of glory? Even a philosopher, if he knows history, will admit that a long peace may fatally weaken the martial muscles of a nation. In the present inadequacy of international law and sentiment a nation must be ready at any moment to defend itself; and when its essential interests are involved it must be allowed to use any means it considers necessary to its survival. The Ten Commandments must be silent when self-preservation is at stake.

It is clear (continues the general) that the United States must assume today the task that Great Britain performed so well in the nineteenth century—the protection of Western civilization from external danger. Communist governments, armed with old birth rates and new weapons, have repeatedly proclaimed their resolve to destroy the economy and independence of non-Communist states. Young nations, longing for an Industrial Revolution to give them economic wealth and military power, are impressed by the rapid industrialization of Russia under governmental management; Western capitalism might be more productive in the end, but it seems slower in development; the new governors, eager to control the resources and manhood of their states, are a likely prey to Communist propaganda, infiltration, and subversion. Unless this spreading process is halted it is only a matter of time before nearly all Asia, Africa, and South America will be under Communist leadership, and Australia, New Zealand, North America, and Western Europe will be surrounded by enemies on every side. Imagine the effect of such a condition upon Japan, the Philippines, and India, and upon the powerful Communist Party of Italy; imagine the effect of a Communist victory in Italy upon the Communist movement in France. Great Britain, Scandinavia, the Netherlands, and West Germany would be left at the mercy of an overwhelmingly Communist Continent. Should North America, now at the height of its power, accept such a future as inevitable, withdraw within its frontiers, and let itself be encircled by hostile states controlling its access to materials and markets, and compelling it, like any besieged people, to imitate its enemies and establish governmental dictatorship over every phase of its once free and stimulating life? Should the leaders of America consider only the reluctance of this epicurean generation to face so great an issue, or should they consider also what future generations of Americans would wish that these leaders had done? Is it not wiser to resist at once, to carry the war to the enemy, to fight on foreign soil, to sacrifice, if it need be, a hundred thousand American lives and perhaps a million noncombatants, but to leave America free to live its own life in security and freedom? Is not such a farsighted policy fully in accord with the lessons of history?

The philosopher answers: Yes, and the devastating results will be in accord with history, except that they will be multiplied in proportion to the increased number and mobility of the engaged forces, and the unparalleled destructiveness of the weapons used. There is something greater than history. Somewhere, sometime, in the name of humanity, we must challenge a thousand evil precedents, and dare to apply the Golden Rule to nations, as the Buddhist King Ashoka did (262 B.C.),[64] or at least do what Augustus did when he bade Tiberius desist from further invasion of Germany (A.D. 9).[65] Let us refuse, at whatever cost to ourselves, to make a hundred Hiroshimas in China. "Magnanimity in politics," said Edmund Burke, "is not seldom the truest wisdom, and a great empire and little minds go ill together." [66] Imagine an American President saying to the leaders of China and Russia:

"If we should follow the usual course of history we should make war upon you for fear of what you may do a generation hence. Or we should follow the dismal precedent of the Holy Alliance of 1815, and dedicate our wealth and our soundest youth to suppressing any revolt against the existing order anywhere. But we are willing to try a new approach. We respect your peoples and your civilizations as among the most creative in history. We shall try to understand your feelings, and your desire to develop your own institutions without fear of attack. We must not allow our mutual fears to lead us into war, for the unparalleled murderousness of our weapons and yours brings into the situation an element unfamiliar to history. We propose to send representatives to join with yours in a persistent conference for the adjustment of our differences, the cessation of hostilities and subversion, and the reduction of our armaments. Wherever, outside our borders, we may find ourselves competing with you for the allegiance of a people, we are willing to submit to a full and fair election of the population concerned. Let us open our doors to each other, and organize cultural exchanges that will promote mutual appreciation and understanding. We are not afraid that your economic system will displace ours, nor need you fear that ours will displace yours; we believe that each system will learn from the other and be able to live with it in co-operation and peace. Perhaps each of us, while maintaining adequate defenses, can arrange nonaggression and nonsubversion pacts with other states, and from these accords a world order may take form within which each nation will remain sovereign and unique, limited only by agreements freely signed. We ask you to join us in this defiance of history, this resolve to extend courtesy and civilization to the relations among states. We pledge our honor before all mankind to enter into this venture in full sincerity and trust. If we lose in the historic gamble, the results could not be worse than those that we may expect from a continuation of traditional policies. If you and we succeed, we shall merit a place for centuries to come in the grateful memory of mankind."

The general smiles. "You have forgotten all the lessons of history," he says, "and all that nature of man which you described. Some conflicts are too fundamental to be resolved by negotiation; and during the prolonged negotiations (if history may be our guide) subversion would go on. A world order will come not by a gentlemen's agreement, but through so decisive a victory by one of the great powers that it will be able to dictate and enforce international law, as Rome did from Augustus to Aurelius. Such interludes of widespread peace are unnatural and exceptional; they will soon be ended by changes in the distribution of military power. You have told us that man is a competitive animal, that his states must be like himself, and that natural selection now operates on an international plane. States will unite in basic co-operation only when they are in common attacked from without. Perhaps we are now restlessly moving toward that higher plateau of competition; we may make contact with ambitious species on other planets or stars; soon thereafter there will be interplanetary war. Then, and only then, will we of this earth be one."

XII. Growth and Decay

We have defined civilization as "social order promoting cultural creation." [67] It is political order secured through custom, morals, and law, and economic order secured through a continuity of production and exchange; it is cultural creation through freedom and facilities for the origination, expression, testing, and fruition of ideas, letters, manners, and arts. It is an intricate and precarious web of human relationships, laboriously built and readily destroyed.

Why is it that history is littered with the ruins of civilizations, and seems to tell us, like Shelley's "Ozymandias," that death is the destiny of all? Are there any regularities, in this process of growth and decay, which may enable us to predict, from the course of past civilizations, the future of our own?

Certain imaginative spirits have thought so, even to predicting the future in detail. In his Fourth Eclogue Virgil announced that some day, the ingenuity of change having been exhausted, the whole universe, by design or accident, will fall into a condition precisely the same as in some forgotten antiquity, and will then repeat, by deterministic fatality and in every particular, all those events that had followed that condition before.

87

Alter erit tum Tiphys, et altera quae vehat Argo
delectos heroas; erunt etiam altera bella,
atque iterum ad Troiam magnus mittetur Achilles—

"there will then be another [prophet] Tiphys, and another Argo will carry [Jason and other] beloved heroes; there will also be other wars, and great Achilles will again be sent to Troy." [68] Friedrich Nietzsche went insane with this vision of "eternal recurrence." There is nothing so foolish but it can be found in the philosophers.

History repeats itself, but only in outline and in the large. We may reasonably expect that in the future, as in the past, some new states will rise, some old states will subside; that new civilizations will begin with pasture and agriculture, expand into commerce and industry, and luxuriate with finance; that thought (as Vico and Comte argued) will pass, by and large, from supernatural to legendary to naturalistic explanations; that new theories, inventions, discoveries, and errors will agitate the intellectual currents; that new generations will rebel against the old and pass from rebellion to conformity and reaction; that experiments in morals will loosen tradition and frighten its beneficiaries; and that the excitement of innovation will be forgotten in the unconcern of time. History repeats itself in the large because human nature changes with geological leisureliness, and man is equipped to respond in stereotyped ways to frequently occurring situations and stimuli like hunger, danger, and sex. But in a developed and complex civilization individuals are more differentiated and unique than in a primitive society, and many situations contain novel circumstances requiring modifications of instinctive response; custom recedes, reasoning spreads; the results are less predictable. There is no certainty that the future will repeat the past. Every year is an adventure.

Some masterminds have sought to constrain the loose regularities of history into majestic paradigms. The founder of French socialism,

Claude-Henri de Rouvroy, Comte de Saint-Simon (1760–1825), divided the past and the future into an alternation of "organic" and "critical" periods:

> The law of human development . . . reveals two distinct and alternative states of society: one, the organic, in which all human actions are classed, foreseen, and regulated by a general theory, and the purpose of social activity is clearly defined; the other, the critical, in which all community of thought, all communal action, all coordination have ceased, and the society is only an agglomeration of separate individuals in conflict with one another.
>
> Each of these states or conditions has occupied two periods of history. One organic period preceded that Greek era which we call the age of philosophy, but which we shall more justly call the age of criticism. Later a new doctrine arose, ran through different phases of elaboration and completion, and finally established its political power over Western civilization. The constitution of the Church began a new organic epoch, which ended in the fifteenth century, when the Reformers sounded the arrival of that age of criticism which has continued to our time. . . .
>
> In the organic ages all basic problems [theological, political, economic, moral] have received at least provisional solutions. But soon the progress achieved by the help of these solutions, and under the protection of the institutions realized through them, rendered them inadequate, and evoked novelties. Critical epochs—periods of debate, protest, . . . and transition, replaced the old mood with doubt, individualism, and indifference to the great problems. . . . In organic periods men are busy building; in critical periods they are busy destroying.[69]

Saint-Simon believed that the establishment of socialism would begin a new organic age of unified belief, organization, co-operation, and stability. If Communism should prove to be the triumphant new order of life Saint-Simon's analysis and prediction would be justified.

Oswald Spengler (1880–1936) varied Saint-Simon's scheme by dividing history into separate civilizations, each with an independent life span and trajectory composed of four seasons but essentially two periods: one of centripetal organization unifying a culture in all its phases into a unique, coherent, and artistic form; the other a period of centrifugal disorganization in which creed and culture decompose in division and criticism, and end in a chaos of individualism, skepticism, and artistic aberrations. Whereas Saint-Simon looked forward to socialism as the new synthesis, Spengler (like Talleyrand) looked backward to aristocracy as the age in which life and thought were consistent and orderly and constituted a work of living art.

> For Western existence the distinction lies about the year 1800—on one side of that frontier, life in fullness and sureness of itself, formed by growth from within, in one great, uninterrupted evolution from Gothic childhood to Goethe and Napoleon; and on the other the autumnal, artificial, rootless life of our great cities, under forms fashioned by the intellect. . . . He who does not understand that this outcome is obligatory and insusceptible of modification must forgo all desire to comprehend history.[70]

On one point all are agreed: civilizations begin, flourish, decline, and disappear—or linger on as stagnant pools left by once life-giving streams. What are the causes of development, and what are the causes of decay?

No student takes seriously the seventeenth-century notion that states arose out of a "social contract" among individuals or between the people and a ruler. Probably most states (i.e., societies politically organized) took form through the conquest of one group by another, and the establishment of a continuing force over the conquered by the conqueror; his decrees were their first laws; and these, added to the customs of the people, created a new social order. Some states of Latin America obviously began in this way. When the masters organized the work of their subjects to take advantage of some physical boon (like the rivers of Egypt or Asia), economic prevision and provision constituted another basis for civilization. A dangerous tension between rulers and ruled might raise intellectual and emotional activity above the daily drift of primitive tribes. Further stimulation to growth could come from any challenging change in the surroundings,[71] such as external invasion or a continuing shortage of rain—challenges that might be met by military improvements or the construction of irrigation canals.

If we put the problem further back, and ask what determines whether a challenge will or will not be met, the answer is that this depends upon the presence or absence of initiative and of creative individuals with clarity of mind and energy of will (which is almost a definition of genius), capable of effective responses to new situations (which is almost a definition of intelligence). If we ask what makes a creative individual, we are thrown back from history to psychology and biology—to the influence of environment and the gamble and secret of the chromosomes. In any case a challenge successfully met (as by the United States in 1917, 1933, and 1941), if it does not exhaust the victor (like England in 1945), raises the temper and level of a nation, and makes it abler to meet further challenges.

If these are the sources of growth, what are the causes of decay? Shall we suppose, with Spengler and many others, that each civilization is an organism, naturally and yet mysteriously endowed with the power of development and the fatality of death? It is tempting to explain the behavior of groups through analogy with physiology or physics, and to ascribe the deterioration of a society to some inherent limit in its loan and tenure of life, or some irreparable running down of internal force. Such analogies may offer provisional illumination, as when we compare the association of individuals with an aggregation of cells, or the circulation of money from banker back to banker with the systole and diastole of the heart. But a group is no organism physically added to its constituent individuals; it has no brain or stomach of its own; it must think or feel with the brains or nerves of its members. When the group or a civilization declines, it is through no mystic limitation of a corporate life, but through the failure of its political or intellectual leaders to meet the challenges of change.

The challenges may come from a dozen sources, and may by repetition or combination rise to a destructive intensity. Rainfall or oases may fail and leave the earth parched to sterility. The soil may be exhausted by incompetent husbandry or improvident usage. The replacement of free with slave labor may reduce the incentives to production, leaving lands untilled and cities unfed. A change in the instruments or routes of trade—as by the conquest of the ocean or the air—may leave old centers of civilization becalmed and decadent, like Pisa or Venice after 1492. Taxes may mount to the point of discouraging capital investment and productive stimulus. Foreign markets and materials may be lost to more enterprising competition; excess of imports over exports may drain precious metal from domestic reserves. The concentration of wealth may disrupt the nation in class or race war. The concentration of population and poverty in great cities may compel a government to choose between enfeebling the economy with a dole and running the risk of riot and revolution.

Since inequality grows in an expanding economy, a society may find itself divided between a cultured minority and a majority of men and women too unfortunate by nature or circumstance to inherit or develop standards of excellence and taste. As this majority grows it acts as a cultural drag upon the minority; its ways of speech, dress, recreation, feeling, judgment, and thought spread upward, and internal barbarization by the majority is part of the price that the minority pays for its control of educational and economic opportunity.

As education spreads, theologies lose credence, and receive an external conformity without influence upon conduct or hope. Life and ideas become increasingly secular, ignoring supernatural explanations and fears. The moral code loses aura and force as its human origin is revealed, and as divine surveillance and sanctions are removed. In ancient Greece the philosophers destroyed the old faith among the educated classes; in many nations of modern Europe the philosophers achieved similar results. Protagoras became Voltaire, Diogenes Rousseau, Democritus Hobbes, Plato Kant, Thrasymachus Nietzsche, Aristotle Spencer, Epicurus Diderot. In antiquity and modernity alike, analytical thought dissolved the religion that had buttressed the moral code. New religions came, but they were divorced from the ruling classes, and gave no service to the state. An age of weary skepticism and epicureanism followed the triumph of rationalism over mythology in the last century before Christianity, and follows a similar victory today in the first century after Christianity.

Caught in the relaxing interval between one moral code and the next, an unmoored generation surrenders itself to luxury, corruption, and a restless disorder of family and morals, in all but a remnant clinging desperately to old restraints and ways. Few souls feel any longer that "it is beautiful and honorable to die for one's country." A failure of leadership may allow a state to weaken itself with internal strife. At the end of the process a decisive defeat in war may bring a final blow, or barbarian invasion from without may combine with barbarism welling up from within to bring the civilization to a close.

Is this a depressing picture? Not quite. Life has no inherent claim to eternity, whether in individuals or in states. Death is natural, and if it comes in due time it is forgivable and useful, and the mature mind will take no offense from its coming. But do civilizations die? Again, not quite. Greek civilization is not really dead; only its frame is gone and its habitat has changed and spread; it survives in the memory of the race, and in such abundance that no one life, however full and long, could absorb it all. Homer has more readers now than in his own day and land. The Greek poets and philosophers are in every library and college; at this moment Plato is being studied by a hundred thousand discoverers of the "dear delight" of philosophy overspreading life with understanding thought. This selective survival of creative minds is the most real and beneficent of immortalities.

Nations die. Old regions grow arid, or suffer other change. Resilient man picks up his tools and his arts, and moves on, taking his memories with him. If education has deepened and broadened those memories, civilization migrates with him, and builds somewhere another home. In the new land he need not begin entirely anew, nor make his way without friendly aid; communication and transport bind him, as in a nourishing placenta, with his mother country. Rome imported Greek civilization and transmitted it to Western Europe; America profited from European civilization and prepares to pass it on, with a technique of transmission never equaled before.

Civilizations are the generations of the racial soul. As life overrides death with reproduction, so an aging culture hands its patrimony down to its heirs across the years and the seas. Even as these lines are being written, commerce and print, wires and waves and invisible Mercuries of the air are binding nations and civilizations together, preserving for all what each has given to the heritage of mankind.

XIII. Is Progress Real?[72]

Against this panorama of nations, morals, and religions rising and falling, the idea of progress finds itself in dubious shape. Is it only the vain and traditional boast of each "modern" generation? Since we have admitted no substantial change in man's nature during historic times, all technological advances will have to be written off as merely new means of achieving old ends—the acquisition of goods, the pursuit of one sex by the other (or by the same), the overcoming of competition, the fighting of wars. One of the discouraging discoveries of our disillusioning century is that science is neutral: it will kill for us as readily as it will heal, and will destroy for us more readily than it can build. How inadequate now seems the proud motto of Francis Bacon, "Knowledge is power"! Sometimes we feel that the Middle Ages and the Renaissance, which stressed mythology and art rather than science and power, may have been wiser than we, who repeatedly enlarge our instrumentalities without improving our purposes.

Our progress in science and technique has involved some tincture of evil with good. Our comforts and conveniences may have weakened our physical stamina and our moral fiber. We have immensely

95

developed our means of locomotion, but some of us use them to facilitate crime and to kill our fellow men or ourselves. We double, triple, centuple our speed, but we shatter our nerves in the process, and are the same trousered apes at two thousand miles an hour as when we had legs. We applaud the cures and incisions of modern medicine if they bring no side effects worse than the malady; we appreciate the assiduity of our physicians in their mad race with the resilience of microbes and the inventiveness of disease; we are grateful for the added years that medical science gives us if they are not a burdensome prolongation of illness, disability, and gloom. We have multiplied a hundred times our ability to learn and report the events of the day and the planet, but at times we envy our ancestors, whose peace was only gently disturbed by the news of their village. We have laudably bettered the conditions of life for skilled workingmen and the middle class, but we have allowed our cities to fester with dark ghettos and slimy slums.

We frolic in our emancipation from theology, but have we developed a natural ethic—a moral code independent of religion—strong enough to keep our instincts of acquisition, pugnacity, and sex from debasing our civilization into a mire of greed, crime, and promiscuity? Have we really outgrown intolerance, or merely transferred it from religious to national, ideological, or racial hostilities? Are our manners better than before, or worse? "Manners," said a nineteenth-century traveler, "get regularly worse as you go from the East to the West; it is bad in Asia, not so good in Europe, and altogether bad in the western states of America";[73] and now the East imitates the West. Have our laws offered the criminal too much protection against society and the state? Have we given ourselves more freedom than our intelligence can digest? Or are we nearing such moral and social disorder that frightened parents will run back to Mother Church and beg her to discipline their children, at whatever cost to intellectual liberty? Has all the progress of philosophy since Descartes been a mistake through its failure to recognize the role of myth in the consolation and control of man? "He that increaseth knowledge increaseth sorrow, and in much wisdom is much grief." [74]

Has there been any progress at all in philosophy since Confucius? Or in literature since Aeschylus? Are we sure that our music, with its complex forms and powerful orchestras, is more profound than Palestrina, or more musical and inspiring than the monodic airs that medieval Arabs sang to the strumming of their simple instruments? (Edward Lane said of the Cairo musicians, "I have been more charmed with their songs . . . than with any other music that I have ever enjoyed." [75]) How does our contemporary architecture—bold, original, and impressive as it is—compare with the temples of ancient Egypt or Greece, or our sculpture with the statues of Chephren and Hermes, or our bas-reliefs with those of Persepolis or the Parthenon, or our paintings with those of the van Eycks or Holbein? If "the replacement of chaos with order is the essence of art and civilization," [76] is contemporary painting in America and Western Europe the replacement of order with chaos, and a vivid symbol of our civilization's relapse into confused and structureless decay?

History is so indifferently rich that a case for almost any conclusion from it can be made by a selection of instances. Choosing our evidence with a brighter bias, we might evolve some more comforting reflections. But perhaps we should first define what progress means to us. If it means increase in happiness its case is lost almost at first sight. Our capacity for fretting is endless, and no matter how many difficulties we surmount, how many ideals we realize, we shall always find an excuse for being magnificently miserable; there is a stealthy pleasure in rejecting mankind or the universe as unworthy of our approval. It seems silly to define progress in terms that would make the average child a higher, more advanced product of life than the adult or the sage—for certainly the child is the happiest of the three. Is a more objective definition possible? We shall here define progress as the increasing control of the environment by life. It is a test that may hold for the lowliest organism as well as for man.

We must not demand of progress that it should be continuous or universal. Obviously there are retrogressions, just as there are periods of failure, fatigue, and rest in a developing individual; if the present stage is an advance in control of the environment, progress is real. We may presume that at almost any time in history some nations were progressing and some were declining, as Russia progresses and England loses ground today. The same nation may be progressing in one field of human activity and retrogressing in another, as America is now progressing in technology and receding in the graphic arts. If we find that the type of genius prevalent in young countries like America and Australia tends to the practical, inventive, scientific, executive kinds rather than to the painter of pictures or poems, the carver of statues or words, we must understand that each age and place needs and elicits some types of ability rather than others in its pursuit of environmental control. We should not compare the work of one land and time with the winnowed best of all the collected past. Our problem is whether the average man has increased his ability to control the conditions of his life.

If we take a long-range view and compare our modern existence, precarious, chaotic, and murderous as it is, with the ignorance, superstition, violence, and diseases of primitive peoples, we do not come off quite forlorn. The lowliest strata in civilized states may still differ only slightly from barbarians, but above those levels thousands, millions have reached mental and moral levels rarely found among primitive men. Under the complex strains of city life we sometimes take imaginative refuge in the supposed simplicity of pre-civilized ways; but in our less romantic moments we know that this is a flight reaction from our actual tasks, and that the idolizing of savages, like many other young moods, is an impatient expression of adolescent maladaptation, of conscious ability not yet matured and comfortably placed. The "friendly and flowing savage" would be delightful but for his scalpel, his insects, and his dirt. A study of surviving primitive tribes reveals their high rate of infantile mortality, their short tenure of life, their lesser stamina and speed, their greater susceptibility to disease.[77] If the prolongation of life indicates better control of the environment, then the tables of mortality proclaim the advance of man, for longevity in European and American whites has tripled in the last three centuries. Some time ago a convention of morticians discussed the danger threatening their industry from the increasing tardiness of men in keeping their rendezvous with death.[78] But if undertakers are miserable progress is real.

In the debate between ancients and moderns it is not at all clear that the ancients carry off the prize. Shall we count it a trivial achievement that famine has been eliminated in modern states, and that one country can now grow enough food to overfeed itself and yet send hundreds of millions of bushels of wheat to nations in need? Are we ready to scuttle the science that has so diminished superstition, obscurantism, and religious intolerance, or the technology that has spread food, home ownership, comfort, education, and leisure beyond any precedent? Would we really prefer the Athenian agora or the Roman comitia to the British Parliament or the United States Congress, or be content under a narrow franchise like Attica's, or the selection of rulers by a praetorian guard? Would we rather have lived under the laws of the Athenian Republic or the Roman Empire than under constitutions that give us habeas corpus, trial by jury, religious and intellectual freedom, and the emancipation of women? Are our morals, lax though they are, worse than those of the ambisexual Alcibiades, or has any American President imitated Pericles, who lived with a learned courtesan? Are we ashamed of our great universities, our many publishing houses, our bountiful public libraries? There were great dramatists in Athens, but was any greater than Shakespeare, and was Aristophanes as profound and humane as Molière? Was the oratory of Demosthenes, Isocrates, and Aeschines superior to that of Chatham, Burke, and Sheridan? Shall we place Gibbon below Herodotus or Thucydides? Is there anything in ancient prose fiction comparable to the scope and depth of the modern novel? We may grant the superiority of the ancients in art, though some of us might still prefer Notre Dame de Paris to the Parthenon. If the Founding Fathers of the United States could return to America, or Fox and Bentham to England, or Voltaire and Diderot to France, would they not reproach us as ingrates for our blindness to our good fortune in living today and not yesterday—not even under Pericles or Augustus?

We should not be greatly disturbed by the probability that our civilization will die like any other. As Frederick asked his retreating troops at Kolin, "Would you live forever?" [79] Perhaps it is desirable that life should take fresh forms, that new civilizations and centers should have their turn. Meanwhile the effort to meet the challenge of the rising East may reinvigorate the West.

We have said that a great civilization does not entirely die—*non omnis moritur*. Some precious achievements have survived all the vicissitudes of rising and falling states: the making of fire and light, of the wheel and other basic tools; language, writing, art, and song; agriculture, the family, and parental care; social organization, morality, and charity; and the use of teaching to transmit the lore of the family and the race. These are the elements of civilization, and they have been tenaciously maintained through the perilous passage from one civilization to the next. They are the connective tissue of human history.

If education is the transmission of civilization, we are unquestionably progressing. Civilization is not inherited; it has to be learned and earned by each generation anew; if the transmission should be interrupted for one century, civilization would die, and we should be savages again. So our finest contemporary achievement is our unprecedented expenditure of wealth and toil in the provision of higher education for all. Once colleges were luxuries, designed for the male half of the leisure class; today universities are so numerous that he who runs may become a Ph.D. We may not have excelled the selected geniuses of antiquity, but we have raised the level and average of knowledge beyond any age in history.

None but a child will complain that our teachers have not yet eradicated the errors and superstitions of ten thousand years. The great experiment has just begun, and it may yet be defeated by the high birth rate of unwilling or indoctrinated ignorance. But what would be the full fruitage of instruction if every child should be schooled till at least his twentieth year, and should find free access to the universities, libraries, and museums that harbor and offer the intellectual and artistic treasures of the race? Consider education not as the painful accumulation of facts and dates and reigns, nor merely the necessary preparation of the individual to earn his keep in the world, but as the transmission of our mental, moral, technical, and aesthetic heritage as fully as possible to as many as possible, for the enlargement of man's understanding, control, embellishment, and enjoyment of life.

The heritage that we can now more fully transmit is richer than ever before. It is richer than that of Pericles, for it includes all the Greek flowering that followed him; richer than Leonardo's, for it includes him and the Italian Renaissance; richer than Voltaire's, for it embraces all the French Enlightenment and its ecumenical dissemination. If progress is real despite our whining, it is not because we are born any healthier, better, or wiser than infants were in the past, but because we are born to a richer heritage, born on a higher level of that pedestal which the accumulation of knowledge and art raises as the ground and support of our being. The heritage rises, and man rises in proportion as he receives it.

History is, above all else, the creation and recording of that heritage; progress is its increasing abundance, preservation, transmission, and use. To those of us who study history not merely as a warning reminder of man's follies and crimes, but also as an encouraging remembrance of generative souls, the past ceases to be a depressing chamber of horrors; it becomes a celestial city, a spacious country of the mind, wherein a thousand saints, statesmen, inventors, scientists, poets, artists, musicians, lovers, and philosophers still live and speak, teach and carve and sing. The historian will not mourn because he can see no meaning in human existence except that which man puts into it; let it be our pride that we ourselves may put meaning into our lives, and sometimes a significance that transcends death. If a man is fortunate he will, before he dies, gather up as much as he can of his civilized heritage and transmit it to his children. And to his final breath he will be grateful for this inexhaustible legacy, knowing that it is our nourishing mother and our lasting life.

Guide to Books

mentioned in the Notes

ARISTOTLE, *Politics*. Everyman's Library.

BAGEHOT, WALTER, *Physics and Politics*. Boston, 1956.

CARTER, THOMAS F., *The Invention of Printing in China and Its Spread Westward*. New York, 1925.

COXE, WILLIAM, *History of the House of Austria*, 3v. London, 1847.

DURANT, WILL, *The Mansions of Philosophy*. New York, 1929.

DURANT, WILL and ARIEL, *The Story of Civilization*:

    I. *Our Oriental Heritage*. New York, 1935.

    II. *The Life of Greece*. New York, 1939.

    III. *Caesar and Christ*. New York, 1944.

    IV. *The Age of Faith*. New York, 1950.

    V. *The Renaissance*. New York, 1953.

    VI. *The Reformation*. New York, 1957.

    VII. *The Age of Reason Begins*. New York, 1961.

    VIII. *The Age of Louis XIV*. New York, 1963.

    IX. *The Age of Voltaire*. New York, 1965.

    X. *Rousseau and Revolution*. New York, 1967.

Encyclopaedia Britannica, 1966 edition.

GIBBON, EDWARD, *The Decline and Fall of the Roman Empire*, ed. Milman, 6v. New York: Nottingham Society, n.d.

GOBINEAU, J. A. DE, *The Inequality of Human Races*. London, 1915.

GOMME, A. W., *The Population of Athens in the Fifth and Fourth Centuries B.C.* Oxford, 1933.

GOWEN, H. H., AND HALL, JOSEF, *Outline History of China*. New York, 1927.

GRANET, MARCEL, *Chinese Civilization*. New York, 1930.

ISOCRATES, *Works*. Loeb Library.

KAUTSKY, KARL, *Communism in Central Europe in the Time of the Reformation*. London, 1897.

LANE, EDWARD, *Manners and Customs of the Modern Egyptians*, 2v. London, 1846.

LEMAÎTRE, JULES, *Jean Jacques Rousseau*. New York, 1907.

PASCAL, BLAISE, *Pensées*. Everyman's Library.

PAUL-LOUIS, *Ancient Rome at Work*. London, 1927.

PLATO, *Dialogues*, tr. Jowett, 4v. New York: Jefferson Press, n.d.

PLUTARCH, *Lives*, 3v. Everyman's Library.

RENAN, ERNEST, *The Apostles*. London: Methuen, n.d.

———, *Marc Aurèle*. Paris: Calman-Lévy, n.d.

Sédillot, René, *L'Histoire n'a pas de sens.* Paris, 1965.
Seebohm, Frederick, *The Age of Johnson.* London, 1899.
Siegfried, André, *America Comes of Age.* New York, 1927.
Spengler, Oswald, *The Decline of the West,* 2v. New York, 1927.
Thucydides, *History of the Peloponnesian War.* Everyman's Library.
Todd, A. J., *Theories of Social Progress.* New York, 1934.
Toynbee, Arnold J., *A Study of History,* 10v. London, 1934f.

Notes

CHAPTER I

1. Sédillot, René, *L'Histoire n'a pas de sens.*
2. Durant, *Our Oriental Heritage,* 12.
3. *Age of Faith,* 979.
4. Sédillot, 167.
5. *The Reformation, viii.*
6. *The Age of Reason Begins,* 267.

CHAPTER II

7. Pascal, *Pensées,* No. 347.
8. Plato, *Phaedo,* No. 109.

CHAPTER III

9. *Caesar and Christ,* 193, 223, 666.

CHAPTER IV

10. Gobineau, *Inequality of Human Races, xv,* 210.
11. *Ibid.,* 211.
12. *Ibid.,* 36–7.
13. In Todd, A. J., *Theories of Social Progress,* 276.
14. See *Our Oriental Heritage,* 934–38.

CHAPTER VI

15. *Caesar and Christ,* 211.
16. *The Renaissance,* 576.

17. *Our Oriental Heritage,* 275.
18. *The Reformation,* 761.
19. *The Age of Reason Begins,* 394.
20. *The Age of Voltaire,* 64.
21. *Our Oriental Heritage,* 265.
22. *The Reformation,* 763.
23. *The Age of Voltaire,* 487.
24. Gibbon, Edward, *Decline and Fall of the Roman Empire,* I, 314.

CHAPTER VII

25. *Caesar and Christ,* 296–97.
26. *The Age of Faith,* 525–26.
27. Plato, *Laws,* No. 948.
28. *Our Oriental Heritage,* 205–13.
29. *Ibid.,* 416–19, 434, 504.
30. Renan, *The Apostles, xxxiii.*
31. Lemaître, *Jean Jacques Rousseau,* 9.
32. Durant, *The Mansions of Philosophy,* 568.

CHAPTER VIII

33. *The Reformation,* 752.
34. *The Age of Louis XIV,* 720.
35. Plutarch, *Life of Solon.*
36. *The Life of Greece,* 112–18.
37. Plutarch, *Tiberius Gracchus.*
38. *Caesar and Christ,* 111–22, 142–44, 180–208.

CHAPTER IX

39. *Encyclopaedia Britannica*, II, 962b.
40. *Our Oriental Heritage*, 231. We have revised the date there given for Hammurabi.
41. *The Life of Greece*, 587–92.
42. Paul-Louis, *Ancient Rome at Work*, 283–85.
43. *Caesar and Christ*, 641f.
44. Szuma Ch'ien in Granet, Marcel, *Chinese Civilization*, 113.
45. *Ibid.*
46. *Our Oriental Heritage*, 700f. The dates there given are being revised for a new edition.
47. Gowen and Hall, *Outline History of China*, 142.
48. In Carter, Thomas, *The Invention of Printing in China and Its Spread Westward*, 183.
49. *Our Oriental Heritage*, 724–26.
50. *The Age of Reason Begins*, 249–51.
51. Kautsky, Karl, *Communism in Central Europe in the Time of the Reformation*, 121, 130.
52. *The Reformation*, 383, 391, 398–401.

CHAPTER X

53. Renan, *Marc Aurèle*, 479.
54. Gibbon, *Decline and Fall*, I, 31.
55. Gomme, A. W., *The Population of Athens in the Fifth and Fourth Centuries B.C.*, 21, 26, 47; *Life of Greece*, 254.
56. Thucydides, *Peloponnesian War*, iii 10; *Life of Greece*, 284.
57. Plato, *The Republic*, Nos. 560–64.

58. *Ibid.*, No. 422.
59. Aristotle, *Politics*, No. 1310.
60. Isocrates, *Works*, "Archidamus," No. 67.
61. This paragraph has been copied from *The Life of Greece*, 464–66.
62. *Caesar and Christ*, 128–30.
63. *Ibid.*

CHAPTER XI

64. *Our Oriental Heritage*, 446.
65. *Caesar and Christ*, 218.
66. In Seebohm, *The Age of Johnson*, xiii.

CHAPTER XII

67. *Our Oriental Heritage*, 1.
68. See *The Mansions of Philosophy*, 355; Toynbee, *A Study of History*, IV, 27f.
69. Quoted from Bazard's *Exposition de la doctrine Saint-Simonienne*, in Toynbee, I, 199.
70. Spengler, *Decline of the West*, I, 353, 90, 38.
71. This is the initial theory of Toynbee's *Study of History*, I, 271f.

CHAPTER XIII

72. This section appropriates some passages from an essay on the same subject in *The Mansions of Philosophy*.
73. Anon. in Bagehot, *Physics and Politics*, 110.
74. Ecclesiastes, i, 18.

75. Lane, Edward, *Manners and Customs of the Modern Egyptians*, II, 66.
76. *Our Oriental Heritage*, 237.
77. Todd, *Theories of Social Progress*, 135.
78. Siegfried, André, *America Comes of Age*, 176.
79. *Rousseau and Revolution*, Ch. II, Sec. iii, William Coxe, *History of the House of Austria*, III, 379.

Index

Dates in parentheses following a name are of birth and death except when preceded by *r.*, when they indicate duration of reign for popes and rulers of states. A single date preceded by *fl.* denotes a *floruit*. A footnote is indicated by an asterisk. All dates are A.D. unless otherwise noted.

Abélard, Pierre (1079–1142), 53
Achaeans, 27
Actium, 57
Aeschines (389–314 B.C.), 100
Aeschylus (525–456 B.C.), 97
Africa, 30, 84
agriculture, 16–17, 100; mechanization, technological advances, 22, 54, 58; a stage in economic history, 37, 38, 39, 41, 47, 88; state ownership or control of, 59–64 *passim*
airplane, impact on civilization, 16
Alcibiades (c. 450–404 B.C.), 39, 99
Alexander the Great, King of Macedon (r. 336–323 B.C.), 12
Alexandria, 60
Alpine peoples, 27, 28
America, 28, 39, 40, 53, 94; contemporary painting in, 97; progress in, 97–99; *see also* NORTH AMERICA; SOUTH AMERICA; UNITED STATES
American Revolution, 76
Amon, religion of, 49
Anabaptists, 65
anarchism, 65

Angkor Wat, 29
Angles, 27, 30
Anglican Church, 50
Anglo-Saxon law, 76
Anglo-Saxons in America, 23, 27, 31, 48
Antoninus Pius, Emperor of Rome (r. 138–161), 69
Antony, Mark (83–30 B.C.), 39, 56–57
Arabs, 97
architecture, 97
Aretino, Pietro (1492–1556), 40
Argos, 75
Ariosto, Lodovico (1474–1533), 40
aristocracy, 70–71, 75, 76, 82; and French Revolution, 57; and government, 70, 73, 75, 76, 90; and the arts, 70, 73, 78
Aristophanes (450?–385 B.C.), 100
Aristotle (384–322 B.C.), 74, 93
art and artists, 29, 31, 70–71, 78, 95; of Periclean Athens, 73; an aspect of civilization, 87, 97, 100, 102
Aryan race, 25–28 *passim*
Ashoka, King of Magadha (r. 273–232 B.C.), 82, 84
Asia, 15, 53, 84, 90, 96